The Long Way Back

The Long Way Back

Afghanistan's Quest for Peace

CHRIS ALEXANDER

HARPER

An Imprint of HarperCollins*Publishers*
www.harpercollins.com

HarperCollins books may be purchased for educational, business, or sales promotional use. For information, please write: Special Markets Department, Harper-Collins Publishers, 10 East 53rd Street, New York, NY 10022.

The epigraphs on pages 15, 83, 85 and 204 are reprinted, with permission, from *The Baburnama: Memoirs of Babur, Prince and Emperor*, Wheeler M. Thackson, ed. and trans. Copyright 1996, Freer Gallery of Art and Arthur M. Sackler Gallery, Smithsonian Institution. All rights reserved.

The epigraph on page 183 is from *Shahnameh: The Persian Book of Kings*, translated by Dick Davis (courtesy of Mage Publishers: www.mage.com).

Published in Canada in 2011 by HarperCollins Publishers Ltd.

FIRST U.S. EDITION   958.1047

Library of Congress Cataloging-in-Publication Data has been applied for.

ISBN: 978-0-06-202037-6

11 12 13 14 15   OFF/RRD   10 9 8 7 6 5 4 3 2 1

To all the people of Afghanistan,
and to Hedvig Christine and Selma Zolaykha

A true believer loves for his brother what he loves for himself.
—The Prophet Muhammad, as reported by Anas bin Malik

CONTENTS

A DECADE OF AFGHAN LEADERS (2001–11)

Abdullah, Dr. Abdullah. Born in Kabul. Foreign minister under Rabbani and Massoud, then under Karzai until 2005. Contested 2009 presidential elections, placing second.

Ahady, Anwar ul-Haq. Born in Surobi. Degrees from Beirut and Northwestern. Head of Afghan Mellat. After 2001, central bank governor, finance and commerce minister.

Akhundzada, Sher Mohammad. Scion of leading Helmand mujahidin family. Governor until 2005. Member of Meshrano Jirga. Close to Karzai.

Aloko, Mohammad Ishaq. Born in Kandahar. Served as prosecutor and intelligence officer under Daoud Khan. Author, resident in Germany. Attorney general since 2008.

Alokozay, Abdul Rahman. Head of leading Mohmand merchant family from Nangarhar, resident in Dubai. Global trading operations. Strong political role.

Anwari, Sayed Hussain. Shia Harakat-i Islami commander from Parwan. Minister of agriculture, then governor of Kabul and Herat provinces.

Arghandiwal, Abdul Hadi. From Kabul. Civil war finance minister. Reconciled in 2005, elected to Wolesi Jirga. Head of new Hezb-i Islami. Economy minister since 2010.

Arsala, Hedayat Amin. Aristocrat. PhD. Career in World Bank. Foreign minister when Karzai was deputy. After 2001, vice-president, commerce minister and senior minister.

Atmar, Mohammad Haneef. Mohmand from Laghman, with Kandahari mother. After 2001, human rights commission chair, minister of rural development, education and interior.

Atta Mohammed Noor, Ustad. Born in Balkh. Strongest Jamiat commander in the north. Displaced Dostum from Mazar after Taliban fall. Governor of Balkh since 2004.

Azimi, Abdul Salam. Born in Farah. PhD. Legal advisor to president, then chief justice starting in May 2006. Author of justice-reform and anti-corruption strategy.

Berader, Mullah Abdul Ghani. Popalzai from Deh Rawud. Taliban governor, commander. Led southern front after 2007. Arrested by ISI in 2010 after making overtures to Kabul.

Bismullah Khan Mohammadi. Tajik from Panjshir. Shomali commander under Massoud. Chief of general staff from 2003. Interior minister in 2010.

Dadullah Lang, Mullah. Kakar from Oruzgan. Scourge of Hazarajat. From Quetta, commanded Taliban southern front. Killed in Helmand on May 12, 2007.

Danesh, Mohammad Sardar. Shia with MA in Islamic jurisprudence. Born in Daikundi, first governor of new province. After 2004, minister of justice, then of higher education.

Daudzai, Mohammad Umar. Hezb-i Islami from Qarabagh. UNDP Kabul head during Taliban. Karzai chief of staff from 2003 to 2005 and 2007 to present, with interlude in Tehran.

Din Mohammad, Haji. Born in Fatehbad, Nangarhar. Elder brother of Haji Qadir and Abdul Haq. Under Karzai, governor of Nangarhar and then Kabul provinces.

Dostum, Abdul Rashid. Notorious Uzbek commander from Jawzjan. Pivotal in fall of Najib and Taliban regimes. Since 2005, despite occasional periods of exile, chief of staff to the general staff.

Ehsan Zia, Mohammad. From Kabul. MA from York. Capable NGO manager. With MRRD from 2002—minister from 2006–2009.

Fahim, Mohammad Qasim. Military commander of United Front after Massoud's death. First post-Taliban defence minister. Vice-president from 2001 to 2004 and 2009 to present.

Farhang, Mir Mohammad Amin. From prominent Kabul family. Doctorate from Cologne. Minister of three portfolios: reconstruction, economy and commerce. Impeached due to fuel corruption scandal in 2008.

Farooqi, Khalid. Former Hezb-i Islami intelligence chief from Paktika. Led return of several activists to Kabul in 2005. Member of Wolesi Jirga.

Fitrat, Abdul Qadir. From Badakhshan and Kabul. Lived in US after 1996. Central bank governor from 2007 to 2011. Resigned citing threats from Kabul Bank scandal.

Ghani (Ahmadzai), Dr. Ashraf. Born in Logar. Educated at Beirut and Columbia. World Bank official. Advisor to Brahimi on Bonn Agreement. Finance minister from 2002 to 2004. Chancellor of Kabul University. Consultant. Presidential candidate in 2009.

Gilani, Fatima. Daughter of Pir Syed Ahmad Gilani. Influential in jihad. Head of Afghan Red Crescent Society from 2004 to 2010. Married to Anwar ul-Haq Ahady.

Gilani, Pir Syed Ahmad. Born in Surkhrud. Son of Sayed Hassan Gilani, leader of Qadiriyya Sufism in Afghanistan, who came to Nangarhar from Baghdad in 1905.

Haqqani, Sirajuddin. Son of Jalaluddin Haqqani, Khalis commander in jihad. Major Taliban backer since 1996. Brutal Taliban tactician. Bases in North Waziristan.

Hekmatyar, Gulbuddin. Founder of Hezb-i Islami. Returned to Peshawar area in 2001. At ISI insistence, forged alliance with Taliban and al Qaeda. Lives semi-covertly.

Ibrahim Spinzada, "Engineer" Mohammed. Barakzai from Farah. Former UNHCR official in Kandahar and Quetta. Close Karzai advisor. Deputy national security chief.

Ismail Khan, Mohammad. Jamiat commander from Shindand who famously led Herat uprising against Soviets. Herat governor to 2004, then energy minister and water minister.

Jawad, Said Tayeb. Born in Kandahar. Studied in Germany and US. Karzai's chief of staff from 2002 to 2003. Afghan ambassador to Washington from 2003 to 2010.

Juma Khan, Haji. Baluch from Nimruz from key drug-trafficking family. Major Taliban ally with ties to Kabul. Controlled Baramcha drug bazaar before arrest by US in 2008.

Kabir, Mullah Mohammad Abdul. Zadran from Paktia. Major Taliban commander in east, based after 2001 in Peshawar. "Captured" by Pakistan in 2005 and again 2010.

Karzai, Hamid. Son of Afghan senator killed by ISI in 1999. Deputy foreign minister. Pro-Western conciliator. President since 2001.

Khalid, Haji Asadullah. From Nawa in Ghazni, where he was governor from 2001 to 2005. Governor of Kandahar from 2005 to 2008. Minister of borders and tribal affairs from 2010.

Khalili, Abdul Karim. Shia from Behsud district in Wardak province. Key leader of Hezb-i Wahdat. Vice-president since 2001. Oversaw DDR and DIAG.

Khalili, Masood. Son of famous poet, and grandson of courtier and landowner. With Massoud at time of death. Ambassador to India, Turkey and Spain.

Khoram, Abdul Karim. Educated in France. Hezb-i-Islami loyalist. Controversial minister of culture, information, tourism and youth (2006–09), now Karzai chief of staff.

Lodin, Azizullah. From prominent Herat family. Academic in Germany. Feud with Ismail Khan. Led anti-corruption office, parliamentary secretariat and election commission.

Ludin, Jawed. Pashtun with strong links to UK. Karzai's chief of staff from 2003 to 2005. Ambassador to Nordic countries, then Canada. Now deputy foreign minister.

Mangal, Mohammad Gulab. Educated Mangal tribesman from Gardez. Served with distinction as governor of Paktika, Laghman and (since 2008) Helmand.

Mansour, Mullah Akhtar Mohammad. Former Taliban chief of aviation. Shadow Kandahar governor who promoted suicide attacks. Imposter came to Kabul in 2010.

Massoud, Ahmad Shah. Born in Bazarak, Panjshir, in 1953. Jamiat commander starting in 1970s. Held out against Taliban onslaught until his death on September 9, 2001.

Massoud, Ahmad Zia. Born in Muqur, Ghazni, in 1956. Elder brother of Ahmad Shah. Ambassador to Russia from 2001 to 2004, then vice-president from 2004 to 2009.

Mohaqiq, Ustad Haji Mohammad. Shia mujahidin commander active in Balkh. Minister of planning. Presidential candidate in 2004. Member of Wolesi Jirga.

Mohseni, Saad. Afghan-Australian founder of Tolo TV, Lemar TV and the MOBY Group—Afghanistan's largest media outfit. Based in Dubai and Kabul.

Mojadeddi, Hazrat Sebghatullah. From prominent Kabul family. Spiritual leader of Afghan Naqshbandi Sufism. President in 1992. Speaker of upper house from 2006.

Moqbel, Zarar Ahmed. From Parwan. Served in Tehran embassy. First deputy minister, then minister (2005–08) of interior. Counter-narcotics minister in 2010.

Mostapha Zahir, Shahzada. Royal prince, grandson of Zahir Shah. Educated at Queen's University, Canada. Ambassador to Rome. Director general of environmental protection.

Naderi, Professor Mohammad Ishaq. Economics professor at NYU. Senior economic advisor to Karzai and co-chair of JCMB.

Nadery, Ahmad Nader. Commissioner of Afghan independent human rights commission. Election activist. Civil society leader.

Naeemi, Abdul Jabbar. From Kandahar. Led Karzai campaign in Pakistan in 2004. Later made governor of Wardak, then Khost.

Najafi, Dr. Daoud Ali. Chief electoral officer for 2009 presidential elections. Accused of yielding to pressure from Karzai camp. Acting transport minister since 2010.

Noorzai, Haji Bashir. Leading drug trafficker in the south. One of the first to bankroll the Taliban movement. Related to Aref Noorzai. Arrested by US in 2005.

Noorzai, Mohammad Aref. Key ally of Karzai family in the south. Former minister of borders and tribal affairs, as well as first deputy Wolesi Jirga speaker.

Nuristani, Dr. Ahmad Yusuf. Early Karzai spokesman. Irrigation, water and environment minister. First deputy defence minister from 2005, then governor of Herat from 2009 to 2010.

Obaidullah Akhund, Mullah. From Panjwayi. Former Taliban defence minister. Captured in late 2001, then released. "Arrested" by ISI prior to Cheney visit in 2007.

Popal, Ghulam Jilani. Skilled NGO manager. Deputy minister for customs and revenue under Ashraf Ghani. Since 2007, director general for local governance under Karzai.

Qadir, Haji Abdul. Khalis commander later allied with United Front. Vice-president. Killed on July 6, 2002, in payback for political or drug-related dispute.

Qanuni, Younis. Northern Alliance official. Interior minister in 2002. Minister of education, then runner-up presidential candidate in 2004. Wolesi Jirga speaker.

Rabbani, Ustad Burhanuddin. Jamiat leader from Badakhshan. Born in 1940. President after 1992. Wolesi Jirga member. Leader of high council for peace after 2010.

Raheen, Sayed Maktoum. Professor of Persian literature. Twice minister of culture (from 2002 to 2004 and 2009 to present); ambassador to India in interim. Architect of modern media law.

Rahimi, Muhammad Asif. Born in Kabul in 1959. Educated at Omaha. Resident in Canada after 2001. Head of NSP from 2005. Agriculture minister since 2008.

Rassoul, Dr. Zalmai. Key member of Rome group. National security advisor to Karzai. Foreign minister since early 2010.

Saba, Mohammad Daoud. Born in Gozara. PhD in geology from India. Lived in US and Canada. Author of first Afghan human development report. Governor of Herat.

Sabit, Abdul Jabar. Jurist and human rights activist from Nangarhar. Controversial attorney general from 2006 until 2008.

Salangi, Abdul Basir. First police chief of Kabul after fall of Taliban. Implicated in Sherpur scandal. Police chief of Wardak until 2005. Governor of Parwan since 2008.

Saleh, Amrullah. Born in 1972. Key liaison for Massoud with US and other countries. Director general of NDS starting in 2004. Key architect of counter-insurgency.

Samar, Dr. Sima. Born in Jaghori. Fled to Pakistan in 1984. Vice-president and women's affairs minister after 2001. Human rights commission chair since 2002.

Sangin, Amirzai. A Wazir tribesman educated in Urgun and Gardez. Studied as telecom engineer in London. Communications minister since 2006.

Sarabi, Habiba. Born in Mazar-e-Sharif. Minister of women's affairs. Named governor of Bamiyan in 2005—first woman to hold such a position.

Sayyaf, Abdul Rasul. From Paghman. Leader of Ittehad-i Islami. Supported by ISI, Saudi Arabia and (after 2001) US. Chair of Wolesi Jirga foreign affairs committee.

Shahrani, Nimatullah. Uzbek from Badakhshan. Vice-president from 2002 to 2004, then minister of hajj and awqaf (religious affairs) until 2009.

Shahrani, Wahidullah. Son of Nimatullah, educated in UK. Deputy finance minister, then commerce minister in 2008 and mines minister in 2009. A reformer.

Sherzoi, Gul Agha. Barakzai commander from Kandahar. Twice named governor of his home province. Urban development minister. Nangarhar governor since 2005.

Shinwari, Fazl Hadi. Ittehad supporter from Shinwar district of Nangarhar. Chief justice from 2001 to 2006, countering Taliban influence. Died in 2011.

Spanta, Dr. Rangin Dadfar. From land-owning family in Karokh district. Professor and green activist in Aachen. Foreign minister (2006–10), then national security advisor.

Stanekzai, Mohammad Masoom. From Logar. Communications minister (2002–04), then responsible for DIAG (after 2005) and reconciliation (after 2010).

Taniwal, Hakim. Strong administrator. Governor of Khost, then governor of Paktia until killed by suicide bomber on September 10, 2006.

Usmani, Mullah Akhtar Mohammad. Major Taliban commander in Helmand. Killed in late 2006 by targeted airstrike.

Wafa, Assadullah. Born in Kandahar. A Karzai family friend. Governor of Paktia (2004–05), Kunar (2005–06) and Helmand (2006–08).

Wahidi, Sayed Fazlullah. Born in Surkhrud. A successful NGO manager before becoming governor of Kunar province in 2007.

Wardak, General Abdul Rahim. Eminent senior officer. Jihadi commander. Chief of army staff in 1992. Defence minister since 2004.

Wardak, Ghulam Farouk. From Chak in Wardak. With NGOs and UNDP in Peshawar. Ran election commission and cabinet office before becoming education minister in 2008.

Yasini, Mirwais. From Kama in Nangarhar. Headed Afghanistan's first anti-drug office. Elected to Wolesi Jirga in 2005. Ran against Karzai in 2009, placing fifth.

Yasir, Mullah Ustad Mohammad. A former Taliban commander in Kabul. Released in the deal to free an Italian journalist in 2007. Plays a key liaison role.

Zahir Shah, Mohammad. Reigned as king from 1933 to 1973. Returned to Afghanistan in April 2003, but died in Arg presidential palace on July 23, 2007.

Zakhilwal, Omar. Educated in Canada. Founded Afghan Investment Support Agency. Finance minister since March 2009.

Zakir, Mullah Abdul Qayyum. From Helmand. Transferred from Guantanamo to Poli-Charkhi, then released in 2007. In Quetta, gifted Taliban organizer of southern front.

Regional Map of Afghanistan and Surrounding Nations

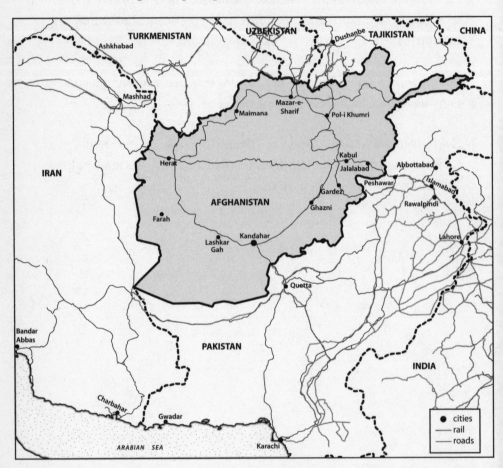

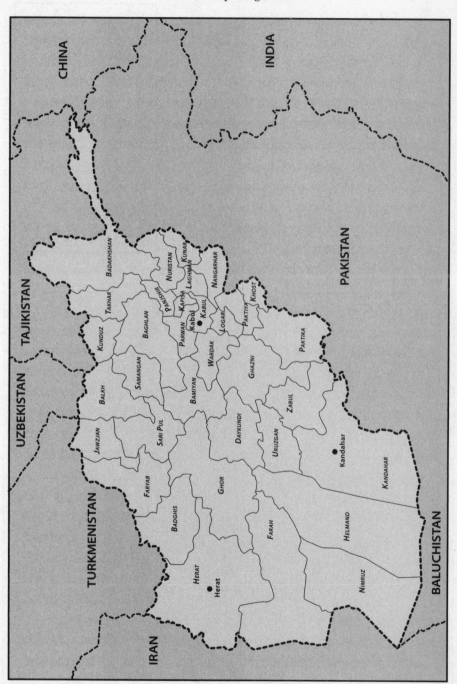

Taliban and Al Qaeda withdrawal to Pakistan in 2001 and 2002 and Establishment of First Provincial Reconstruction Teams in 2003

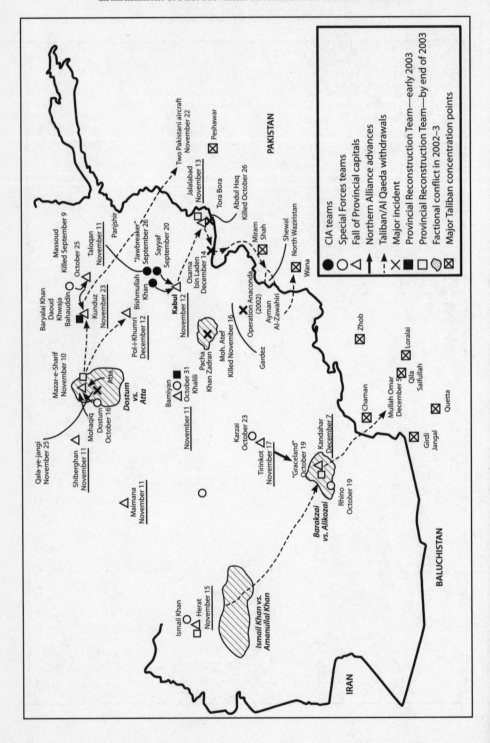

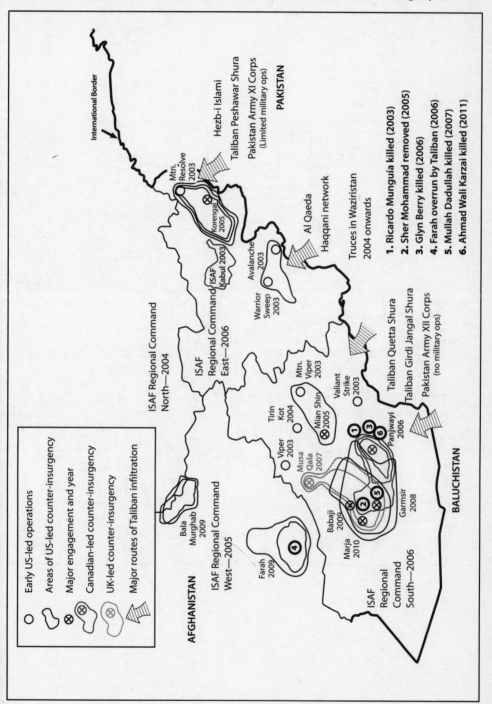

Kabul City

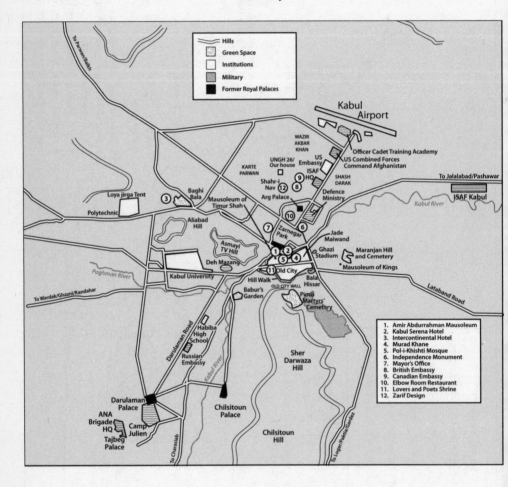

Legend:
- Hills
- Green Space
- Institutions
- Military
- Former Royal Palaces

Map labels:

Kabul Airport

To Parwan/Bakh

WAZIR AKBAR KHAN

Officer Cadet Training Academy

US Embassy

US Combined Forces Command Afghanistan

UNGH 26/ Our house

ISAF HQ

KARTE PARWAN

SHASH DARAK

To Jalalabad/Peshawar

Shahr-i-Nav

Defence Ministry

ISAF Kabul

Baghi Bala

Loya jirga Tent

Kabul River

Mausoleum of Timur Shah

Arg Palace

Polytechnic

Aliabad Hill

Zarnegar Park

Jade Maiwand

Maranjan Hill and Cemetery

Asmayi TV Hill

Ghazi Stadium

Mausoleum of Kings

Deh Mazang

Paghman River

Kabul University

Old City

Hill Walk

OLD CITY WALL

Bala Hissar

To Wardak/Ghazni/Kandahar

Latahand Road

Babur's Garden

Pious Martyrs' Cemetery

Habiba High School

Russian Embassy

Sher Darwaza Hill

Darulaman Road

Kabul River

Darulaman Palace

ANA Brigade HQ

Camp Julien

Chilsitoun Palace

Tajbeg Palace

Chilsitoun Hill

To Charasiab

To Logar/Paktia/Gardez

1. Amir Abdurrahman Mausoleum
2. Kabul Serena Hotel
3. Intercontinental Hotel
4. Murad Khane
5. Pol-i-Khishti Mosque
6. Independence Monument
7. Mayor's Office
8. British Embassy
9. Canadian Embassy
10. Elbow Room Restaurant
11. Lovers and Poets Shrine
12. Zarif Design

SIX WINTERS IN KABUL

The body of the air is lapis, and
Where it falls
Beyond the soft horizon
The light turns back to Heaven.

—Christopher Logue, *War Music*

There arguably has never been a more willing partner for American-led nation building than Afghanistan in the immediate wake of 9/11. In Afghanistan, as elsewhere, al Qaeda's attacks on the US mainland were recognized as a catastrophe, but the aftermath of the American invasion at least held the prospect of an end to the country's isolation and civil war. Afghanistan had been without a national army or police force since 1992. It had known no peace since 1978. It had lacked a legitimate government since 1973. For nearly three decades, Afghans had been hungry for sustained engagement from the international community. And then came 9/11: the ashes of ground zero had thrown up a phoenix of hope for a beleaguered country hemmed in by a phalanx of evils—from poverty and warlordism to impunity and heroin production.

A new era of stability for Afghanistan never seemed so tantalizingly close as in December 2001, when prominent Afghans hammered out the Bonn Agreement, which envisaged both a transitional government for the country and the fielding of a NATO-led International Security Assistance Force (ISAF). The Taliban had fled Kabul, Kandahar and every other provincial capital. In the old royal palace in Kabul, used by all Afghan leaders since the 1880s, Hamid Karzai was inaugurated as chairman of the interim administration—president in all but name— under the watchful gaze of ministers and diplomats from abroad. The seal of legitimate rule had been restored.

It was a little more than a year later when my role in Afghanistan's evolution began. It was February 2003. I was sitting at my desk in Moscow, where I worked as minister counsellor in Canada's embassy. A call came in from Ottawa. Would I agree to take the new post of Canada's first resident ambassador in Afghanistan? It took me all of seconds to agree.

A few months later, an Azerbaijan Airlines Tupolev-154, originating from Baku, deposited me in Kabul. Afghan Protocol met me on the tarmac, as did Canadian charge d'affaires Keith Fountain and ISAF deputy commander Major General Andrew Leslie, commander of Canada's Task Force Kabul. My immediate task was to enlarge our diplomatic mission—teasing more office and living space out of Kabul's bombed-out cityscape. It would soon grow to be one of Canada's largest. Our instructions were to integrate defence, development and diplomacy functions. With a large budget for assistance and 2,500 troops in Afghanistan (40 percent of ISAF strength at the time), we had the resources to make an impact.

Canada made a substantial commitment to Afghanistan partly by default: the Liberal government of Jean Chrétien had decided, in early 2003, not to take part in the invasion of Iraq, which most Canadians regarded as an unnecessary and divisive war of choice. The campaign in Afghanistan, on the other hand, had been forced on the United States and its allies by 9/11 and had been explicitly backed by the United Nations Security Council. Participating in the Afghan conflict allowed Canadians to assist the US-led war on terrorism, while staying true to our country's dominant foreign policy principles.

At a more basic level, Canadian leaders—including Chrétien's successors, Paul Martin and Conservative prime minister Stephen Harper—simply realized that the Afghan mission was critically important from both a military and a humanitarian perspective. Afghanistan needed a fresh start.

This book is about the two years I spent in Afghanistan as Canada's ambassador—and the following four years I spent serving the United Nations as deputy special representative of the secretary-general within its civilian mission (United Nations Assistance Mission in Afghanistan). It is a story of both historic achievements and bitter disappointments, chronicling the initial euphoria of the early years, followed by the resurgence of the Taliban and their allies. This book pays tribute to ordinary Afghan citizens, who've done much to build a better future, and to the Western troops who risk their lives to protect that enterprise, as well as to the thousands of civilians from all over the world who have toiled to alleviate humanitarian suffering, lighten the heavy yoke of poverty or bring enterprise, development and hope to Afghan communities.

I also describe the crucial yet oft-ignored multilateral diplomacy that has been going on behind the scenes in that country since late 2001. Many nations have sent their best and brightest to take on key civilian and military roles in Afghanistan. The quality of their effort too often has been obscured amid the frustrations and disappointments of a difficult mission. I want to emphasize how the United Nations, NATO, the United States, the European Union, Canada, Japan, Russia, China, Turkey, India and Afghanistan's other neighbours all have contributed substantially to the recovery of Afghan institutions, as well as to a political process that still stands a chance of one day bringing national reconciliation.

The case for pessimism may seem strong. Wounds left by thirty years of war still are raw. Terrorism is a daily menace. Roads are often littered with Taliban bombs. Regional warlords, drug barons and corrupt government officials all flout the conceit of a functional and unified nation. Yet my own confidence in Afghanistan's future has never flagged. Every visit to a village mosque bedecked in green flags, signifying a new building, or a school with new windows and a dirt floor, rough-hewn desks and fifty smiling faces, has shown me what tenacity and hard work can accomplish.

Readers interested in Afghanistan will find no shortage of books on the subject—going back to the sixteenth-century *Baburnama*, written by the founder of the Mughal Empire, and even far beyond. Afghan history most often has been told in dynastic chronicles—a tradition that metamorphosed into the nineteenth-century imperial chronicles authored by British and Russian military officers. In the twentieth century, the trend shifted to travel memoirs, in which the country was described as an exotic anachronism, but the intrigue and drama of the end of Empire and of the Cold War was never far to seek.

It wasn't until 2001 that writers began subjecting Afghanistan to urgent geopolitical scrutiny: the current events sections of bookstores now bulge with works about al Qaeda, the Taliban and all aspects of the American-led military mission. The best of these, such as Ahmed Rashid's 2001 bestseller, *Taliban*, and his 2008 follow-up, *Descent into Chaos*, explain how the seeds of the current war were sown in the region's history. Yet I feel the picture could be made clearer if more of us who have laboured in the country for extended periods would give their account of the events we witnessed. This book is written in that spirit.

I begin with an introduction providing a thumbnail history of Afghanistan, with a focus on episodes that foreshadowed the country's current traumas. In the history of religion, Afghanistan is one of the great wellsprings and transmission lines—for Hinduism, Buddhism and the Abrahamic faiths. Afghanistan was also central to the rise of the Mughal Empire, its conflicts with Safavid Persia and the formation of the Durrani Empire in the eighteenth century. This provides a background to the frontier policies of British India, which in turn provided the template for Pakistan's modern doctrine of "strategic depth." As I argue in later chapters, it is this doctrine—under which Pakistan's security apparatus continues to subsidize all manner of anti-Indian and anti-Western jihadis, even at the risk of Pakistan's own security—that remains the main engine of instability in Afghanistan.

The story since 2001 is divided into three parts. The first describes the Bonn process from 2001 to 2004, which restored Afghanistan's political authority. There is a chapter on the role of Afghanistan's neighbours in these early post-9/11 years, and another on Kabul as royal capital.

The second part of the book covers the years 2005 to 2007, focusing on the resurgent conflict with the Taliban and the partial breakdown in the partnership between the international community and President Karzai. It describes our shared failure to fund adequate courts, prosecutors, investigators and prisons. I also present a close profile of the western province of Herat, home to one of Afghanistan's most advanced cities, now caught between its proud ancient legacy, a Taliban resurgence and strategic meddling from neighbouring Iran.

The third part of the book covers the response to this crisis, from 2008 to 2010, including the US military surge and the drive to support large-scale institution building. I present two case studies: the province of Nangarhar, where the insurgency mostly has been tamed, and Kandahar, where it rages on. The conclusion looks ahead to an eventual peace process—one that must end the pattern of armed external interference in Afghanistan once and for all.

Even the most intractable conflict inevitably grinds to a halt. The Korean War (1950-53) ended with an armistice after two years of negotiations. The Vietnam War (1955-75) ended with the Paris Peace Accords. The Bosnian War (1992-95) ended with the Dayton Accords. Afghanistan's conflict (1978 to present) likely will end in a similar way, with a peace treaty whose terms are subject to international supervision in both Afghanistan and Pakistan.

—•—

My six winters in Afghanistan passed quickly, even without central heating or a watertight roof. On February 18, 2009—twenty years to the day after the last regular Soviet forces departed, as it happened—my wife and I drove out of the city, heading north. I will never forget the moment. The light that day bathed Kabul in a vivid winter radiance. It had snowed for four days, and the city's mud walls seemed like canvases stretched on alabaster frames.

We ventured north through Khairkhana Pass, onto the Shomali Plain of Parwan province. Snaking our way upward from the Ghorband River toward the notorious Soviet-built Salang Tunnel that is Kabul's northern lifeline, we passed buses jammed with workers and tractors unsteadily ploughing snow.

We had been crazy to think of driving from Kabul to Moscow in February—across the frozen Kazakh Steppe. But my wife, Hedvig Christine, insisted upon it. Seven years in Kabul (we met during my first year in the city) had left her taste for adventure undiminished, even though she was seven months pregnant.

Unfortunately, in Afghanistan, tragedy is never far away. On the eve of our departure, at least a dozen people were killed in avalanches in Salang; scores more were trapped for hours. A friend later recounted how his vehicle had filled with snow to his shoulders, leaving a narrow margin for escape. A year later, the snows came again in February. This time, over one hundred were killed—not victims of war, but victims of the primitive infrastructure whose improvement war prevents.

A senior member of Afghanistan's National Directorate of Security (NDS) had assigned us an escort for our drive. We thought it unnecessary. But hospitality declined in this culture is friendship refused and occasionally undone. New teams met us at every provincial boundary, smiling as they bounced along with their AK-47s in the back of Toyota Surf half-ton trucks. One of the security trends being tracked that year was Taliban infiltration into northeast Afghanistan—along the very route we were using. On September 2, 2009—just six months after we had left—NDS deputy director Abdullah Laghmani was killed by a suicide attacker in his native Laghman.

He joined dozens of friends Hedvig and I had both lost—every one convinced the risks they were running were justified by the goals we all shared. It was impossible to leave the country without a heart full of sorrow for its people. As we passed out of Afghanistan, on the same Friendship Bridge between Hairatan and Termez that Major General Boris Vsevolodovich Gromov had crossed with his son twenty years previous, I clung tightly to the hope that our daughter—Selma Zolaykha Alexander, born two months later—might grow up to see Afghanistan at peace.

Afghanistan's principal challenge is one of underdevelopment, which ultimately is a consequence of its position as a buffer state— a pawn, essentially, over two centuries of Great Game, Cold War and Indo-Pakistani manoeuvring. The past decade has seen many generous and principled nations make a start at undoing this legacy: releasing Afghans from the bonds of history and geopolitics in which they have languished for too long. Will we have the perseverance to continue this slow but necessary process? This book was written after I had ceased to be a UN staff member and before my election as Member of Parliament for Ajax-Pickering. It represents neither the policy of the government of Canada nor of the United Nations. In fact, I have sought to protect the confidences entrusted to me during my six years in Afghanistan, and for this reason I sought to re-interview in 2010 those individuals whose views are given at length. As a result, this account of Afghanistan's story since 2001 is a personal, not an official, perspective. My aim has been to provide a compelling and intelligible narrative of these often bewildering events to as wide an audience as possible, especially since so many countries and organizations have contributed so much to the multinational effort to stabilize and rebuild Afghanistan. By the time my story is done, I hope readers will agree that the country's long way back remains a worthy cause.

THE LONG WAY BACK

Introduction

BABUR'S GARDEN

Und solang du das nicht hast,
Dieses: Stirb und werde!
Bist du nur ein trüber Gast
Auf der dunklen Erde.

—Goethe, *West-östlicher Diwan*

Afghanistan's history has been one of great empires rubbing up against one another—of Persians, Mongols, Arabs, Greeks, Russians, Britons and countless others fighting for Central Asia's landlocked lynchpin in the shadow of the Hindu Kush. What follows is a brief summary of how these epic civilizational conflicts have dictated Afghanistan's modern shape and character. Many of the country's current problems reflect events that took place decades, or even centuries, ago. You can't fix Afghanistan's present without studying its past.

Perhaps the best place to begin the story is Babur's Garden in Kabul, the burial place of Zahir ud-Din Muhammad Babur (1483–1531), the first Mughal emperor. For Westerners, the garden's splendour was captured by Victorian war artist James Atkinson, who included an image of the spot in his series of lithographed plates, *Sketches in Afghaunistan*. His depiction of Babur's Garden shows a dense grove, with men in flowing robes holding forth in unspecified transactions and disputes. In the background lie picturesque fields and mountains, as well as the distinctive ornamentation of the mosque built by Emperor Shah Jahan, Babur's great-great-grandson. It is 1839. The British Army has just arrived in Kabul, and the first bloodbath is months away.

Even before Babur's rise to power in the early sixteenth century, Kabul and adjacent kingdoms had been cradles of religion, bastions of culture, seats of empire. The spot chosen for Babur's *charbagh*—a traditional Timurid quadrilateral garden—had been a Buddhist monastery dating to as early as the fourth century. It faces a floodplain beyond which the Baba mountain range marches north to Bamiyan, Balkh and Badakhshan, its passes having witnessed the armies of Kanishka, Genghis Khan, Tamerlane and the Soviet Union. At their foot, an ancient artery of trade snakes south to Kandahar. Indo-Iranian authors of the Vedas travelled this road, as did Alexander the Great, Arab armies proselytizing for Islam, Iranian conqueror Nadir Shah Afshar and later the British. Behind the garden, a rocky headland—Sher Darwaza, the Lion's Gate—guards a narrow gorge through which the Kabul River flows down to the city's western gates. From Old Kabul, roads fan out to India. Few places in the world have witnessed so much history.

Babur was raised in the town of Andijan, in today's Uzbekistan. At the age of twelve, in the year 1495, he became ruler of the fertile Fergana Valley, when his father, the incumbent, fell to his death from a dovecote. Pugnacious uncles gave the adolescent Babur no peace. Eventually, he lost both Fergana and the Silk Road city of Samarkand. At twenty-one, weary and landless, he crossed the Hindu Kush with a handful of loyal retainers. After becoming inspired by a sighting of Canopus in the heavens on his way down the Ghorband Valley, he reclaimed Kabul's citadel from a usurper. Padshah Babur, as he now called himself, would remain prince of Kabul until his death in 1531.

With a mother descended from Genghis Khan and his father a great-great-grandson of Tamerlane, founder of Central Asia's fourteenth-century Timurid Empire, Babur was no pretender to Kabul's throne. His love of the city was genuine. At his own request, his remains would be reburied in Babur's Garden by his son, the emperor Humayun—himself born in Kabul's citadel. Though Babur's Mughal Empire expired 150 years ago, his final resting spot persists as a symbol of Afghanistan's recurring place at the heart of Asia.

———

From the earliest days of human settlement, the plains and valleys of what is now Afghanistan teemed with Stone Age settlements. Animals were domesticated on the northern pastures of the Hindu Kush in the early Neolithic Age. Balkh, the Mother of Cities, is reckoned to be among the world's oldest outside the Fertile Crescent.

Over the millennia, this land came under the influence of different faiths and empires. The two-and-a-half-millennium-old Avesta, Zoroastrianism's sacred book, mentions nine different Afghan provinces, from Balkh in the north to Kandahar in the south. According to the Achaemenid inscriptions at Behistun in modern-day Iran, six satrapies comprising today's Afghanistan accounted for a third of Darius's Persian Empire. Greco-Bactrian and Kushan dynasties launched the modern Silk Road through Afghan soil, joining the Mediterranean with the Pacific, transmitting Judaism and Christianity eastward, Buddhism northward and Islam in both directions. After the decline of the Abbasid caliphate in Baghdad, the arts and sciences flourished in Afghanistan under the Samanid and Ghaznavid empires.

Then, as now, Afghanistan often bore witness to tragedy and cataclysm. In 1149, Ghorid ruler Alauddin Jahansuz—known as the World Burner—put Ghazni to the torch: the Afghan city and its treasures burned for seven days and seven nights. In the thirteenth century, the country became a battleground for Genghis Khan. In 1381, the conqueror Tamerlane, Babur's great-great-grandfather, slaughtered the population of Herat in what is now western Afghanistan.

This was Babur's legacy as his Mughal Empire took shape in the sixteenth century. His reign was steeped in traditions that combined Mongol, Turkic and ancient influences. Like Tamerlane, he practised the Turkic code of tribute and taxation known as *yasaq*, alongside Islamic sharia law. Babur was determined to live up to the ideals encoded in the *Shahnameh*, the epic Persian poem written by Ferdowsi at Ghazni in AD 1000—as well as by poets such as Sanai, Attar, Jami and Nawai, who, like Babur himself, wrote in Chagatai, a Turkic language. In taking the conqueror's path south and east to Hindustan—Lahore, Delhi and the rest of India—he was following in the footsteps of Alexander the Great.

As Babur took power in Kabul, a major new power was rising to his west, where Shah Ismail had brought most of Persia under his sway. For the next two centuries, the frontiers of two new empires—Babur's Mughal dynasty and Persia's Safavid—met along a north–south axis through the Hindu Kush. The Mughal emperors who succeeded Babur—Humayun, Akbar, Jehangir, Shah Jahan and Aurangzeb— would visit Kabul from their centre of power in India, anxious over- lords retaining their Afghan dominions only with difficulty.

Much like Britain and Russia during the Great Game centuries later, Safavid Persia and Mughal India vied over two centuries for power around the Hindu Kush. The rivalry played out on many battlefields, nowhere more spectacularly than at Kandahar, which, at one point, changed hands eight times in the space of just one and a half centuries.

It was at the beginning of the eighteenth century, with both empires weakened and the region's once-scattered tribes becoming an increas- ingly cohesive force, that the idea of a distinct Afghan state began to emerge. The predominant Pashtuns—who spoke the Pashto language and practised the ancient societal tribal code of Pashtunwali—had played major roles under both Mughals and Safavids. With the rise of the Hotaki dynasty, and then the Durrani Empire in 1747 under Ahmed Shah Durrani, these Pashtun tribes became sovereigns in their own land of an empire stretching from Delhi to Isfahan.

From the beginning, the emerging nation of Afghanistan was fraught with many of the same problems that vex the country to this day, including incessant squabbling among various regional power brokers, doctrinal conflict between the Sunni and Shiite branches of Islam, and the mismatch between Afghanistan's borders and the lands historically controlled by Pashtun tribes. The first decades of the nineteenth century comprised a particularly chaotic stretch of revolts, invasions, restorations and bloody family feuds—ending only in 1843, when the amir of Afghanistan, Dost Mohammad Khan, consolidated power and systematically tamed most of the provinces of modern-day Afghanistan.

Despite his success, Dost Mohammad was forced to confront a growing problem: the rise of Western influence and colonial meddling in the region. His relations with Britain and its East India Company improved steadily, but the price was an erosion in Afghanistan's sphere of influence. There was no Afghan resistance to Charles Napier's conquest of Sind in 1843. When the British formally annexed the Punjab in 1849—including Peshawar, a centre of Pashtun intellectual life that is now the modern-day capital of one of Pakistan's four provinces—the amir looked the other way. Afghanistan had lost its footing in India, with consequences that persist into our own time.

By the middle of the nineteenth century, the Afghan state had become dependent on British largesse. When the Persians reoccupied Herat in 1856, Delhi concluded an Anglo-Afghan Treaty of Friendship, providing for a subsidy and steady weapons supply. As in the 1840s, this came with a price. When the Indian Mutiny struck in 1857, Dost Mohammad resisted pressure to retake Peshawar and adjoining areas, a decision that would leave Pashtuns divided between Afghanistan and Muslim India to this day. As the last quarter of the nineteenth century opened, British India had annexed and absorbed virtually all the territories making up today's Pakistan.

Thanks to Russian advances in the north, the alliance between Afghanistan and England eventually broke down. When a Russian envoy arrived at Kabul in 1878 and a British force was refused entry, a new Anglo-Afghan war began. British forces reached Kabul by January 1879, and the Afghan leader, Sher Ali Khan, fled northward, dying later in the northern Afghan city of Mazar-e-Sharif. The British then signed an agreement (grandly titled the Treaty of Eternal Peace and Friendship) with Sher Ali's son Yaqub Khan, under which Afghanistan surrendered control over its foreign relations in return for the traditional subsidy and support against invasion.

The new alliance was short-lived. After little more than a month in the country, the British representative to Kabul (the wonderfully named Pierre Louis Napoleon Cavagnari) was killed by a mob. The country was thrust into chaos until power was consolidated under Amir Abdurrahman Khan, a grandson of Dost Mohammad Khan, who would go on to rule the country for two decades, putting down numerous rebellions in the process. Under his rule, Afghanistan's modern borders took their recognized shape, with the creation of the so-called Durand Line (demarcated by Sir Mortimer Durand in 1893) to the south and east, and the Amu River as the northern border, separating Afghanistan from the Russian sphere of Central Asia (what is now Uzbekistan, Tajikistan and Turkmenistan).

In 1907, the Great Game formally ended with the conclusion of an Anglo-Russian convention. London's long-standing Frontier and Forward Policies had finally been vindicated: a century of British manoeuvring had succeeded in keeping Russia and other foreign powers on the far side of the Hindu Kush, away from India, and had permitted the development of an increasingly stable indigenous Afghan monarchy.

But the Forward Policy also had created a reservoir of anti-Western resentment among many Afghans, who bristled under Britain's quasi-colonial yoke. Not until 1919 was Afghanistan permitted to control its own foreign policy. Even into the 1930s, Britain continued to meddle in the country's affairs.

———

As India underwent partition in 1947, Afghan grievances found a new outlet in Pakistan. Kabul wanted Pakistan's North West Frontier province to have the option to join Afghanistan. When this proposal was rejected, Afghanistan became the only country to vote against Pakistan's membership in the United Nations. In 1949, a loya jirga—Pashto for "grand assembly"—in Kabul endorsed the idea of a united "Pashtunistan," a Pashtun homeland that would comprise Pashtun tribal areas on both sides of the Durand Line. In 1961, Afghan prime minister Mohammad Daoud Khan went so far as to send soldiers across the border—a force that was promptly defeated by Pakistan.

The ensuing diplomatic crisis and economic blockade crippled Afghanistan's economy, and Daoud was removed from office. Increasingly isolated, Afghanistan was denied US military support and was excluded from regional trade and diplomatic organizations. Turning to Moscow was Kabul's only option, and Soviet influence began to grow markedly.

But the Russians weren't alone. Just as it had jousted with Britain for control of the country throughout most of the nineteenth century, Moscow now found itself competing against a nascent jihadist movement supported from Pakistan. When Mohammad Daoud Khan returned to power in 1973, transforming Afghanistan from a monarchy into a republic, Pakistan was already pursuing its own version of Britain's Forward Policy, backing regional Afghan warlords fomenting armed rebellions against Daoud's regime. Pakistan's military establishment, endlessly fixated on the Indian threat to the east, saw Afghanistan, to the northwest, as a source of strategic depth, both a citadel in case of attack and a gateway to the hinterland of Central Asia. Pakistan's goal was to prevent Indian influence in Afghanistan at all costs. Thus was born the monster that, eventually, would blow back across the border to threaten Pakistan itself.

During the anti-Soviet jihad in Afghanistan—prosecuted mainly by the Inter-Services Intelligence (ISI), the Pakistani equivalent of the CIA—"strategic depth" was Pakistan's guiding doctrine. The country's leaders believed that Russia's invasion of Afghanistan was ultimately doomed to failure (just as they now have similar doubts about the current American-led campaign). By supporting the Islamist mujahidin fighting the USSR, Pakistan's generals believed they could dictate Afghanistan's future following the Soviets' departure and thereby keep India out.

When Mikhail Gorbachev announced in early 1988 that Soviet forces would withdraw from Afghanistan, Pakistan was confident it had won the battle for Kabul. Though it would take several more years of warfare, most of Afghanistan eventually would be conquered by jihadi warriors trained and indoctrinated in Pakistan.

On April 17, 1992, as the mujahidin were at the gates of Kabul, ready to deliver the knockout blow to the pro-Soviet regime that had clung to power following the Soviets' departure, a dark limousine pulled into the main UN compound. A burly man stepped out with his brother, wife, two children, a close advisor and bodyguards. The man and his family had been turned back on their way to the airport en route to India. He already had stepped down as leader of the country's ruling party. Now, he was a prisoner in his own country.

The man was Dr. Mohammad Najibullah, president of Afghanistan since 1986. He would remain a guest at these UN buildings for four years and five months, until finally being killed by the Taliban in 1996. (His body was hung from a traffic police guard post, a perfect symbol of the Taliban's medieval approach to law and order.) Najib's fragile regime had been fatally undermined by the economic collapse caused by the Soviet Union's dissolution over New Year's 1991. Subsidies to Afghanistan, including fuel, had evaporated overnight. The army and air force couldn't continue operating. Najib's best officers began to switch sides. Afghanistan was broke, desperate and sliding into its pre-9/11 status as a rogue haven for al Qaeda.

In one of his last interviews, to the *New York Times* in March 1992, the former Afghan president declared: "We have a common task, Afghanistan, the United States of America, and the civilized world, to launch a joint struggle against fundamentalism. . . . If fundamentalism comes to Afghanistan, war will continue for many more years . . . Afghanistan will turn into a centre of world smuggling for narcotic drugs. Afghanistan will be turned into a centre for terrorism." Prescient words—but no one was listening. The attention of the international community was focused elsewhere—on the breakup of the Soviet empire, on unifying Europe and on preventing new conflicts in the Balkans. Few cared about Afghanistan, or even militant Islam, and the idea that the United States would be fighting a war in this obscure part of the world within a decade's time was unthinkable.

———•———

As the Americans and so many others have learned in recent decades, the crux of Afghanistan's instability is its eastern border with Pakistan, which many Afghans regard as provisional until the creation of a united Pashtunistan and which many Pakistanis regard simply as meaningless, given the imperatives of strategic depth, a doctrine borne of rivalry with India. As the indirect authors of the jihadis' victory over the Soviet Union, Pakistan's generals thought they had earned the right to call the shots at Kabul. Many still do—echoing the same arrogance exhibited by the British who helped Afghanistan fight off Russian influence during the Great Game.

The principal difference between the two eras is that, thanks to the march of technology, the terrorist threat is now global. For the first time in Afghan history, the whole world—not just the neighbours—has a critical stake in the country's internal conflicts. And increasingly, the leaders whose countries are most engaged are realizing that their main obstacle to victory lies across the border, in Pakistan.

It is ordinary Afghans who have paid the highest price for this continuing violence—not only with their lives and livelihoods but with the erosion of their country's rich heritage and history, only a tiny fraction of which I have described in this introduction. Until they were ousted in 2001, the Taliban worked hard to obliterate the pre-Islamic and dynastic history of Afghanistan, including, most famously, the giant Buddhas of Bamiyan. It is a miracle that such treasures as Babur's Garden survived at all.

Afghanistan's surviving literature and artifacts are important because they remind us that the country is hardly a primitive backwater. For much of its history, it was the seat of empires and high culture. Long before al Qaeda sought to pervert the Muslim faith in this region, Afghan scholars and poets were leading lights of the Islamic world. Afghanistan was one of the first Islamic states to have a written constitution. It was one of the first members of the League of Nations and the United Nations. It remains a country of enormous creative potential, one with justified pride in its history and achievements.

I dedicated much of my professional life to serving in Afghanistan because I truly do believe it can reclaim a glorious and civilized past. This book is dedicated to the same premise.

PART ONE
TREADING LIGHTLY

Equip man with a sword, remove his infirmities,
and see what he will be: a brave knight or a devious thief?

—Rumi, *The Mathnawi*

CHAPTER ONE

PRICE OF ENTRY

*Put out a fire today while you can, for when
it blazes high it will burn the world.*

—*The Baburnama*

For Americans, the 9/11 attacks began when Mohamed Atta took the controls of American Airlines Flight 11 and flew it into the North Tower of the World Trade Center. But al Qaeda's autumn terrorist offensive actually began two days earlier, in the furthest place imaginable from New York's financial district: a remote militia headquarters deep in northeastern Afghan. What happened there on 9/9 would fundamentally alter the balance of power in Afghanistan on the eve of the subsequent American invasion.

One of the few surviving witnesses to the event was Afghan poet-turned-diplomat Masood Khalili. In 2010, eight years later, I learned his story as the two of us shared a car trip through central Turkey en route to the shrine of the great Sufi poet Jalal ud-Dīn Balkhi, or Rumi.

It was early September 2001 when he'd got the call on his satellite phone, Khalili told me. He was in Delhi, working as an ambassador for the shadow government of Afghanistan's Northern Alliance, which by that time was the only serious force still fighting the Taliban and its al Qaeda allies. The caller summoned him to Khwaja Bahauddin, in Afghanistan's Takhar province, near the Tajikistan border, to discuss the Northern Alliance's increasingly difficult campaign.

The news that Khalili received there wasn't good. Foreign fighters were swelling Taliban ranks. No longer a mere circle of fanatics, Osama bin Laden's organization had become part of Afghanistan's power structure—a missionary force to export jihad to neighbouring countries. Why was the West doing nothing? Khalili wondered. How could the Northern Alliance make the world understand Afghanistan's plight? Then Khalili and his hosts spoke of more banal things, grousing about money as they ate chocolate.

The next morning, a tray containing a breakfast of grapes and Nescafé was waiting for Khalili. After his meal, he learned there were new visitors at the compound. Two Arabs had arrived—journalists, they said—to interview Ahmad Shah Massoud, the legendary anti-Soviet mujahidin leader who now served as military commander of the Northern Alliance. Such outsiders did not come often.

It was a rare opportunity for Massoud to argue his case to the world.

"For whom do you work?" Khalili asked the Arab men. "A newspaper?"

"We belong to Islamic organizations based in London, France—all over the world," one replied vaguely.

Islamic organizations . . . Khalili laughed at the euphemism. "They belong to the other side," he whispered to his host. Nevertheless, Massoud went ahead with the interview.

Khalili and a group of others sat down to watch as one of the Arab visitors, a giant of a man, set up a camera. Then his partner, a smaller Tunisian, leaned in close to Massoud and began methodically asking questions in Arabic.

Most of these questions concerned bin Laden. "Why did you say in Paris that Osama bin Laden was not a Muslim?" "Why did you say that he was a terrorist?" "What is moderate Islam?" "Why have you not joined the Taliban?" And so on. The burly Arab cameraman rolled his tape as his partner put his questions to Massoud.

Then, suddenly, a question in English, a language Massoud did not understand: "What is the situation of Islam in Afghanistan?" Khalili began to translate the words for Massoud's benefit. He remembers that it was precisely when he got to the Dari word for "situation"—*waza*—that a bright light flared.

The whoosh of the blast filled the air. The room was burning. A vest of explosives had ripped the interviewer into three parts. The second Arab, the cameraman, tried to flee but was caught. Khalili was heavily sprayed by the rain of shrapnel. One fragment, he remembers, seemed aimed at his heart but was blunted by the passport Massoud had earlier slipped into his breast pocket.

But Ahmad Shah Massoud, the bomb's intended target, was dead. So, it seemed, was the fragile Northern Alliance movement that this legendary warrior—the Lion of Panjshir—held together by force of fear and personality. For a few weeks, at least, until the Americans arrived, the Taliban would have Afghanistan all to themselves.

Massoud's multi-ethnic Northern Alliance had represented Afghanistan's last hope for a decent and moderate government. After his death, one of his commanders, Mohammad Qasim Fahim, took charge. But all expected the Taliban to exploit the transition with a final military offensive into the small rump of northeastern Afghanistan still controlled by Northern Alliance forces.

Across the border, in Pakistan, there was rejoicing. For years, Massoud had been the main thorn in the Taliban's side—he was a man with friends in India and Iran, even Russia and the United States. Now he was gone.

Then, two days later, came 9/11—a tragedy for America but a potential deliverance for Afghanistan. At least 2,669 American citizens perished, as did 329 foreign nationals from fifty-three countries. By 3:30 p.m. that same day, President George W. Bush was satisfied al Qaeda was behind the attacks. In his evening TV address, he pledged to "find those responsible and bring them to justice." Crucially, he said the United States would "make no distinction between the terrorists who committed these acts and those who harbour them."

The next day, the United Nations Security Council condemned the attacks as a "threat to international peace and security." NATO invoked Article 5 of the North Atlantic Treaty—deeming 9/11 to be an attack against all its members. With the eyes of the world on al Qaeda's base of operations in Central Asia, no one could ignore Afghanistan any longer.

The Pentagon had no off-the-shelf plan for war in Afghanistan. But Washington had been in touch with Massoud since 1996, modestly supporting his anti-Taliban United Front since 1998, mostly in the service of its half-hearted campaign to capture or kill bin Laden. On September 14, the CIA ordered operatives to the Panjshir Valley to partner with their Northern Alliance contacts against the Taliban. The first CIA team, code-named Jawbreaker, landed on September 26, armed not only with guns but also with stacks of cash for Fahim and his lieutenants.

Two weeks later, air strikes began, and the enemy's morale began to slacken. By November 11, just two months after the 9/11 attacks, the Taliban and al Qaeda were abandoning Kabul, withdrawing east toward Jalalabad. The first US personnel entered the Afghan capital the next day.

All at once, Kabul sprang back to life. Despite dead bodies in the streets and a few cases of lynching, there was no looting. The atmosphere was one of liberation. Commerce resumed, with music CDs, videos and other once-banned consumer items flowing into the city. Northern Alliance forces took up policing functions, as well as the levers of political power. Some American officials worried that Fahim's men, a force dominated by Uzbeks, Tajiks and other minorities, would alienate the majority Pashtun population. Yet there was little protest on the ground: events were moving too quickly for any coherent opposition to form. In any case, the rule of the Northern Alliance was to be temporary. An international conference would decide permanent power-sharing arrangements. Already the name of Hamid Karzai, a prominent Pashtun militia leader who'd been operating across the Pakistani border, in Quetta, was being put forward as a potential leader.

On November 13, the UN negotiator for Afghanistan, Lakhdar Brahimi, briefed the Security Council. He called Afghanistan a collapsed and destitute state and raised the challenge of creating a legitimate Afghan government, noting the "special role" of Iran and Pakistan in stabilizing the country. Two ingredients were essential, he said: regional consensus and "a massive commitment, politically and financially, to the long-term stability of Afghanistan." He called for an interim government, followed by a transitional administration. Brahimi informed the council that a conference would be convened to bring together "a wide cross-section of Afghan parties."

The conference took place in Bonn and included twenty-eight Afghan delegates. In a dramatic gesture, Hamid Karzai addressed the meeting by satellite phone. "We are one nation, one culture; we are united and not divided," he said. "We all believe in Islam, but in an Islam of tolerance."

Expected to last five days, the conference ran to December 5—a total of nine days. The final agreement was signed by twenty-three Afghan participants, witnessed by Brahimi. It provided for an interim administration headed by Karzai, with five vice-chairmen and twenty-four members who were to function as ministers.

The next day, the Taliban began to withdraw from Kandahar city. British prime minister Tony Blair declared the Taliban regime "effectively now disintegrated." As for bin Laden, he and his entourage headed east, making a stand in an area called Tora Bora—"black dust" in the Pashto language—whose foothills contained a cave complex the young Saudi had built in the 1980s during the war against the Soviets. As bombing intensified, bin Laden was overheard giving a December 10 radio address, expressing regret that he had allowed his followers to be trapped and granting them permission to surrender. On December 12, his side proposed a ceasefire, which was rejected by the United States. But his apparent desperation was a ruse. According to the report of the US Senate Committee on Foreign Relations, on or about December 14, bin Laden was able to walk unmolested into Pakistan accompanied by trusted Saudi and Yemeni guards—the same path followed by numerous Taliban commanders. General Tommy Franks, who led the US war effort, later took responsibility for declining to send a larger contingent of Rangers to encircle the al Qaeda leader's position, having instead depended on local Afghan militia commanders.

———

With the Taliban routed, many of Afghanistan's smartest and most successful exiles began to trickle back into the country to help with the rebuilding process. One of these people was Ashraf Ghani, an ethnic Pashtun who had travelled the world as an academic and World Bank official during the 1980s and 1990s. He returned to Kabul in December 2001 and would go on to become a cabinet minister in the early years of the Karzai government. Years later, he told me in an interview that he was shocked at the post-Taliban condition of his country. "Logar province, from which I come, bore no resemblance whatever to my childhood or youth years," he told me. "I went to my village, embraced six hundred men: they were just bones." As the month wore on, the political situation became precarious. The problem, as the Americans had feared, was that the power structure that took over was a loose collection of outsiders and old-guard Northern Alliance militia commanders—men who had little grassroots connection to the country beyond their isolated power bases. "The country was made a gift to people who had been ousted and who did not have any social base," Ghani explained to me. "These people were brought in helicopters. . . . Whole provinces of Afghanistan were made gifts to them."

Ghani joined the government, first as chief advisor to the president, on February 1, 2002, then later as finance minister. At the first Afghanistan Development Forum in April, he presented his country's National Development Framework. At home, his ministry began the difficult task of trying to turn Afghanistan into a modern country.

"Paper is more powerful than the gun, if you know how to use it," he observed to me. "Monday cabinet meetings began with a report on finances—and an envelope with details for each minister. The budget began to steer policy. At first it was [just] me. By 2003, we had a team."

Abdul Salaam Rahimi, Ghani's deputy, was part of that team. Now a not-for-profit media mogul in Kabul, he remembers the period as one of institutional culture shock. "They had brought computers to the Treasury Department," he recalled to me in an interview. "People literally started breaking them because they hated them. They [had never] touched computers." In a country that had been carved up by warlords for decades, the strictures of accountable governance did not sit well with the old power brokers. "When we stopped a transaction from the Ministry of Defence, people came with armoured vehicles and big guns. They threatened to take me away from the ministry," Rahimi told me. "The Ministry of Defence was huge—big people, bad people. The Ministry of Interior was another one," he added. "Gul Agha Sherzoi [a Soviet-era mujahidin leader and governor of Kandahar] was so powerful, he was promising he would throw Ashraf Ghani out of a plane window." Fahim, who now served as defence minister, was another bully. In one case, Rahimi recalls, one of Fahim's associates stormed in and declared, "You are stopping my money. I will cut you in pieces, like meat in a butcher shop." (He later apologized.)

Amid such threats, the management team at the Finance Ministry chose its battles and phased in its reforms. In just two months, they managed to computerize the revenue and budget departments—small miracles in a country where accounts typically were unsteadily kept with ink and paper.

But at first the bureaucrats in Kabul could not at first control the provinces, where local governors, many of them Soviet-era mujahidin who'd retained their own loyal militias, would impose their own customs duties on trade in and out of their jurisdictions, remitting little or nothing to Kabul.

Eventually, however, some progress was made even on this front. With the arrival of Jilani Popal as deputy minister for customs, annual revenue climbed in three years from $200 million to over $700 million. For the first time in Afghan history, treasury and budget departments were headed by women.

Much of their work concerned institutions that just about every other country on earth takes for granted—like a unified national currency. Officials of the International Monetary Fund, the US Treasury and other Western bodies advocated a two-year process of conversion to the greenback. But Karzai's political instincts were sound on this. He knew the Afghan public wouldn't accept it. In the end, an Afghan-led plan was implemented, and four unstable currencies were unified into a newly minted Afghani. The exchange rate has remained stable ever since.

Afghanistan's first full year without the Taliban, 2002, is remembered for the new freedoms that Afghans enjoyed. But life remained difficult. Everything was in short supply, including food and basic construction materials for homes and schools. The reconstruction support pledged by the international community arrived in paltry quantities. Under a resolution passed by the Security Council in March 2002, the International Security Assistance Force (ISAF) deployed to Kabul under British major general John McColl, who had been in the country since December. His troops began to patrol Kabul, training the first local Afghan army and guard units. But scattered violence continued unabated. In several cases, US bombing attacks against suspected Taliban remnants struck innocents. An attack on a convoy carrying elders to the inauguration of President Karzai killed dozens. On February 14, Civil Aviation Minister Abdul Rahman was killed at Kabul Airport, allegedly by angry pilgrims, but more probably by a warlord he had crossed.

Amid all this, Afghanistan was taking important diplomatic and symbolic steps toward becoming a member of the community of nations. President Karzai made his first visit to the United States

and United Kingdom in January 2002. The next month, he travelled to Abu Dhabi, Tehran and Delhi. The new Afghan flag had been
raised over the presidential palace on February 5. Women's Day was
celebrated in Kabul on March 9, and a nationwide back-to-school
campaign brought 3 million children, including an unprecedented
number of girls, back into the education system at the start of the
school year on March 21. A week later, the Security Council authorized the establishment of the United Nations Assistance Mission
in Afghanistan (UNAMA), to be led by Brahimi, which would bring
together its existing political and humanitarian operations under one
structure. On April 2, Pakistani president Pervez Musharraf arrived
in Kabul—the first visit by a Pakistani leader since Nawaz Sharif a
decade earlier. "We have also vowed that we will not allow each other's
countries, ever, to be used against interests of ours," he said, pledging
support for Karzai's efforts. "Our plan is his plan," Musharraf said.
In early March, elements of the US 101st Airborne and 10th Mountain
divisions, supported by soldiers from nine allied nations, undertook
Operation Anaconda against over five hundred Taliban and foreign fighters in the Shahi-Kot mountains above the Zurmat Valley
in Paktia province. Hundreds of Taliban were killed; others escaped
eastward into Pakistan. At the time, it was seen as a mere mop-up
operation. The Americans, believing the war to have been largely
won, began withdrawing units, a prelude to the invasion of Iraq a
year later.

Afghanistan's loya jirga (grand assembly) began in June 2002 under
a huge tent near the Soviet-built Polytechnical University of Kabul. It
was opened by Mohammad Zahir Shah, a unifying figure who'd served
as Afghanistan's monarch from 1933 until he was deposed and exiled
by Mohammad Daoud Khan in 1973. Such was the nostalgia for that
golden age that many of the 1,500 delegates in Kabul actually supported naming the returned eighty-seven-year-old as head of state.

Zahir Shah himself seemed oblivious, and nothing came of it, but the development threw a mild panic into the organizers.

After 6 p.m., June 11, Aziz Ahmad, head of the jirga secretariat, kissed His Majesty's hand as he alighted from his vehicle. The king walked slowly into the main tent. When he appeared before the delegates, the room burst into loud shouts of "Zahir Shah, *zindabad*!"— "Long live Zahir Shah!" There was deafening applause. The king waved his hand in the movie-star gesture he had used when visiting the Kennedy White House. He then sat down behind a microphone. "Hello?" he said. But the sound was dead, switched off to pre-empt impromptu remarks. What's more, Zahir Shah had nothing to say: the official who'd been charged with carrying the transcript of his speech had gotten delayed at the security post. Finally, the text was placed in His Majesty's frail hands. At first Zahir Shah paused, as if reviewing it for accuracy. Then he began, *"Bismillah-i rahman-i rahim . . ."* At that point, some in the audience expected him to claim the role of head of state with his own lips. Instead, His Majesty said: "I introduce Hamid Karzai as my son, I respect him, and as president of Afghanistan." The air was sucked out of the room, as if a feast had been followed by a funeral. The former king quickly concluded his remarks. He then listened politely to Karzai's speech and left. There was no applause.

———

Despite arousing little in the way of popular enthusiasm, Karzai was elected unopposed by the jirga as everyone's compromise candidate, becoming chairman of the Transitional Administration by a resounding vote. On June 19, he named his cabinet, most of whose members had been agreed to at the jirga.

But this show of political unanimity did little to shore up the country's security. On July 1, a wedding party was mistakenly hit by bombers in the Deh Rawud district of Zabul. Dozens were killed. On July 27, a seven-hour firefight erupted around the Jalalabad compound of the Arab-Canadian Khadr family, whose links to al Qaeda were well known. On August 9, a car bomb in the same city killed thirty-five. On September 5, 2002, there was an assassination attempt against President Karzai in Kandahar—Governor Gul Agha Sherzoi was injured. The same day, a huge car bomb exploded in Kabul near the Ministry of Information and Culture, killing over thirty and leaving more than a hundred injured. In informal remarks to the Security Council on October 30, Brahimi warned of an emerging alliance among al Qaeda, remaining Taliban forces and the Islamist Hezb-i Islami militia of warlord Gulbuddin Hekmatyar.

Who was supporting these forces? In a telling incident on December 29, a Pakistani border guard shot and wounded a US soldier a few hundred metres from the border in Paktika province. When the United States threatened hot pursuit, Pakistan moved additional forces to the area. Notwithstanding Musharraf's declaration of solidarity with Karzai, Pakistan's policy of exploiting Afghanistan for purposes of strategic depth was alive and well.

CHAPTER TWO

FRIEND FOR A SEASON

A man asked the Prophet, "What sort of deeds [or what qualities of]
Islam are good?" The Prophet replied, "To feed [the poor] and greet
those whom you know and those whom you do not know."

—Hadith narrated by Abdullah bin Amr, as related by
al-Bukhari

W hen I arrived in Baku in August 2003, en route from Russia to
my new posting in Afghanistan, I caught a fleeting glimpse of
a Central Asian country in the course of full-blown moderniza-
tion—the same dream we all had for Afghanistan. All around, I saw
the vast sweep of oil fields that powered much of this former Soviet
Republic's economy, the landscape illuminated by the neon glow of the
commercial districts that the nation's petrodollars had bankrolled.

At the airport, the "VIP Hall" manager was asleep, though inky coffee
appeared all the same. Travelling with me were other Afghanistan-bound
colleagues: a French counsellor for Cooperation and Cultural Affairs, a
US State Department desk officer, a French doctor-cum-photographer,
and a street-smart, Paris-based, Moscow-hardened Iranian hack (I like
to think he would take the term as a compliment). Our flight to Kabul
took off late but got us to Afghanistan quickly, lifting us over the Caspian,
Amu Darya and Hindu Kush in less than a hundred minutes.

The descent was steep into the valley that cupped Kabul. The geog-
raphy I saw out the window looked bleak. Here and there, a lattice-
work of foundations peered through the sand. It seemed a land-locked

Atlantis. Surely, no people lived here. But at 500 metres, life exploded into view: a herd of goats by a pond, a clutch of children on a roof waving. Bright print dresses were drying on bushes. Plumb lines of smoke rose out of brick kilns. As we rattled down the potholed runway, we passed the wrecked fuselages of decades-old Soviet aircraft—into another world.

With doors flung open, the dry heat of Kabul's plain rose to greet us. Canadian foreign-service officer Keith Fountain and Andrew Leslie, the ISAF deputy commander, gave me warm welcomes. Leslie (the grandson of *two* Canadian defence ministers) was also commanding the 2,500-strong battle group and brigade headquarters Canada had deployed that summer.

On the drive downtown, I was struck by the devastation. Civil war had left a royal mess. Yet amid ruined neighbourhoods, ordinary Afghans cut a vivid figure. In turbans and baggy kameezes, they had a proud, even biblical, aspect as they wrestled carts laden with propane or trudged uphill with sacks of fruit. Horns clamoured like elephants. Bustle and toil were universal. Far from being erased, the Silk Road, with roots beyond even the Old Testament, seemed on the mend.

Entering my room at the Global Guest House off Flower Street, the temporary home for embassy staff, I found two doves perched above the hall, amid ruby curtains and patchwork wall hangings—harbingers of peace, I naively hoped.

Such illusions were challenged by the early briefings I received from diplomatic colleagues. From my first meetings, UN mission head Lakhdar Brahimi made it clear he was preoccupied with two problems: the inability of member states to cough up enough forces to pacify Afghanistan's still-simmering violence, and the distraction of Iraq, which was then still monopolizing world attention.

In mid-2003—a time when Saddam Hussein still had not yet been captured—US forces in Afghanistan numbered fewer than 10,000; ISAF provided only about 7,000 more, all confined to Kabul. Apart from the United States, only Canada and Germany had substantial contingents. A score of new diplomatic missions had reopened along-side Pakistan's, which had never closed, but the assistance numbers didn't add up. Donors had not yet shown any sign of providing funding on the scale required.

In the wake of the diplomatic train wreck that had preceded the invasion of Iraq, the international consensus on Afghanistan that had underpinned the Bonn Agreement was breaking down. The day before my arrival in Kabul—August 19, 2003, which happened to be Afghanistan's Independence Day—Brahimi's UN counterpart for Iraq, the charismatic Brazilian Sergio Vieira de Mello, had been killed, along with twenty other UN staff members, in their Canal Hotel office in Baghdad. Al Qaeda in Mesopotamia had taken responsibility.

It was a tragic precursor of violence to come, in Afghanistan as much as Iraq: thanks to the Internet-facilitated globalization of jihad, the nihilistic tactics employed in the Middle East were spreading to Central Asia, triggering fresh waves of devastation.

Prior to his deployment to Afghanistan, Brahimi had reinvented UN peacekeeping, overseeing successful nation-building operations in East Timor, Kosovo and elsewhere. In the wake of 9/11, Brahimi had helped lead the UN effort to cobble together a roadmap for Afghanistan at Bonn. But there still was no coherent vision for domestic governance or economic development. Trust levels in the region were low. A comprehensive peace deal with the parties to the conflict, including the Taliban and the country's various regional warlords, many still estranged even after the Bonn conference, had not even been attempted.

By 2003, the UN was engaged in a difficult balancing act: indulging Afghan nationalism with a "light footprint" while urging donors to do and spend more in the name of nation building; calling for troops to deploy outside Kabul while refusing to lead a national police mission. The greatest threat to Afghanistan's peace—from Taliban networks regrouping across the border in Pakistan—lay beyond either US or UN control. For Brahimi, the situation was rich with dark irony: Pakistan was among the largest troop contributors to global UN peacekeeping operations. Yet it simultaneously played host to al Qaeda and the Taliban, the two groups doing more than any other to destabilize and terrorize the world.

There was an unsettling intimacy to diplomatic life in Kabul. The same set of people met constantly to discuss different problems—too often, fruitlessly.

My first days and weeks in Kabul were full of meetings with a recurring cast of Afghan ministers, NATO generals and foreign ambassadors, sometimes with President Karzai himself in attendance. The first time I had a direct conversation with him was when I formally presented my own ambassadorial credentials. My colleagues and I passed under crenellated gatehouses into Amir Abdurrahman's late-nineteenth-century Gul Khana ("Flower Palace") on a sunny day in early September. The square in front of his office was shaded with enormous plane trees—an elegant mosque presenting an island of calm in the roiling sea of Kabul's chaos. An honour guard lined the path to the palace door.

After a military band rolled unsteadily through "*O Canada*," we walked up the steps into the palace. Karzai was waiting at the top of the stairs. An old hand at protocol himself, the president unsheathed my letters with a flourish, then feigned disappointment. "Oh, you too are from Elizabeth II," he joked, pointing to the fact that my letters had formally been addressed to him by the Queen of Canada. "I already have one of those!" (It was true: my British colleague had arrived almost a year earlier.) In all my years dealing with the Afghan president, his sense of humour and courtesy, the good manners that Afghan society values so highly, never deserted him—even in his darkest moments.

Karzai's enthusiasm for his job was evident. He was warm and talkative, waxing lyrical about Canada's generosity to Afghan refugees over the previous two decades. Like many in his government, he had relatives in Toronto, Vancouver and other large North American cities. He also paid tribute to the international presence taking shape in Kabul. He referred to Afghanistan as a crossroads of civilizations, a coded riposte to Samuel Huntington's then-much-discussed theory that the Muslim and Western worlds were doomed to endure a clash of civilizations.

There was a can-do attitude about the president—an echo of the euphoria fuelled by the Taliban's fall in 2001. He was accessible and active, and made the most of his status as darling of the global media. Yet I also could detect a Potemkin-village quality to what he showed me. The machinery of Afghan government was in most areas non-existent. Beneath a veneer of competence, there was a great void within the civil service. From the palace kitchen to the furthest classrooms, millions of Afghans were doing jobs for which they were unprepared.

After meeting Karzai, I was taken to the oldest part of the Dilkusha Palace to meet His Majesty Mohammad Zahir Shah, former king of Afghanistan, who, as mentioned earlier, had returned as Baba-i-Millat, Father of the Nation. Even at eighty-eight, Zahir Shah was a picture of vitality, as handsome as he had been in photographs from President Kennedy's White House. A flame of intellect still burned brightly on his expressive face. He had been on his throne when FDR announced his New Deal. Here was a survivor, his outlook hardened by experience, but also made supple by a prediliction for Sufism.

In his conversation with me, he did not dwell on his role in Afghanistan's rebuilding, preferring to speak of my own country—in polished French, no less. During his decades in exile, he told me, he'd dreamed of living in Canada. Friends had told him it was a hunter's paradise. His son and grandson had lived in Montreal and Kingston, conveying Canada's vastness and the warmth of their welcome. But his family had insisted on settling in Rome, which is where he spent his years outside Afghanistan.

He wanted to see the country reconnect with the world on a grand scale. As we spoke, it became clear to me why this man had been so valuable as a peacemaker, bringing Afghanistan's established families into partnership with the hard-nosed Northern Alliance, all within the framework established at Bonn. Karzai owed this aging patriarch a huge debt, and still sought his advice.

A few days later, the Canadian embassy had a splashy opening. Bill Graham, then Canada's Liberal foreign minister, appeared and used the occasion to recall his first visit to Kabul, when he and a friend had driven overland from Europe through Iran in 1960—this before Canada even had opened diplomatic relations with Afghanistan. Foreign Minister Abdullah Abdullah paid tribute to Canada's commitment, noting we were among the largest donors.

Privately, Graham was devastated by the level of destruction and poverty all around us in Kabul. The Kabul Graham knew in the 1960s was a clean, modern city, with paved streets and many amenities. Canada was determined to do its part to rebuild the country to something approaching its one-time glory. Six weeks after Graham's visit, then prime minister Jean Chrétien himself made his first trip, praising President Karzai, the troops in Kabul and the new embassy with his characteristic vigour.

That fall, Canada also became the first country to make a substantial contribution to Afghanistan's coming electoral process by donating $10 million in voter-registration kits. These included printed booklets and Polaroid cameras that were used to generate a laminated photo-ID card for each eligible Afghan elector. This was important because Afghanistan then had no voters' list and no census data. Many people didn't even have reliable identity documents. The Joint Electoral Management Body, appointed during this period, had only a skeleton staff. Many doubted whether Afghanistan would hold elections at all. But we persevered, and 9.7 million Afghans eventually would be registered for the first presidential election, though no voters roll was compiled.

Canada's early focus had been on humanitarian needs, rural development and the Bonn process, including the new constitution, disarmament and elections. But the place of women in post-Taliban

Afghanistan also needed special attention. In late October, I travelled to Herat to launch Radio Sahar, a station run entirely by women, with provincial governor Ismail Khan.

He received us in the governor's mansion, hidden in a glade of pines, in his usual white robes and turban. Though he was courteous, it did not take him long to recite his list of grievances. He made it clear that he was still smarting from the wrist-slapping he had endured over customs revenues: like every other regional leader in Afghanistan, he wanted control over the tax money that originated in his jurisdiction. He did not think it the business of foreigners to pay Afghanistan's bills—even if there was no functioning state.

At the opening ceremony for the radio station, the governor urged women to know their place, and to avoid lewd spectacles such as fashion shows. Ismail Khan, who had been jailed by the Taliban for three years, was a gradualist when it came to the benefits of liberation. But I'll give the man some credit for that day. Despite political roadblocks, regular threats to staff and his own reservations, he let the station operate. In this part of the world, that counted as progress.

———

Our car was spinning counter-clockwise. We didn't know why, but in this land of roadside explosives, one always suspected the worst.

When the dust settled, we breathed a sigh of relief. With our driver blinded by a cloud of dust, an oncoming truck had glanced off our car's engine block, deflecting us onto the road's shoulder. As our Toyota Surf completed a dusty arc, bodyguards spilled out onto the rutted field. We were outside Kunduz Airport, surveying the same runways that Pakistani aircraft had used to flee—with cargo unknown—as the Taliban regime was crumbling in late 2001. The morning sun was a blotted stain to the east. It was October 25, 2003.

The Dutch ambassador and I were soon on our way again, with apologies from our Afghan hosts. We were about to witness a new beginning: a ceremony to mark the start of the first disarmament campaign in the thirty-year history of Afghanistan's conflict.

At the local buzkashi field, bleachers had been set up. Grizzled old men were formed in untidy rows, antiquated rifles at their sides. As they marched off to be inspected by their president, it was difficult not to be moved by their weather-beaten faces. These guerrilla fighters had lived to see the backs of the Taliban. They had come as they were—in striped *chapans*, drooping *patous* and mangled boots.

It had been an ordeal to get to this point. Mohammad Fahim, who'd taken over the Northern Alliance following the assassination of his boss, Ahmad Shah Massoud, had been Afghanistan's first vice-president and defence minister since June 2002. He had dragged his heels both on restructuring his ministry and on the UN-backed Disarmament, Demobilization and Reintegration (DDR) program, which had been part of the Bonn Agreement. His subordinates also were wary; no local commander had wanted to be the first to submit to the new regime.

Mohammad Daoud Daoud, the former Northern Alliance military commander who'd helped US Special Forces liberate Kunduz in November 2001 (the last major battle against the Taliban), was the first to fall in line. He was brash but presentable—and came as close to calling the shots in Afghanistan's northeast as anyone. His brother was reportedly into drugs, lending a rich irony to Daoud's subsequent appointment as deputy interior minister for counter narcotics. But whatever his failings, Daoud displayed courage by being the first to disarm after a quarter century of conflict.

The day began with three speeches. President Karzai repeated his appeal for Afghanistan to resume its status as a "crossroads of civilizations." Lakhdar Brahimi reminded Afghans of their duty to prepare the way for peace. First Deputy Defence Minister Abdul Rahim Wardak described DDR as an activity vital to securing our victory over terrorism. The weapons collected from the soldiers were packed into a small moving truck—and then confusion reigned briefly over who was to be given the key. Would the UN or the Afghan Ministry of Defence have control? The latter, it turned out.

The journalists in attendance were underwhelmed. They told me that it seemed like a token gesture, an ornamental ceremony designed to please foreigners. After all, new arms were flowing into the country. If Afghanistan was to succeed, we all realized, it would have to do so as a state in control of the weaponry within its borders. But for now, the warlords still had a virtual monopoly of violence. In the west, two bitter rivals, Ismail Khan and Amanullah Khan, had been openly jousting for power over the summer. In Maimana, near the Turkmenistan border, forces loyal to Uzbek militia leader Abdul Rashid Dostum had chased an unfriendly governor out of town, and Karzai's representative in the area was forced to seek refuge in Turkmenistan. Across the north, there were now regular skirmishes between leaders allied to Dostum and those allied to Tajik general Atta Mohammed Noor. Kandahar and Paktia too were up for grabs. In each of these cases, advantage was being pursued not only with the usual ragtag militias but with the additional leverage afforded by artillery, armoured vehicles, rocket launchers and heavy machine guns, now no longer aimed at the Taliban. This was a standing challenge to the authority of the new government. Action was needed to take the heavy weapons out of the militias' hands.

One of the first meetings dedicated to this subject took place at the British ambassador's residence, a beautiful property north of Kabul's centre. Present at the meeting were the British ambassador Ronald Nash, US charge d'affaires David Sedney, US commander Lieutenant General David Barno and the Office for Military Cooperation for Afghanistan (OMTC-A) commander, Major General Karl Eikenberry, as well as Leslie and me. The subject of the discussion had been proposed by the Canadians in ISAF: a cantonment in Kabul where heavy weapons could be stored. Our American audience was skeptical that now was the right time to proceed. But they reluctantly agreed to back the idea.

Modelled to some extent on similar experience in Bosnia, the cantonment plan began to build up steam over the next few months. In time, it would become one of the most decisive moves to switch the initiative from warlords, who had dominated the country since 1992, back to the weak but legitimate government in Kabul.

The Bonn Agreement had stipulated that "a Constitutional loya jirga shall be convened within eighteen months of the establishment of [Afghanistan's] Transitional Authority." Only a month late, it opened on December 14, 2003, under the big tent at Kabul's Polytechnical University. A draft constitution had been completed a year earlier by a group of eight officials, operating under Vice-President Nimatullah Shahrani, who then opened the document up to consultations led by a thirty-five-member commission.

Security was tight at the main event: five hundred delegates were arriving from across the country. President Karzai had asked me and a few other ambassadors for advice about who should chair the gathering. There were drawbacks to all the available candidates, I thought. The correct choice had to be someone of stature, with strong Islamic credentials, able to quote the Koran, with a capacity for leadership and persuasion, and with broad legal and political experience. I mentioned the one Karzai himself was most likely to favour: former president Hazrat Sebghatullah Mojadeddi—esteemed *mujāhid*, leader of the National Islamic Front of Afghanistan, scholar and multilingual scion of Afghanistan's leading Naqshband family—fitted the bill perfectly.

When the big tent finally opened we were met by a tide of turbans, with subtle differences in colour and style depending on who was wearing them and where they came from. There were black masses of coiled silk on Zabuli and Helmandi khans. The most notable jihadi leaders, in the front row, wore yellow-and-white fabric twisted tightly around sparkling gold skullcaps, flaunting their status as sheikhs of Islam. Hazara leaders sported more modest grey *lungi*, obscuring white caps. The northerners displayed a mix of *pakols*, *karakuls* and onion-shaped offerings in dark brown. The most splendid were the creamy yellow heaps, defying gravity—the width of a door jamb—on Zadran, Katawaz and Suleimankhel elders from Khost and Paktika. One of the few without headgear was Abdul Rashid Dostum, whose militia had jockeyed for power in the centre of Kabul and who, thanks to his most recent power plays, had almost not been included, in a vast blue and green *chapan*.

The meeting was called to order. Children sang. Then the jirga was officially opened by Father of the Nation Zahir Shah, who called the gathering a chance to establish a constitution for the future, an anchor for enduring peace and stability. He called on delegates to "set the destiny of the nation." They had a responsibility: "Work hard and faithfully," Zahir Shah enjoined. "Be flexible." Look to the "high interest of the nation." He prayed for the prosperity and high-mindedness of Afghanistan.

Pir Syed Ahmad Gilani—along with Mojadeddi, one of the country's top spiritual leaders—took the floor as interim chair, in white turban with yellow feather. He said Afghanistan was seeking a constitution "with all the ingredients for development and accountability." This would be a new path—putting aside the tragedies of two and a half decades. It would give an active role to the international community. It also would bring peace.

President Karzai began speaking in Dari, the variant of Persian spoken in Afghanistan. (Dari is one of Afghanistan's two main languages, the other being Pashto, the language of Pashtuns. Uzbek, Turkmen and many other languages are also spoken by sizeable minorities.) A constitution gave order to society, he reminded his audience. It could either open the door to prosperity and tranquility or set the stage for the opposite. Afghanistan's constitution should be based on Islam, tradition and native culture. It would be a founding law—a choice about how to live in the future. It should provide for independence of the judiciary, and for legitimate, elected, representative institutions.

Thousands of public submissions had been received by the country's constitutional commission, he noted. The draft presented took Islam as a true guide. But it also provided for an independent human rights commission and a vibrant civil society. The rights of pensioners, orphans and the disabled would be respected. And there would be an Islamic presidential system.

The president had good news to report about Afghanistan's situation: freedom of speech and of the media were a reality. The Bonn Agreement was being successfully implemented. An election law had been enacted. The rights of women were improving. Afghanistan's flag had again been raised abroad at reopened embassies. Afghans were coming home, including many of the wealthy, educated citizens who had emigrated to escape the country's violence. Within Afghanistan, the internally displaced were returning to their homes.

Afghanistan had reintroduced a stable currency. New notes had been delivered—without mishap—to the country's banks. Karzai singled out Anwar ul-Haq Ahady, governor of the country's independent Central Bank, for this success. Wages were rebounding. Foreign workers were helping to rebuild infrastructure. In 2004, 1,400 kilometres of roads would be refurbished with US assistance, including the all-important Kabul–Kandahar highway, which was almost complete. Ten million children had been vaccinated. Two new mobile phone operators were now active. Ariana, one of Afghanistan's airlines, had resumed flights. Kabul had new buses. Three thousand schools had reopened, putting 4.2 million students back at their studies, with 20 million new textbooks. Universities had absorbed 35,000 young men and women. In one year, 20,000 police had been trained, plus 2,000 for the Counter Narcotics Police of Afghanistan (CNPA).

Karzai then went on to describe Afghanistan's failings. Terrorists were returning from across the border. Forests were being illegally cut. Corruption was rampant in government. Millions of refugees remained outside the country. Then there was the drug problem. Poppy crops would "kill this country," he said, if this threat was not addressed.

In the days that followed, political consensus remained elusive. Some power brokers wanted to implement a parliamentary system so they could vote in a prime minister of their choosing. Islamists pressed for more robust mention of sharia in the national constitution. The questions of national anthem (Pashto only, or bilingual?), the definition of official languages and the question of whether to permit dual nationality for national ministers proved divisive. No one could even reach agreement on election dates.

UN envoy Lakhdar Brahimi, together with his deputy, Jean Arnault, and US special envoy Zalmay Khalilzad, brokered the wheeling and dealing, securing compromises. They shuttled among power centres, building alliances. The president's own agents on the floor of the jirga—Ashraf Ghani, Farouk Wardak, Haneef Atmar, Omar Zakhilwal and others—struggled valiantly to keep their original constitutional draft intact as much as possible.

The scheduled ten days stretched into two weeks; at New Year's, the session had still not concluded. President Karzai intervened, pressuring key jihadis and leading a large group to Wardak province for the opening of the newly rebuilt Kandahar–Kabul highway. By January 4, they had a final draft.

The result, which in Ghani's view had the support of most Pashtuns plus the entire Northern Alliance, justified all the soul-searching and brinkmanship. By making Dari, Pashto and Uzbek official languages and offering to give service in others where numbers warranted, Afghanistan had embraced pluralism, an effect strengthened by the mention of civil liberties and women's rights. Ad hoc groups had emerged to champion other principles, with Pashtun tribal elders joining northern intellectuals to promote a presidential system and southern Communists making common cause with mujahidin commanders from western Afghanistan on human rights. The jirga's outcome had been an expression of national unity. Just as important, there had been no security incidents, despite fears that disagreements might lead to civil war.

If the battle for human rights and gender equality had been advanced, freedom of religion had not. There were 150 signatures gathered in favour of a secular republic—hardly enough to derail the christening of the Islamic Republic of Afghanistan. Article 2 of the 1964 constitution, which allowed non-Muslims to perform their rites "within the limits determined by laws for public decency and public peace," had not been carried over, and so the document contained no explicit protection for Christians, Hindus, Sikhs and other religious minorities, whose numbers were minimal. After thirty years of jihad, beginning with the war against the Soviet occupation, this result was virtually inevitable. In Ghani's verdict, "We were lucky to be getting away with this. If you confronted Islam head on, you lost."

Pakistani prime minister Zafarullah Khan Jamali was the first senior visitor to Kabul after the jirga. His country's civilian government had applauded Afghanistan's new constitution as an achievement of historic proportions. Sporadic attacks, many claimed by the Taliban, had continued in the south and southeast, as well as in Pakistan's adjoining tribal areas. But the insurgency had gone relatively quiet over the winter, particularly during the jirga itself. People still then believed that Pakistan would do its part to bring peace to Afghanistan.

———

By early February, there was concern that voter registration was not progressing quickly enough. As President Karzai manoeuvred for support in the forthcoming elections, he faced pressure to find sinecures, or even positions of genuine responsibility, for some of Afghanistan's violent protagonists. Dostum, for instance, lobbied for the ceremonial position of chief of staff to the commander-in-chief; after feigning indignation, Karzai granted it. Amrullah Saleh, who had been Massoud's Northern Alliance liaison with several countries, became director of the National Directorate of Security.

One afternoon, I climbed to the Bala Hissar, Kabul's ancient hilltop citadel, with British ambassador Rosalind Marsden. We had come to press the case for disarmament and heavy-weapons cantonment with the commander of the 55th Division, a storied unit. Three of Marsden's predecessors—Burnes, McNaughton and Cavagnari—had been killed within sight of our perch. We looked out over the smoggy cityscape. Landmarks to violence were everywhere. But we remained confident about prospects for more progress on the Bonn agenda.

The 55th Division had apparently done its bit in the national weapons purge, or so we were told. But looking down from the high ground, we saw several tarpaulins hiding familiar bulky shapes. On closer inspection, it turned out the division had seen fit to hold some heavy artillery "in reserve"—just in case. It would take until autumn 2004 for heavy-weapons cantonment to be more or less complete across the country. In the end, well over 10,000 tanks, armoured personnel carriers, rocket launchers and heavy guns came under government control, the largest such program ever overseen by the United Nations.

———

The incoming ISAF commander, Canadian lieutenant general Rick Hillier, would assume leadership on February 7, 2004. He invited me to join him on a trip to Pakistan before his arrival in Kabul. It would be the first time either of us had visited Pakistan. Our plan was to tour the border areas and be briefed by Pakistani commanders on their efforts to support security operations in Afghanistan. It was an eye-opening experience, though not in the way our Pakistani hosts intended.

We arrived on the eve of Kashmir Solidarity Day, February 5, when downtown Islamabad, along Jinnah Avenue up to the presidential palace, was festooned with banners reading "Moral Support to Kashmir's Struggle Is Everyone's Duty," "Indian Brutalities in Kashmir Must Stop," "India Must Quit Kashmir" and "Implement UN Resolutions on Kashmir." From the start, Pakistan's perennial wellspring of anxiety was on full display.

The Pakistan Army then took us on a helicopter tour of the Federally Administered Tribal Areas (FATA)—the isolated, unforgiving region of northwest Pakistan abutting Afghanistan that was still beyond the rule of law prevailing in settled areas. To this day, the area is subject to an antiquated Frontier Crimes Regulation and remains a principal hub for al Qaeda and Taliban operations.

We set out in a Russian-made Mi-18 from a government helipad. Our first destination was Mohmand Agency, north of Peshawar. This small territory, whose tribal population was closely linked to roughly an equal number of Mohmands living in Afghanistan's Nangarhar area, began at the plateau above the Kabul River. From this vantage point we could see both the Kunar and the Kabul rivers shining brightly. The Nawa Pass—Alexander's crossing point into India in 327 BC—was now marked with a Pakistan Army post. We also passed the Ghirsal Pass, not far from the position known as Churchill's Picket, the name dating from the British leader's time with the Malakand Field Force.

After receiving a briefing from 11 Corps, we overnighted in the city of Peshawar itself, a jihadi entrepôt that nonetheless had become rich by comparison with Kabul in 2003. Then, as now, the city was a staging area for Pakistani meddling in Afghanistan: as far back as the 1970s, Peshawar's Bala Hissar had been the site of Pakistan army training for Afghan Islamists.

We then flew south over red clay country, crossing a saddle of land near the town of Darra Adam Khel, famed for its arms bazaar, before reaching the town of Hangu. As the terrain turned mountainous, we surveyed forbidding peaks transformed into fortresses. At Bannu, a one-time British base, we stopped at Pakistan's 116 Brigade headquarters to pick up its commander, Brigadier General Shaukat.

A bluff and affable leader, Shaukat was clearly the master of all he surveyed. As we lifted back up and over the fertile and densely populated valley east of Bannu, we headed down-country into Waziristan, a land of castle keeps, with a large, cloistered population hemmed in by vast, achingly arid deserts. Trees were scarce. Houses as massive as small forts were perched at improbable angles on steep slopes. We passed over Razmak, where the 2nd Indian Army Brigade had been stationed before partition. As recently as 2003, there had been only one Pakistani brigade for all Waziristan; now there were two—one in North Waziristan, one in South Waziristan. Together, the two agencies were nearly half the size of Belgium.

As we moved from north to south, metal roofs appeared below us. Our pilots and flight staff chattered continuously into their radios. They were dressed in US flight aviators' uniforms and Tasco ear protectors labelled as originating from East Providence, Rhode Island. As we passed over the town of Wana, situated in the large valley of the same name, enormous four-walled compounds came into view. This was a town literally surrounded by castles. Near a paved road, nomads had camped. Horses ran into their shelters as our helicopter passed.

Originally from Swat, Brigadier Shaukat had been assigned to Waziristan for a year and a half. His tasks were to control entry and exit, to conduct cordon and search operations against infiltrators, to open inaccessible areas and to facilitate development. His forces were now engaged in Operation Mizan, securing lines of communication between major population centres.

Despite US pressure to create "blocking positions" to prevent al Qaeda and Taliban infiltration into Afghanistan, the border with Afghanistan remained porous, he conceded. The South Waziristan Scouts, the unit furnishing many of his detachments, were under his command for military tasks but not for police or anti-smuggling operations. Violence was a constant, if sporadic, presence. On November 2, two Uzbek jihadis had been killed near Angoor Adda; eight more had died in 2002. Four soldiers were lost in a separate incident, apparently in retaliation for a previous operation in which, Shaukat said, "miscreants had been killed."

Terrorism was not "their war"—meaning Pakistan's war—Shaukat told me. The army was not mobile. They lacked night vision. "Our limitations have to be understood," he insisted. Plus, the terrorists were hard to find: since 2001, Osama bin Laden had adopted a low profile, I was told.

There was a simmering, violent quality to life in this area of Pakistan, Shaukat explained. Authorities would demolish houses in response to the killing of Shaukat's soldiers, which in turn would stir up more enmity. Even as he tried to put an upbeat face on Pakistan's campaign, it became clear that Shaukat and the men around him did not believe there was much point in risking life and limb for what they regarded as primarily a foreign cause.

We moved by helicopter westward from Wana toward the Afghan border, crossing immediately into mountains, one topped by a lone barren fortress. Opposite Shkai, a long road appeared to lead directly to Afghanistan's Paktika province. In the town of Rohan, on the border, we saw houses sprouting nests of antennae and dishes, obviously home to sophisticated tenants.

Upcountry the towers, battlements and watchtowers grew more numerous. At the end of the valley that is Waziristan's western border, the helicopter turned right. We now were situated directly opposite Afghanistan's Khost region, near the Qurbas Gate, from which waves of suicide attackers would later flow into Afghanistan. There were many relatively open crossing places into Afghanistan all across this remote region. Nearby, the Kāka Ziārat River flowed directly into Afghanistan, a sluiceway for smugglers. As our Pakistani hosts readily agreed, Durand—the Brit who'd drawn the line separating Afghanistan from Pakistan—"had been a nutter."

We followed one track, then another. At Arawali, there were again many crossings, with one conspicuously large house sitting at the border. We passed Kot-e Bayan and Kot-e Bala. The houses were huge, with the Koh-e Safed mountains glowering over them, forests yielding up above 3,000 metres to alpine meadowlands, now carpeted in snow. The panorama was dotted with more insanely situated houses on steep inclines, with Loire-style watchtowers.

It was obvious to me that the Pakistan Army was going through the motions. It had moved against some al Qaeda elements in FATA, Peshawar and elsewhere—Arabs and other foreigners whose status in Pakistan always had been an irritant. But there was much less action taken against regionally indigenous networks run by the Taliban, as

well as by the Haqqani and Hekmatyar clans. These had been Pakistan's
main proxies in the Afghan conflict for over a quarter century. The
Pakistan military did not see these groups as threats, and some commanders even regarded them as allies. In any event, they were eager
not to incur the wrath of local tribes. When I asked one lieutenant general about the performance of his corps against Taliban leadership, he
dodged the question. His operation had only one overriding purpose:
respond to US pressure to dismantle al Qaeda capacity while opening
FATA to further economic and humanitarian development.

Despite Shaukat's cool demeanour, the mood in Wana had been one
of siege. Later in 2004, the army would begin to negotiate the first
in a series of truces with terrorist networks in Waziristan that would
bring military operations there to a complete standstill. Not coinciden-
tally, this was the period when Afghanistan's insurgency was entering
a period of resurgence.

Shaukat's unit would be withdrawn from the region altogether in
2005: within a year and a half of our visit, much of the FATA had been
surrendered entirely to the very terrorist and insurgent networks that
the US-led coalition and ISAF had deployed to Afghanistan to defeat.
Whether by design or by accident, Waziristan had become the world's
leading sanctuary for global jihadis. They would soon be plotting
attacks in Europe and elsewhere, as well as launching an escalating
campaign of suicide attacks in Afghanistan, and later in Pakistan. The
areas to which the leaders of al Qaeda and the Taliban had withdrawn
in late 2001 remained off limits to military operations.

In other words, the key architects of 9/11—Osama bin Laden,
Ayman al-Zawahiri and Khalid Sheikh Mohammed—were now on the
territory of Pakistan, a country that the Bush administration would
subsequently designate a "major non-NATO ally," a status previously
accorded to Australia, Egypt, Israel and Japan, among others. It was a
chilling paradox that would return to haunt the mission in Afghanistan.

CHAPTER THREE

PALACE RULES

Kings know:
What damages their principality
Endangers all.

—Christopher Logue, *War Music*

The path led upward from Shohada-i-Saliheen, the cemetery of the pious martyrs. Children milled about, laughing. It was a crisp Kabul morning. In the cold winter air, the city's garbage had lost its odour; the breeze was sweetened by burning *sandalis*—coal-fired braziers around which families huddled at night. In the alleyway ahead, a single man tripped lightly along with a bundle.

We passed Bala Hissar, Kabul's storied fifth-century citadel, located south of central Kabul. Here, Babur styled himself *padshah*, or emperor, for the first time in 1504; his son Humayun was born inside. The building remains in use, now serving as a headquarters for Afghan military intelligence.

Continuing along our route, we passed men with henna-hued fighting dogs and climbed onto a pebble-strewn crest of rubble overlooking the city's main burial ground. Among the most famous occupants is Tamim, a companion of the Prophet Mohammed, who was reputedly killed here in 644. He is flanked by the son of Abdullah Ansari, the revered saint of Herat, whose grandsons Abdus Samad and Abdus Salaam are Kabul's patrons. Legendary singer Ahmad

Zahir, Kabul's heartthrob in the 1970s, is also buried here. It is as if all of Afghan history has been compressed into a stony hillside. The surrounding neighbourhood, Arsheqan wa Arefan, named for a shrine dedicated to lovers and poets, is a carpet of fern and olive hues.

As we climbed, the air became clearer, and we could see the dirty pillow of smoke hovering over the city below. Our ascent continued over mud-plastered masonry, a wall built by the nomadic Hephthalites fifteen centuries ago. One of Kabul's early kings, Zamburak Shah, was famously bricked into this structure: legend has it that the beautiful slave girl to whom he yielded his throne for a day had tricked him.

After passing sluggishly over a series of ruined watchtowers, we reached the top of the mountain known as Sher Darwaza, the Lion's Gate. Babur's Garden lay below, and west Kabul spread out across our field of vision—from the Charasiab district, Gulbuddin Hekmatyar's headquarters during the civil war of the early 1990s, when life was nearly choked out of the city, to Asmayi, or TV hill, standing above the sprawling campus of Kabul University.

As we progressed on our tour, the rising sun set Kabul's few glass buildings ablaze with orange fingers of light. The call of the muezzin competed with riotous horns on buses ferrying clerks to offices. To the northwest lay the town of Paghman, once a district of royal gardens, and a road bending west toward Kandahar. To the east lay the roads to Jalalabad and Lataband. An ominous sight was the panopticon of Pol-i-Charkhi, a prison and Communist-era mass-burial site where an estimated 27,000 political prisoners had been executed. Monuments to Afghanistan's suffering were never far from our route.

Nor were monuments to its glories. This valley once had been thick with poets, seers, sages and, especially, merchants. Kabul's strength, in times of prosperity, has been its caravans—travellers who set out across this ring of mountains for the emporia of India, the bazaars of Persia, the warehouses of Cathay. Kabul's commerce was the backdrop for Kipling's *Kim* (and, of more local appeal, Rabindranath Tagore's Bengali classic *Kabuliwala*). Its lifeblood was the Grand Trunk Road, India's backbone, stretching eastward from the Lahore Gate in Kabul's

Old City. Routes extended west too, to the Middle East and Africa. "In the bazaars, Egypt's caravans pass by," poet Sa'ib Tabrizi sang of Kabul in the time of the Mughal emperor Shah Jahan.

It was Amir Abdurrahman, Afghanistan's ruler during the last two decades of the nineteenth century, who created modern Kabul. Despairing of the city's desolate, ancient fortress, Bala Hissar, which had been destroyed during the Second Anglo-Afghan War, the Iron Amir began construction of the Arg presidential palace, using foreign architects. Eid Gah Mosque and its parade grounds were his grandest commission. He also built an armaments factory, a summer pavilion north of the city, a palace in Babur's Garden and the city's first prison. Kabul's most famous high school, Habibia, was named for his son, Amir Habibullah, who would succeed his father. By 1901, the year of Amir Abdurrahman's death, Kabul had a population of 150,000.

In many ways, it is still Abdurrahman's city today. Kabul's airport, parliament and other more modern additions have simply book-ended the city's original core, an old metropolis teeming with trade, opposite a presidential palace drenched in power politics. City life revolves around Abdurrahman's tomb in Zarnegar Park—adjoining the Arg, flanked by the mayor's office and the city's leading hotel, within sight of Timur Shah's Durrani-era mausoleum, itself mobbed by stalls.

Kabul's first suburb, Shahr-i-Nau, initially known as Shahabuddin Maidan to honour a Ghorid prince, was planned in 1930, extending northwest from the palace. Prime Minister Mahmud Khan punched Jade Maiwand, now Kabul's main street, through the Old City in 1949. Karte Wali and Wazir Akbar Khan, where embassies now cluster, were added north of the Arg in the 1950s and 1960s. Kabul University moved to a new campus in 1964.

By this time, Kabul had grown to 400,000. President Mohammad Daoud Khan, the man who would definitively overthrow Afghanistan's monarchy in 1973, approved a plan for the city that would accommodate a population as large as 800,000. Including adjoining areas, the Kabul metropolitan area now holds more than 3 million.

In 1992, Kabul became a central battleground in the war that, eventually, would bring the Taliban to power. After a first burst of fighting near the Ministry of Interior, the city was carved up between warlords. The Islamist Jamiat-i Islami faction dominated the north of the city, Hekmatyar's Hezb-i Islami the south. Abdul Rashid Dostum's militia controlled the airport, and all three jockeyed for power in the centre. Hezb-i Wahdat, a group founded and supported by the country's ethnic Hazara Shiite Muslim minority, was pre-eminent in the city's west, Mohammad Younis Khalis's militia in the east.

All parts of the city were hit in this chaotic battle. Casualties ran into tens of thousands. Many abandoned the city, draining the population back to 1950s levels. The marks of Jangi-ye Kabul—the "Kabul wars," as they're now called—are still everywhere. Even since the Taliban's ouster in 2001, Kabul's reconstruction has been patchy. Five mayors have come and gone; apart from a few roads, no major infrastructure has been built. Most people still lack clean water and sanitation.

As for the rule of law, much depends on whom you know. When the United Front entered Kabul on the heels of the fleeing Taliban on November 14, 2001, many drew parallels with 1929, an interregnum that was quickly succeeded by a period often described as "the rule of the brothers" in reference to the power struggles involving five great-grandsons of Sultan Muhammad Khan Telai—one of whom was the father of King Zahir Shah. Like their forebears from eight decades previous, Mohammad Fahim's forces treated Kabul as their property, taking over real estate vacated by the fleeing Taliban. Thousands of houses fell into the hands of Fahim's commanders.

Fahim, who'd become defence minister and vice-president in Afghanistan's new post-Taliban regime, supervised this process personally. In one case, a Defence Ministry property in Kabul's Sherpur area, coinciding in part with old British cantonments, was seized and subdivided. With only one or two exceptions, every government member of the rank of deputy minister or above received a parcel.

It was a sign of things to come.

As described in Chapter 1, King Zahir Shah—the man deposed and exiled by Mohammad Daoud Khan in 1973—arrived back in Kabul in mid-April 2002, having accepted the title of Baba-i-Millat, Father of the Nation. Just two months later, his wife and queen consort, Princess Humaira Begum, passed away. My first meeting with him was on the day I presented credentials as ambassador; it was the first of several chats. He had the reputation for sometimes referring to the president as "his prime minister"—in mild protest at the slights he felt he received.

At one of our meetings, His Majesty Zahir Shah met me in the same Dilkusha Palace where his father, Mohammad Nadir Shah, had been murdered in 1933 at an awards ceremony for graduating high school students. Zahir Shah's cousin Sardar Wali was at his side, confined to a wheelchair. (The two men were inseparable.) I remember that we spoke about the first coats of arms of Afghanistan's kings, dating back to ancient, pre-Islamic days: two eagles in profile. Then the swords of the medieval Ghorid dynasty had been added. Images of mosque and flags, which grace the current coat of arms, had come later.

The conversation then swung around to the current state of Afghan politics. *"Je suis sûr qu'il était un patriote,"* the king said, referring to US ambassador Khalilzad, who had played a crucial role in ensuring that a presidential system, not a renewed monarchy, emerged from the two loya jirgas. *"Il a beaucoup fait. C'est un homme capable, mais . . ."*

At this point, Sardar Wali interrupted to note the importance of state stability—the need, impressed upon everyone at Bonn, to avoid any rupture among the key participants in Afghanistan's reconstruction. *"Le roi lui-même a dit qu'il était prêt à servir son pays au titre qu'on demandait de lui,"* assured Sardar Wali. *"Il avait insisté que ce statut soit approuvé par le biais d'une loya jirga."*

Clearly, the king had concerns about Afghanistan's direction. But his cousin was keeping him on message.

But the royals were still part of the political landscape. Prince Mostapha Zahir, grandson of King Zahir Shah and director general of the National Environmental Protection Agency in President Karzai's government, took me to another palace on the outskirts of Kabul, Darulaman, the site of his birth.

Modelled on Karlsruhe in Germany and built in the 1920s by Amanullah Khan, Darulaman gave the city and its royal family a European sheen. But like many historic Kabul buildings, the castle now lies in ruins. To the north stands the aforementioned Communist gravesite, the final resting place of President Mohammad Daoud Khan following his 1978 assassination by Communists, as well as of his brother and one-time foreign minister, Mohammad Naim Khan. (Daoud's remains had been identified on the basis of dental records kept in Vienna. More than seven years after the Taliban's ouster, he was properly buried, with national pomp.)

The halls of Darulaman are laced with Taliban graffiti where they'd sat on the floor under its Baroque mouldings, plotting their attacks. In the days of the Russian occupation, the building also had been the headquarters for General Gromov's 40th Army. In the foyer, under the stairs, I found a memento of circles closed: "Moscow–Kabul. 1979–2002. We have returned." It had been written in Russian by KGB veterans of 1979 vintage who'd returned with Russian Federal Security Service (FSB) Director Nikolai Patrushev on his 2002 visit. The Russian embassy nearby was once again the largest in Kabul—but would be surpassed again by that of the United States after Barack Obama's surge.

We turned back from Darulaman toward downtown. During our drive, Prince Mostapha began on a familiar theme, Afghanistan's tortured relations with its neighbour Pakistan. As prime minister, Daoud had described the Durand Line separating the two nations as "an acrobatic of cartography—arbitrarily a line was drawn, kith and kin were divided." Mostapha and his generation understood the dangers unleashed by Daoud's policy of seeking to unify Pashtuns by gobbling up Pakistani territory. How could you on the one hand say to Pakistan that you are my friend and on the other hand stoke the fires of an imaginary Pashtunistan?

"My grandfather [Zahir Shah] told me," Mostapha recalled, "when he returned from Rome [in 2002], that after forty years on the throne [from 1933 to 1973], he was going to give the people three choices. Would you like me to continue—stay on as your king—or step down as your king, and have another king, elect that king—either from this family or from another? That was one choice. The other choice was a referendum: Do you want the continuation of the monarchy, or do you want the presidential system of government? Three choices: either I stay, or you elect another king, or you bring the monarchy peacefully to an end and declare a republic."

In the end, the republic created by the man who overthrew the monarchy in 1973, Mohammad Daoud, survived—albeit in a never-ending state of polarization and conflict. No Afghan leader since Amir Habibullah, the son of Abdurrahman who ruled Afghanistan for the first two decades of the twentieth century, had succeeded in having a stable relationship with his powerful neighbour to the east. And even he could not avoid being assassinated during a hunting trip in Laghman.

Nadir Shah, his son Zahir Shah and Daoud Khan all had been blasted out of office by rivals who thought they were too soft on Britain, and later Pakistan. Each had been found wanting by the pious martyrs. Yet over half a century, they had kept a certain balance—an achievement that had so far eluded their successors in the Arg.

CHAPTER FOUR

SECRET HEART

The "Forward Policy" has brought an increase of territory, a nearer approach to what is presumably a better frontier line and—war.

—Winston Churchill, *The Story of the Malakand Field Force*

Nowruz ("new day") is not an Islamic holiday. It originates in the Zoroastrian celebration of the vernal equinox. But when it comes to cherished traditions, old ways die hard. In Iran, where Nowruz has an ancient lineage, even the ayatollahs have not been able to stamp out its observance. In Afghanistan, the holiday remains a joyous time of special meals, seasonal treats and buzkashi, the Central Asian game that involves men on horseback manoeuvring to place the carcass of a headless goat, by hand, in a chalk circle on a dusty pitch.

In 2004, Kabul's Nowruz celebrations kicked off on March 21 under a scorching sun. Near the Old City, alongside a famous buzkashi field, well-wishers were thronging Ghazi Stadium, King Amanullah's 1923 vintage showcase, now showing its age from under a colourful new paint job. The field was dark with police, army and militia uniforms—a kaleidoscope of geometric formations whose veneer of discipline failed to hide a charming dishevelment. The band belted out marches. Horses from the eastern city of Gardez reared. Wrestlers unlimbered beside turbaned men on unicycles. There was an agricultural fair on the grounds, and the whole event had an old-fashioned carnival feel to it.

This gathering was a show of nostalgia but also an act of defiance, for it was humans, not goats, who'd met their end in this place under the Taliban. As everyone in attendance knew, Mullah Omar's men had staged public executions in Ghazi Stadium only a few years earlier, including the stoning of women.

The country's troubles never were far from people's minds. That very day in Herat, Governor Ismail Khan's son, a former minister of civil aviation, was fatally shot. By nightfall, the governor (and Tajik warlord) was screaming bloody murder, vowing revenge, imagining conspiracies against his family. (But more on that saga later.)

Karzai's Nowruz speech was poignant, though mostly off-the-cuff. Recent achievements were elevated into heroic deeds in the president's soaring rhetoric. A nation bowed by war was putting its promise—youth, athletes, farmers—on display on the stadium floor.

Afghanistan's economy was improving rapidly, Karzai could report. The private sector had roared back to life, pumping out 15 percent growth in 2003. The Iranian ports of Bandar Abbas and Charbahar were choked with goods bound for western Afghanistan. In Mazar-e-Sharif, Afghanistan's northern export hub, construction was booming. In the south, trade with Pakistan was on an upswing as eager traders in Jalalabad, Kabul and Kandahar sought to cash in on the new foreign presence and—something Karzai did not mention—a surging supply of opium. A new caste of drug barons was casting long shadows, with garish villas in Afghan cities, backed by fortunes channelled through Iran, Pakistan and Dubai.

Kabul, meanwhile, remained a city broken by war. Afghans returning from Peshawar in northwestern Pakistan, or escaping rural drought, now lived in makeshift shantytowns—patchworks of UNHCR (United Nations High Commissioner for Refugees) tarpaulins and muddy puddles. Yet even here, pink mansions and wedding halls now dotted the bombed-out landscape. As was the case everywhere in the country, the new money was coming from a combination of opium, legitimate trade and free-spending military and NGO visitors from abroad.

In the key poppy-growing areas, the narco-barons were a political force unto themselves. Some had bankrolled the Taliban's rise to power, and had stuck by Mullah Omar's lieutenants even after their ouster in 2001. All were busily translating fortunes into banks, airlines and shopping centres. Meanwhile, the non-opium nouveaux riches— whose new-found wealth was built on imports, security contracts, bottling plants and the like—mostly were old hands from the Northern Alliance or scions of well-known merchant families.

By this time, Canadian general Rick Hillier had been in command of ISAF for six weeks. The mission of his predecessor, German lieutenant general Götz Gliemeroth, had been limited to Kabul. Hillier's challenge was to expand ISAF's reach. But even in the capital, the gangs of Kabul, even those who'd nominally pledged allegiance to Karzai, were still wary of giving up their turf. In the meantime, US-led coalition forces were launching Operation Mountain Storm, a series of actions aimed at routing remaining pockets of Taliban fighters from the southern and eastern portions of Afghanistan. At the time, many believed these engagements would be mere formalities—the last nails in a Taliban casket. Few beyond the most wary Afghan observers had any premonition of the resurgent conflict to come.

In the months following Nowruz, it became clear that all was not well on the electoral front. Voter registration was off to a slow start. Population assessments were complete for only twenty of thirty-four provinces. An estimated 8 to 9 million more voters remained to be registered, including many who had not yet returned to Afghanistan from their refuges in Pakistan and Iran. With border areas already blossoming into colourful no-go zones on UN maps, Karzai, who had announced his own presidential candidacy on January 10, 2004, was not at all convinced the elections would even take place. But Washington couldn't wait: George W. Bush would be seeking re-election in November. Amid the continuing dust-up over Iraq, his campaign team wanted to show that democracy at least had been achieved in Afghanistan.

There also was a lively debate over whether to hold presidential and parliamentary elections together or separately. Zakim Shah, the new chair of the Joint Electoral Management Body, wanted to push the latter off until 2005. Karzai too counselled patience, in part for self-interested reasons. Without a legislature in place, he was in a stronger position to enact necessary reforms and control the political agenda. Most Afghan political leaders, however, believed simultaneous elections were necessary to bestow legitimacy on the country's political process.

As was often the case, it was Karzai's view that eventually prevailed. Presidential elections were set for October 9—just before fasting was to begin for the holy month of Ramadan. Parliamentary elections would not be held until September 18, 2005.

In his critical analysis of what it would take to make these two electoral projects a success, ISAF's General Hillier had identified one overriding priority: the creation of credible Afghan institutions. To achieve this goal, Hillier opened a remarkable partnership with key ministries. He and Finance Minister Ashraf Ghani, a principled reformer, would meet whenever the need arose—often late in the evening. Joined by other ministers, they would coat whiteboards with critical paths, mapping dependencies, brainstorming new forms of community mobilization, matching foreign donors with needed programs. The sessions were part rolling seminar, part policy shop and at times part command centre. Much of the early progress that Afghanistan made in the post-Taliban period was directly due to such meetings.

Ghani's vision for his country was set out in *Securing Afghanistan's Future,* a report prepared by his Finance Ministry team in early 2004. As the document noted, most of the Afghans who'd stayed home under the Taliban remained unemployed. At the other end of the socio-economic spectrum were urban professionals with English and computer skills, who were facing a "sellers' market." The government, still weak and broke, could not afford to hire these well-educated workers. High-paying NGOs and firms could compensate them well, but in so doing, took them out of the indigenous Afghan job market. Only in a few sectors were well-educated job seekers building up any semblance of an Afghan knowledge economy. The shining exception in this respect was wireless telecom, which had reached 2 million subscribers by 2004. The sector already was the country's largest employer—outside of government itself.

The roadmap Ghani and his team had laid out was ambitious. In each district, grassroots development would focus on supporting new investments in village-level rural infrastructure, including economic initiatives for women, from horticulture and animal husbandry to handicrafts. This, he hoped, would start to tip rural economies away from poppy and back into legitimate crops. Eventually, Ghani hoped, impoverished rural workers would find opportunities not only in agriculture but also in oil, gas and mining development.

At the international level, the Afghan government had little or no economic leverage with its neighbours. So the work of knitting Afghanistan's regional trade relationships back together was falling to entrepreneurs. Up to one-third of the carpet industry, displaced by the conflict to Pakistan, had returned to Kabul and its environs, spreading its cottage-industry approach through the villages of the north and northwest. Although still a pale shadow of their prosperous 1970s-era pre-war forebears, Afghan grape, raisin, pistachio and pomegranate farmers also began to take their first tentative steps back into South Asian markets.

—◆—

On March 31, 2004, representatives from sixty-five governments and international organizations met in Berlin for a donor conference. It was spring in the German metropolis, now brimming with new construction. The contrast with broken Kabul was stark. Nevertheless, Afghan officials went into the meetings with high hopes: confidential World Bank estimates pegged the anticipated new commitments at $27 billion.

German chancellor Gerhard Schröder opened the event, soberly discussing recent violence in Herat while emphasizing the fresh hopes aroused by forthcoming elections, new freedoms and the framing of a constitution. A "free and democratic Afghanistan," he said, benefited the region and all who stood against terror. The Madrid train station bombings, which had taken place just weeks earlier, were cited as a reminder of this important goal.

In his own speech, Karzai quoted Allama Iqbāl, Pakistan's national poet, who had described Asia as a body of soil and water, with Afghanistan as its heart. After reciting a list of his country's achievements since the Taliban's ouster, the Afghan president took pains to stress his nation's gratitude for the help it had received from the international community. "Not for one second do we think we would be where we are without your partnership," he told the assembled dignitaries. In seven to ten years, he said, Afghanistan would be able to cover its budget from its own revenues, and stand on its own feet militarily—a prediction that is still within reach, even if barely.

As he often did when addressing foreigners, Karzai emphasized the threat from drugs. The underlying problem, he explained, was one of limited economic opportunities: when an Afghan farmer destroyed his pomegranate orchard to replace it with poppy, it signified that he was truly desperate. The country could not face the drug threat alone. Eradication, destruction of drug labs, interdicting smuggling routes, providing alternatives to farmers—all this would require joint efforts.

On the question of financial transparency, Karzai told donors what they wanted to hear: Afghanistan would account for every penny of taxpayers' generosity. He would continue implementing financial reforms aggressively, vowing efficiency, clean hands, honesty and a commitment to market principles and human rights. "Our ideal," he said, "is a small government, and a big society." It was a pledge his government would fail in the end to fulfill—in spectacular style.

The principal donors next gave their verdict on the previous two and a half years. Japan's envoy on Afghanistan issues, Sadako Ogata, saluted the United Nations Assistance Mission in Afghanistan, and envoy Lakhdar Brahimi in particular. She noted that 5,500 former combatants had been disarmed and demobilized in four regions, with 4,300 already entering reintegration programs. But this was far from enough: she called on donors to make human security a reality for the country.

It was then the turn of US secretary of state Colin Powell, who emphasized the advantages of burgeoning trade, declaring that the Silk Road was bringing prosperity to the region, as it had in the distant past. He also raised his country's Afghanistan development pledge for 2004 to $2.2 billion.

British foreign secretary Jack Straw, Canada's Bill Graham, Russia's Sergey Lavrov and China's Li Zhaoxing also took the podium to make similarly upbeat statements—as did His Highness the Aga Khan, already the largest private investor in Afghanistan, and EU high representative Javier Solana.

From the steady stream of leaders who had come to address this conference, it was clear to one and all that Afghanistan's future had become a priority for the world's most powerful nations. As Solana said, no one in the room would have guessed that Afghanistan would be the source of the first attack against the NATO alliance—and no one wanted such an attack to happen again.

But for these goals to be met, everyone in the room knew, Pakistan would have to share the same goal. On this subject, Pakistani foreign minister Khurshid Kasuri had encouraging words. Afghanistan's constitutional loya jirga had been "an epoch-making event," he said. Kasuri also claimed that Pakistan "has not and will not allow its territory" to be used by any forces threatening peace. After all, Pakistan had the largest number of troops deployed of any nation—over 70,000 along its border alone. They had not yet eliminated "Taliban and al Qaeda remnants," but he described this as a realistic goal.

Of all the nations represented in Berlin, Pakistan was among the poorest and most unstable. Yet everyone in attendance took what Kasuri had to say very seriously, since building a stable and prosperous Afghanistan would be impossible unless Pakistan controlled its side of the border. Sadly, Kasuri was neither the first nor the last Pakistani politician to fail to be true to his word on this score.

Tariq Azizuddin, Pakistan's former ambassador to Afghanistan and a descendant of the region's Sadozai dynasty, knows the border between the two countries about as well as any diplomat. In 2008, he was taken hostage by the Pakistani Taliban as he travelled overland from Peshawar to Kabul. He was released a few months later, as part of a rumoured prisoner swap, and I later caught up with him in Istanbul for an interview.

When he was a teenager growing up in Pakistan, Azizuddin remembers, travelling between the two countries was safe and common: "I first went as a fifteen-year-old from Peshawar with my elder brother and two friends. There used to be a bus service [to] Kabul, called the Afghan Post Bus Service." For fifteen rupees, they got a ride to remember up the Khyber on a North American–style school bus.

As discussed earlier, the problems that later emerged were bound up with the dream of Pashtunistan, an idealized union of all Pashtun tribes on both sides of the Pakistan–Afghanistan border. Mid-1970s-era Afghan president Mohammad Daoud Khan was "the architect of that issue," Azizuddin told me—"always on the instigation of the Indians." Even as early as 1948, Afghanistan had been the only country to oppose Pakistan's membership in the United Nations: many Afghans believed there should be only one Pashtun nation, and Afghanistan was it.

Azizuddin returned to Kabul in 1992, shortly after the murder of Mohammad Najibullah, Afghanistan's last Soviet-backed president. (During the 1990s, Pakistan was the only country to keep its Kabul embassy open continuously.) In the following months, Azizuddin witnessed the destruction of the Afghan capital amid combat involving would-be dictator Gulbuddin Hekmatyar and northern military commander Ahmad Shah Massoud—two leaders who had worked together to eject the Soviets. "Afghans do not and cannot accept even a brother in a higher position; they would like to take that away from him," Azizuddin lamented, summarizing Pakistan's view of the country's pre-Taliban carnage.

It was impossible to say who bore the larger share of blame for the Afghan civil war of the early 1990s, Hekmatyar or Massoud. But one intangible had been crucial in Azizuddin's view: "Massoud suffered from an inferiority complex. He belonged to a minority community [the Tajiks] which was always playing second fiddle. . . . The Pashtun king [and] Pashtun ruling class—all were Pashtuns." On one occasion during the civil war, according to Azizuddin, Massoud had declared to Hekmatyar: "Kabul is now in our hands. For two hundred years Pashtuns have governed Afghanistan. Now we will govern for two hundred years."

But Pakistan's own policies also had been misguided, Azizuddin admitted, and helped lead to the destruction of Kabul. "My own argument with the heads of [Pakistani intelligence] was: 'You people lost focus,'" he explained to me. "'You took your eye off the ball. Your job was . . . to help the [Afghan] mujahidin secure the liberation of their country, and get the Red Army out of there. Once you were close to that, you started having strange delusions of grandeur. . . . The Soviets went anyway because they had decided "no more losses," and it was a bad experiment. But you thought you had engineered it all.'"

Pakistan had provided military support to both Massoud and Hekmatyar as far back as the 1970s. But Massoud, the northern Tajik, never really trusted Hekmatyar, the Pashtun whose support was mostly in the east and south. "Because the Pakistani trainers were either Punjabi or Pashtun, the Pashtuns used to mix freely and easily with Hekmatyar," Azizuddin told me. "And Massoud didn't know how to speak Pashto, so Massoud was feeling a little left out. . . . His bitterness toward Hekmatyar started at that time."

When Massoud became defence minister under Burhanuddin Rabbani in the Islamic State of Afghanistan that briefly emerged in 1992, his relationship with Pakistan remained strained. This fact helped make him a folk hero to non-Pashtun Afghans following the takeover of the Taliban, who were taken as Pakistani proxies—which explains how his ragtag Northern Alliance always found enough popular support to survive right up to 9/11 and the subsequent American invasion.

When Azizuddin returned to Kabul as ambassador in 2005, he noticed immediately that the tensions between Pashtuns and Tajiks remained. "The United States made the Tajiks and the Northern Alliance their closest allies," he said. "[Washington] viewed all Pashtuns as a bunch of evildoers [who] spawned the Taliban and therefore befriended the Northern Alliance. [But] the Northern Alliance was a very small minority in Afghanistan. And [giving] them the primary role in the retaking of Kabul in 2001 . . . gave them power disproportionate to their numbers. They hung on to it for dear life [even though the Pashtun] Karzai was given the presidency, because Khalilzad had said nominally you have to have a Pashtun at the top."

Of all the jaded takes on Karzai's government I'd heard, that was perhaps the most severe indictment. Here was a moderate Pakistani, no friend of Osama bin Laden or the Taliban, who considered the Karzai government of 2004 essentially a tool of the Northern Alliance. Notwithstanding all the gestures of diplomatic goodwill exchanged between Afghanistan and Pakistan, Azizuddin's attitude showed that prospects for Afghan-Pakistani trust remained dim.

But this lack of trust goes both ways, it must be said. Many Afghans, I've learned, take it for granted that Pakistan won't help stabilize Afghanistan without substantial inducements from the international community. Ghani, the finance minister at the time of the Berlin conference, told me that Pakistan's leaders would have to know that the United States and its allies were committed to Afghanistan for the long haul— twenty years was his estimate—before they'd stop playing both sides of the NATO–Taliban fence. "Pakistanis are distrustful," he told me. "Their vision of history is that they are the 'condom of the West'"—a prophylactic against the Soviets, then militant Islam. "That needs to change."

The tragedy of it, Ghani added, was that the region had the potential to become a booming trade hub. "We need to treat this Durand Line as a zone of cooperation," he told me. "We need to have the imagination to come to treat this line that divides families as a twenty-first-century border, and not as a nineteenth-century European frontier." Instead, Pakistan was continuing to use Afghanistan as a source of strategic depth in its drive to counter Indian regional dominance. Cutting deals with the Taliban and other Islamist militias was a short-sighted strategy. But at Pakistan's General Headquarters in Rawalpindi, it was all they knew how to do.

None of these sensitive cross-border issues was raised by anyone in Berlin. But on April 5, 2004, new US ambassador Zalmay Khalilzad was bold enough to observe the obvious fact that Taliban militants continued to "base, train and operate" from Pakistani territory, and he issued a warning to Islamabad: "Either they solve this problem or we will have to do it ourselves."

It was an unprecedented statement for a senior American official, repeated twice that month, and it drew a ferocious counterattack from Pakistani information minister Sheikh Rashid and Pakistan's Foreign Ministry. But the evidence was incontrovertible. On April 30, Taliban fighters in the Panjwayi district of southern Afghanistan killed Afghan army soldiers who'd been searching for the killers of a downed Australian pilot. In the melee, a Pakistani national had been captured. Across the south and east, there were similar clues about the role of Pakistani-based militants in reigniting the Afghan insurgency. This pattern of pinprick attacks would culminate in early August with a three-day assault in Khost province. The Taliban were restoring their old pathways back into the country—through Kandahar and Zabul, Paktika and Khost, Kunar and Nuristan.

What's worse, even some of Afghanistan's "loyal" warlords—the ones who were supposed to lay down their arms and submit to Karzai's central government—were still behaving dreadfully. As noted earlier, forces loyal to Uzbek militia leader Abdul Rashid Dostum had overrun the town of Maimana, near the Turkmenistan border, chasing Karzai's governor into neighbouring Turkmenistan. Two weeks later, Abdullah Shah, a notorious Hekmatyar-allied thug who'd preyed on civilians during the civil war period, was executed by firing squad. It was the first case of capital punishment under Karzai's rule, despite the president's declared moratorium on the practice.

Then there was the previously mentioned saga of Ismail Khan, the Tajik warlord known in western Afghanistan as the Lion of Herat, whose son recently had been killed in a neighbouring province. At *fateyah* prayers in Kabul for his departed child, Ismail Khan told me he would hold his enemies responsible. But the autonomy he enjoyed as "Amir of Herat" under the post-Taliban order already was crumbling, in large part because of his failure to pass on customs revenues from goods flowing in from Iran and Turkmenistan. His removal from Herat's governorship had been mooted in the palace as early as mid-2003. Now key Karzai associates, led by Interior Minister Ali Ahmad Jalali and Borders and Tribal Affairs Minister Aref Noorzai, were orchestrating a campaign to cut his support base, even as the man grieved.

By May 2004, a coordinated three-pronged offensive was under way against Ismail Khan. In Ghor province, to the east of Herat, Commander Abdul Salaam Khan took the provincial capital, Chaghcharan, from one of Ismail Khan's allies, gaining a windfall of opium in the process. To the south of Herat, meanwhile, Amanullah Khan, a Pashtun strongman from the large Noorzai tribe, moved north from Shindand district to challenge Ismail Khan's power base. In Badghis province, to the north of Herat, Mohammed Zahir Nayebzada, the commander who'd taken responsibility on behalf of his subordinates for the death of Ismail Khan's son (characterizing it as an accident), moved southward.

On May 10, Karzai visited Herat to mediate. The message to Ismail Khan was "Go peacefully now; later will be harder." But the amir wasn't quite ready to give up.

In June, the situation became more complicated when a Dutch Médecins Sans Frontières delegation was murdered in Badghis. The suspects were former allies of Dostum and Ismail Khan. By mid-August,

Amanullah's group was clashing openly south of Herat with Ismail Khan's irregular force. When the former prevailed, they moved on Herat itself but were held in check by the Afghan National Army with US support.

By now, Ismail Khan's weakness was drawing opportunists into the battle, eager for their share of the spoils. Publicly, he vowed to respect any decision made in Kabul that was consistent with the Bonn Agreement. In private, he was preparing to resist by all means.

Karzai dithered until September, trying to avoid a military confrontation with the remnants of Ismail Khan's once-powerful militia. But after Khalilzad signalled full US support for the governor's removal (along with backing from the United Kingdom, Germany and Canada), Karzai made the official decision to remove Ismail Khan as governor. The next day, September 12, his supporters attacked UN installations, the Afghan human rights commission and various NGO compounds in Herat, killing at least seven and setting fire to many buildings. No one would be prosecuted for these crimes, though it was widely believed that Ismail Khan had set these thugs loose as payback for his humiliation.

When Ismail Khan was offered the Ministry of Mines as his consolation prize, he declined—but he later said yes to the energy and water portfolio. To cushion the blow, his old associate Mohammad Khairkhwa, a recent Afghan ambassador to Teheran, was made Herat's governor.

Other warlords were proving more docile. In Kabul, Abdul Rasul Sayyaf—an Islamist mujahidin leader with reputed links to Osama bin Laden and other Arab terrorists—pledged support for Karzai's leadership. So did Karim Khalili, a leader of Afghanistan's Hazara Shiite Muslim minority. Northern Alliance veteran and Tajik leader Atta Mohammed Noor was tamed with an appointment as governor of Balkh province in north-central Afghanistan. Though Northern Alliance leader Mohammad Fahim was passed over for an expected vice-presidential slot, his commanders were shuffled into positions as police chiefs in Kandahar, Nangarhar and elsewhere. Dostum, meanwhile, became chief of staff to the commander-in-chief of the Afghan army, a sinecure held over from Soviet times.

By August 2004, preparations for elections had kicked into high gear. Security would be the biggest challenge. Of the 45,000 police needed to protect Afghanistan's polling places, only 2,000 had been trained. One thousand Russian UAZ and Japanese Toyota "jeeps" required to transport officials and materials had not yet arrived.

In September, George W. Bush was scheduled to host both Karzai and Pakistani president Pervez Musharraf in New York in a bid to ensure that Pakistan did its part to safeguard the security of Afghanistan's elections. Al Qaeda was eager for the elections to fail. On September 9, 2004, the third anniversary of Massoud's assassination, al Qaeda's second-in-command, Ayman al-Zawahiri, released a video claiming that "the defeat of America in Iraq and Afghanistan has become just a matter of time."

Even by the start of October 2004, 25,000 police had been trained, though most lacked salaries, vehicles and weapons. The fledgling Afghan National Army numbered a mere 7,200 troops. What battalions were available had been deployed to expected hotspots. Quick reaction forces were available in every major region, mostly in the form of US units backed by forces from the United Kingdom, Spain, Italy and Canada. Yet it was feared that these troops could not protect all of the terrorists' prospective targets: 113,000 staff operating 21,886 polling stations.

———

Election day, October 9, dawned quiet and cold, with many parts of Kabul shrouded in a gentle mist. In front of schools and mosques, in fields and in public squares, a great mass of humanity already had gathered in orderly lines—men and women queuing separately—for the first-ever vote for a democratically elected Afghan president.

US ambassador Khalilzad had invited Japanese ambassador Kinichi Komano and me to join him for election observation. We had a quick breakfast in the shipping containers that served as his residence. Then we hit the road, dropping in on polling centres at random. It wasn't long before our telephones began to ring: the ink used to mark voters' fingers wasn't working. Some saw it as a plot. My heart sank—some of the ink had been procured in Canada; even more came from India.

As it turned out, the main culprit was confusion. Instead of the indelible ink bottles, water-soluble black ink pens, included in the kits sent to polling stations, had mistakenly been used to mark fingers. The feared scandal never materialized. With very few exceptions, the day passed in peace. In most cases, weather conditions were excellent. Only the provinces of Baghlan and Samangan, in the northeastern part of the country, had registered low turnout.

In the end, over 8 million Afghans cast their votes, a result that even the optimists hadn't predicted. Women had participated in large numbers, even in the more dangerous south. Karzai won over 4.4 million votes, more than 55 percent of the total cast. Former Northern Alliance functionary Younis Qanuni, a Tajik, had garnered 1.3 million votes, or 16 percent of the popular vote. Mohammad Mohaqiq, a Hazara leader who'd fought the Soviets from his base in Balkh province, captured 12 percent, and Dostum got 10 percent—fewer than 1 million votes each.

The voters had fractured along ethnic lines, with the Uzbek Dostum dominating the Turkic-speaking north and northeast, Qanuni taking Tajik-dominated Badakhshan in the northeast and provinces north of Kabul, and Mohaqiq prevailing in Bamiyan and other areas with Hazara majorities. But overall, the result of the presidential vote was clear. In a field of eighteen, Karzai had won on the first ballot.

Although many had predicted Karzai's victory, the runners-up had trouble accepting it. For several days, they complained of fraud and denied the legitimacy of the announced results.

In fact, there had been some fraud in the provinces of Paktika, Kandahar and Kabul, particularly in Sayyaf's home district of Paghman, mostly in the form of ballot stuffing. Hundreds of ballot boxes were quarantined pending investigation. But fewer than 100,000 votes were deemed to have been affected, meaning that none of these shenanigans had affected the overall outcome. Despite rough-and-ready security, the election had been mostly free and fair, as most observers acknowledged.

I was one of those trying to talk sense to the defeated. Their response was irrational but intelligible in Afghan terms. The country had been run on winner-take-all principles for a generation. There was no habit or tradition of accepting defeat.

But the election also taught me that Afghanistan's traditions might be changing. In Herat, disgruntled former governor Ismail Khan had called for a boycott. Instead, the province had turned out in droves, with many voting for Karzai. Indeed, the election result helped marginalize this warlord: in the weeks before the election, pictures of Ismail Khan had been taken down across Herat; in the weeks after, nearly one hundred truckloads of his ammunition were removed from Herat's ancient Ikhtiyaruddin citadel. Ismail Khan's exclusion from the democratic process had marginalized him. Another brick had been quietly removed from the wall of conflict blocking Afghanistan's path forward.

———

In the weeks following the vote, ISAF detected a downward trend in the insurgency. In the words of British deputy commander Major General John Gilchrist, Gulbuddin Hekmatyar's Taliban-allied Hezb-i Islami was a "busted flush," and the election had been an "operational defeat" for the Taliban and al Qaeda. But everyone knew that the effect would merely be temporary unless Karzai could deliver better lives to Afghan citizens. To accomplish this, he would continue to need plenty of outside assistance. Yet despite billions of dollars in pledges made at several high-profile international conferences, the investments to date had been—in the words of European Commission representative Karl Harbo—"frighteningly small."

According to Finance Minister Ghani, only six countries had ever lifted themselves out of deep poverty at the pace Afghanistan needed.

Doing so would require a massive economic rebuilding program on a
national scale, focusing particularly on roads, energy and water management. But he also realized that Afghanistan was a decentralized country whose provinces had vastly different needs and capabilities. Five
provinces (out of thirty-four in total) were generating three-quarters of
the central government's revenues. The twelve poorest received just 1
percent of spending. The best way to move forward, he believed, was
through the Provincial Reconstruction Teams (PRTs) first established
by US forces in 2002. These PRTs contained military, police, agricultural, engineering and logistics personnel and had become a model for
development not only in Afghanistan but also in Iraq.

When he was not cutting deals with the country's many power brokers, President Karzai focused his attention on the security situation in
the south. His most urgent priorities were the expansion of the army, an
improved police force and the campaign against drugs and warlords—
none of which were going very well. Though buoyed by victory, he was
determined not to be carried away by euphoria. His country was, in
medical terms, a patient who, after recovering from life-threatening
trauma and then paralysis, still could not walk without assistance.

On October 30, 2004, three UN international staff who had worked on
the elections were kidnapped in Kabul. They were taken to the Karte
Parwan neighbourhood, then to a building in a semi-rural area on
Kabul's outskirts, and then finally to a house in western Kabul, where
they were held for nearly three weeks—under the noses of Canadian
soldiers patrolling the area.

They were overlooked for good reason. Initial reports from many
sources indicated they had been taken to Wardak province, then prepared for transfer across the border into Pakistan. This proved to be
disinformation in which an astonishing number of reputable Afghans
were complicit. When British ambassador Rosalind Marsden and I
visited *mujāhid*-turned-political boss Sayyaf to seek his assistance, he

vowed to "scour the hilltops and the riverbeds" for the victims. In fact, at that moment they had been a stone's throw away, in an area under Sayyaf's influence. Eventually, it became obvious that the abduction of the workers was fallout from the election and had been engineered by Karzai's opponents, perhaps even by Sayyaf himself.

The authorized version of the episode ascribed the abduction to a Taliban commander from Wardak province, now operating out of Peshawar, who had engaged a well-known group of Kabul criminals. But the deeper motive for this kidnapping has remained hidden. In any case, the hostages were released on November 23 after their jailors, their brains addled by a steady diet of opium, had gotten careless. Some members of the kidnapping gang were arrested. But others— Habib Istalifi and Rais Khudaidad—would go on to make names for themselves as kingpins of Kabul's post-9/11 underworld.

———

On December 7, 2004, Hamid Karzai was sworn in at the newly restored Salaam Khana—an elegant pavilion in the forecourt of the Arg, the same palace where Zahir Shah and his father had been crowned king. The ceremony was attended by foreign ministers from around the world. Zahir Shah was onstage, frail but alert, as Chief Justice Fazl Hadi Shinwari administered the oath of office. The children of Sitara Sedarat kindergarten sang, "I am prepared to die for you, Afghanistan. You are black and red and green."

Bathed in a soft light, Karzai pledged to uphold Islam, the constitution, Afghan law, independence and sovereignty, human rights, prosperity and progress. He also recounted the story of an elderly woman who had come to a polling station in Farah with two voters' cards—one for herself and one for her daughter, who was on the verge of giving birth. She had been told she could vote only for herself. Later that day, she returned with her daughter and the newborn baby.

Karzai singled out the United States, the UN, the European Union, Canada and Japan for praise, as well as "many other neighbours." Then it was the turn of girls of Rabia Balkhi High School, who sang, "I will repair you, o my homeland—with my flesh as bricks and bones as pillars. I will wash the blood away with my tears, and rebuild you with my soul." Hazrat Sebghatullah Mojadeddi, now head of Afghanistan's peace and reconciliation commission, closed with a prayer for this "poor but upstanding nation."

———

On December 24, Ashraf Ghani—seen by Western leaders as both "glue and vision" for Afghanistan's national programs—left the Finance Ministry. Jealous tongues around Karzai had spread spurious rumours of misappropriated loans. But the truth was more prosaic: with Karzai making good on all the various political deals and promises he'd made during the campaign, Ghani had little opportunity to advance any sort of reform agenda. Indeed, Karzai began to see the principled and obdurate finance minister as something of an obstacle to his own horse-trading and log-rolling.

Karzai offered Ghani any other portfolio except finance. Instead, he left government and became chancellor of Kabul University. Envoy Lakhdar Brahimi, the International Monetary Fund and a few others of us tried to explain how disastrous the consequences might be—for Afghanistan's economy, for institution building, for donor support. Our concerns were disregarded by Karzai and those around him. All at once, Afghanistan's economic reform campaign began to lose altitude.

Power now was highly concentrated in Kabul. Aside from the Taliban and its jihadi allies, all of Afghanistan's power centres were grabbing on to Karzai's coattails, just as Karzai himself began to lose his sense of direction. At the same time, many international players began to lose interest in Afghanistan, believing (falsely) that the success of the 2004 election meant the nation could stand on its own feet.

There was a "perception that we had arrived at a plateau, that people could relax," Ghani remembers. "Victory was being declared. [But] part of it was really smoke and mirrors. . . . We had created an atmosphere of hope, but the institutional transformation had not taken place. What I was telling the international community very honestly was that we had not [yet] arrived. But they were interpreting it as though I was asking for far more resources than this country deserved."

Misunderstood by the international community, beset by drugs and political intrigues, and facing a resurgent Taliban campaign based in Pakistan, Afghanistan was about to enter a period of crisis that even Ghani could not have predicted.

CHAPTER FIVE

HOME FRONT

Some people asked a Sufi master, "Which is better, courage or generosity?"
The Sufi master replied, "Those who are generous have no need for courage."

—Sadi, *The Gulistan*

Every morning, it was there: our window onto Afghanistan's past. We opened our eyes to the sight of our bedroom's carved lantern-roof ceiling, a traditional architectural feature of Bamiyan province's ancient Buddhist monasteries and temples. Such roofs had spread into Turkey and northern China, becoming one of Afghanistan's great contributions to world architecture. The people who had built our house in Kabul clearly understood their country's traditions. Though built as recently as the mid-twentieth century, the house nonetheless carried something of Kabul's ancient elegance.

The bedroom was large, covered by carpets, with heavy linen curtains shading windows on three walls. A door led into a large anteroom. Another opened onto a beautiful flagstone veranda.

From the outside, it looked like a tiny brick-and-mud bungalow. Inside, it was spacious. There were plenty of windows. But the walls were thick and imposing. It was cool in summer. In cold weather, wood-fired *bukharis*—light iron barrel stoves—kept each room warm. We also had a tiny gas stove, which, on Friday mornings, would disgorge Hedvig's homemade bread.

The kitchen had a round window, lending the view of the garden outside a nautical aspect. A large dining table stood on a tile floor; squared beams supported a mud roof. A living room ran along the back, with a study, an open hearth and two steps leading down to a round prayer room. The flat roof was on three planes, topped by a solar-heated water reservoir, our only serious bow to modern technology.

In front of the kitchen was another terrace, with chairs and table under a trellis, facing a broad lawn. A larger sister house stood opposite.

In springtime, the rich soil of our garden would erupt first with roses—some delicate, others gargantuan—then later with sunflowers tall as sweep oars. One year, we had five harvests of rocket, as well as fresh basil, rosemary and tomatoes. Our water was drawn from a sixty-metre-deep well that never failed, despite the plunge in Kabul's water table since the time the house was built. A single mature pine, with two stories of branches stripped away for firewood during leaner years, gave little shade but made the house easier for visitors to find.

Guest House 26, as the two buildings were known to the UN bureaucracy, was a microcosm of the country's broader story. Built by a prominent Kabul family in the time of Zahir Shah, the structures originally had sat on two lots separated by a wall. The owners sold them to the Sabzwari family from Herat, merchants hailing from Shindand whose name meant "green meadows." During the civil war of the 1990s, they retreated across the border to Peshawar.

Our one-storey bungalow had stood vacant throughout the Taliban period. In 2001, it had been a ruin, its roof collapsed, several walls disintegrating. Samantha Reynolds, a visionary from UN-Habitat who had helped devise the country's National Solidarity Programme, decided to restore it. She enlisted the support of Clare Lockhart, an advisor to former finance minister Ashraf Ghani. Together, they salvaged a gem.

UN staff had moved into the larger of the two buildings in 2002. Jean Arnault, a deputy head of UNAMA, was an early tenant. Hedvig had taken over the lease on the two buildings in 2005, when she was working for the UN on elections, effectively becoming landlord to the building's other occupants. Our fellow housemates would include a rotating cast of journalists, businesspeople, diplomats and NGO officials.

Jawed, our house manager, had spent all his life in Kabul. In another life, he might have been a factory owner. Instead, he managed seven Afghans who kept generators, pipes, laundry and a thousand other details humming with efficiency for the nine foreigners living in the two houses.

The three *chowkidars*, or doormen, were Shaqib and Wahed—brothers of Jawed, thin as rails, with willowy smiles—and a man named Reza. Three women cleaned house and did laundry. Meena, who worked mostly for Hedvig and me, had taken up her daughter's position when she went on maternity leave—a novelty for Kabul. Seema and Homa handled the other, larger house. Two were from Hazarajat, one from Kabul. Our gardener, the bearded Shafiq, was sturdily industrious, forever hauling hoses or fastening tender stalks with twine.

It was a cross-section of Afghan society—Tajiks, Hazaras and a lone Pashtun. But ethnic identity was beside the point: all were Kabulis and Afghans first, intensely proud of the green paradise they coaxed to more vibrant life every day. Our pride in house and city was shared.

There were hardships. A generator expired. Our pump failed at awkward moments. A two-week cold snap froze our pipes. Many locals had chronic bronchitis from the low-hanging smog, darker in winter, with its olfactory reminders of Kabul's primitive sewage and sanitation system. (Kabul was a fen of uncollected refuse: standing waste water from thousands of privies poisoned gutters, parks and living areas across the city.) When Jawed fell off a roof one day while clearing snow, the bone of his foot was initially set in Kabul. But the pain continued. Even after he was sent to India for another operation, his old gait did not return.

As ambassador of Canada, I would travel with two armoured cars and four armed guards—military police from the Canadian forces, great guys, raffish in humour, intense about their jobs. Though they were skeptical about the safety of civilian compounds such as this one, we never felt unsafe in the evening.

When I became deputy head of the UN mission, I would have a smaller security team, drawn from Romania's Protection and Guard Service, a reformed component of the infamous Communist-era Securitate. Low key but highly skilled in close protection, they were full of Vlad Dracula lore and curious about Afghanistan.

A vintage 1965 Russian Volga stood inside one of the gates, next to our house. It belonged to our housemate Mathieu Lefevre, one of the best young political officers in UNAMA. He later became our first head of office in Zabul province.

Mathieu's uncle was Richard Holbrooke, who had served as US ambassador to the UN and peacemaker for Bosnia. Holbrooke first visited Afghanistan as president of the Asia Society in spring 2006. We flew him to Herat, where we showed him Ismail Khan's old heavy weapons, now in cantonment near the airport. During his visit, Holbrooke was lectured from all sides about the cross-border dimension to the resurgent conflict, and he became concerned that the Bush White House didn't appreciate the precariousness of Afghanistan's situation.

One night, Hedvig and I hosted Holbrooke, his wife, several top ministers and a few ambassadors at our house in Kabul. The discussion was brutally frank. Amrullah Saleh, the head of the Afghan National Directorate of Security, gave his assessment about sanctuaries in Pakistan—the same presentation he had recently delivered to Musharraf. Tariq Azizuddin, then Pakistan's ambassador to Afghanistan, tried hard to defend his country's record before this well-informed audience.

Holbrooke lobbed several cats among these pigeons, gauging the quality of the Afghan civilian and security team assembled around our dining room table. On the whole, he was impressed by them all.

Most uncharacteristically, Hedvig had been on the verge of a nervous breakdown. Her beef, bought from our trusted butcher, had come out of the oven tasting (in her words) like shoe leather. But it was a fabulous evening nonetheless. Holbrooke met United States Army lieutenant general Karl Eikenberry, whom he would later propose as ambassador to Kabul, for the first time. I can recall Afghan defence minister Abdul Rahim Wardak lounging afterward on the cushions of our prayer room with Tariq, making amends for the hard-edged table talk. "You're trying to kill me," Holbrooke complained to Hedvig as she brought out her famous nut cream–meringue fragilité for dessert.

During Holbrooke's second visit to Afghanistan, in 2007, he met again over dinner with many of these Afghan ministers. This time, Holbrooke had a stern message. He warned starkly that without tougher action to root out corruption, the Afghan government would no longer be able to take US support for granted. Later, he pulled no punches in his meeting with Karzai, privately suggesting there might be other strong candidates in the next presidential election. By this point, it was clear Holbrooke would almost certainly have a role in a future post-Bush administration.

———

Though our work was serious, and at times overwhelming, there was still room for the odd celebration. On one memorable New Year's Eve— December 31, 2006—Aleem Siddique, our dapper UNAMA spokesman, dressed up as a character he called the mysterious Mullah M. On New Year's Day, with our friends Joe and Miles, we braved metre-deep snowdrifts to walk Sher Darwaza, the city wall above Old Kabul.

This path from Bala Hissar to Babur's Garden was our favourite ramble. But we would go to Qala-ye Faitullah Road to visit our friend Rahim at Nomad, the shop where he sold designer carpets and new furnishings. We would prowl through the shops of Flower Street. Or we would have brunch or dinner at L'atmosphère, a restaurant started by friends from the French consulting firm Altai, or at the Flower Street Café, started by our friends Khorshied and Timur.

We also ventured farther afield. The hills above Lake Kargha in the nearby town of Paghman, once crowned with monasteries and Buddhist shrines, offered fabulous views. Like Babur, we enjoyed picnics in Istalif above the great, green basin of Parwan, from which aircraft could be observed landing at Bagram Air Base like distant bees. With Mathieu and another UNAMA colleague, Eckart Schiewek, we walked the valleys above Deh-e Qazi, literally the "judge's village," in Nijrab district, a few hours' drive north of Kabul, where Great Game-era British envoy Alexander Burnes once had shot fowl in 1838.

On our second trip to Nijrab, we hiked up and over a steep pass rising 4,300 metres from the plain, and then found ourselves unable to reach any village by dark. Instead, we slept in a roofless sheepfold, our "10,000-star hotel," as the Romanians quipped. It was cold; we had only woollen *patous* for warmth and little to eat. Early the next morning, we resumed our march. Panjshiri sentries gave us a lukewarm welcome before knocking about our Nijrabi guide, whom they considered a traitor for helping a bunch of Westerners traipse around their backyard. But it could have been much worse. During two decades of conflict in these hills, blood had been spilled in every direction.

On a trip to Ghorband district, farther west, we walked up the long valley behind Istalif, over the ridge beyond which the Taliban had never reached even at the height of their power, then onto a narrow glacier leading deep into the Koh-i-Baba mountain range. We found unexploded cluster munitions along the way, probably from 2001. At the summit, we traversed a snowy bowl before finding our path down into the valley of Fondukistan, home to a Buddhist monastery. From well over 4,000 metres altitude, we slid down over 1,000 metres of snow on our backsides in record time. The villagers below were astonished: we were the first to make the crossing that spring.

On a typical day, we would start work shortly after 8 a.m., then finish with dinner, usually no earlier than 8 p.m. We were in the office almost every day of the week. Business continued to be done most evenings as we briefed visiting delegations, and struggled to convey what we saw and thought to headquarters and capitals around the world. But our exertions paled in comparison with those of the most capable

Afghans. Hamid Karzai, Ashraf Ghani, Haneef Atmar, Amrullah Saleh and many others simply had not taken holidays since entering office.

Every year followed the same pattern. Violence would subside in the winter months, as the "traditional fighting season" came to a close. The number of "security incidents" would decline. Local elders would be quoted saying that the Taliban had "gone home for the season"— meaning back to their families in Pakistan. Overconfident pundits, politicians and proud commanders would declare the insurgency beaten, with better times to come.

But it was never so. In the new year, we would have fresh reports of infiltration. By March, incident levels would be on an upswing. New and more potent asymmetric tactics—learned from instructors in Pakistan over the winter, involving more advanced bomb-making materials and additional techniques for avoiding detection—would be on display.

Many Afghans were stoic in the face of every danger. I can remember one tall, unsteady elder in Kabul province who pledged that he would never allow the Taliban on his soil—that he and his comrades would beat them off with wooden staves if necessary. Many such elders were true to their word. Over the years, local elders, clerics and militia leaders had learned to take matters into their own hands when possible. Their resilience would prove to be the country's greatest defence against a new downward spiral.

Against all expectations, Kabul was becoming a city of culture once again. Its Bollywood-fuelled cinemas and live theatre had reopened. The Soros-funded Foundation for Culture and Civil Society held evenings of film and music. An NGO called Turquoise Mountain sponsored poetry readings and created a contemporary-art prize to help support Afghanistan's many craftsmen. Classical Afghan singers and musicians performed at the French and Indian embassies. Many more were being trained at a new academy established by the Aga Khan Trust for Culture. Afghan writers, artists and musicians were once again in demand.

But they faced obstacles. A woman who showed too much swagger on the hit Tolo TV show *Afghan Star* was hounded by religious authorities in Herat. Visual artists were denounced by mullahs as un-Islamic. Journalists, especially hard-hitting Tolo reporters, were at risk across the board—from the Taliban, government officials and local military commanders alike. The country's Western-style media freedoms and cultural resurgence had created a backlash from traditional patriarchs. Even the country's chief justice went public with his denunciation of female news readers.

As foreigners, we were welcome almost everywhere in Kabul. Despite the enormous culture gap between the West and Afghanistan, I was almost always able to make personal connections with Afghan government officials. On one occasion, for instance, as I was led down a hallway in the Ministry of Planning—a holdover from the Soviet era—with then minister Ustad Mohaqiq, the former Hezb-i Wahdat commander trying to run an agency without either an adequate budget or qualified staff, he gripped my hand in a schoolyard gesture of trust, a sign that, despite our differences, we were on the same side. Such gestures were repeated almost everywhere.

The most important connections often were made in the palace of Zahir Shah himself. Every autumn, Karzai invited ministers and the diplomatic corps to celebrate the king's birthday under the spreading chinar trees. The palace pulsed with honour guards, tribal delegations and emergency meetings. In a city where politics often was done face to face, it was a necessary hub for many spinning wheels of activity.

But it remained a genteel world apart from the rest of Kabul. Organized crime was taking root in the city. Businessmen and their families were never safe from kidnappers. Bank robberies and shake-downs were commonplace. It was dangerous to display property, or to consume conspicuously. As in many developing countries, you had to be wary of police. (That said, the police who inhabited a ramshackle guardhouse on our own street were generally loyal, even if their wild appearance often gave the opposite impression. They held their ground during riots, and were grateful for water from our well and the small improvements we made together to their accommodation.) But Kabul's greatest liability was arguably its garbage, which clogged the landscape at every turn. After spending a day collecting it with the mayor and many others, I must admit it seemed to stretch to the horizon. In the summer heat, the stench had our organs rising into our throats over and over again.

Though I am not a Muslim, I fell in with some of the rhythms of Islamic life in Kabul. Every morning at dawn, the muezzin in our neighbourhood would wake me for a moment. It was often the small mosque in the Taimani neighbourhood that I heard first. But Sherpur Mosque in Chahar-e Ansari could also be heard from my home. During more than one Ramadan, I joined the Afghans in eating nothing from dawn until dusk for an entire month. As anyone who has fasted knows, the joy of the hour of *iftar*, the fast-breaking evening meal, is infectious. It cut across social barriers, giving meaning to our shared hunger. At Eid al-Adha, the Feast of Sacrifice, we would give meat to neighbours, some of whom lived very modestly indeed despite the relative affluence of our neighbourhood.

The mix of social classes was at times surreal. One day, Hedvig returned home after chatting with a neighbour up the street. She was shocked: the woman had just offered to give up her son Shabir to us, assuming he would have a "better fortune" as part of our lives. On the other end of the socio-economic spectrum was the country's attorney general, who had built a new office on our street with US money. To our annoyance, his security light shone directly through our windows.

On another occasion, around the time of the Danish cartoon controversy, Hedvig was engulfed by a surging crowd chanting denunciations against Danes. The taxi driver pushed her head below the seat, then headed out of town. If her nationality had been discovered, it might have been curtains for both of them. There was rioting on a small scale on regular occasions, usually in response to some alleged Western crime against Islam.

The greatest threat began with the suicide attacks in 2006. There was always the risk that colleagues one had sent on some innocent errand might find themselves at the wrong place at the wrong time. It changed our calculus for logistics and security. But it did not stop any major player from getting a job done—even after multiple attackers had literally taken the city's showcase hotel hostage for a few hours.

The Canadian embassy staff was attacked only once during my tenure, with a roadside IED on Jalalabad Road, which shredded the metal shell of their vehicle but left all occupants unharmed inside the armour that shielded them. Such vehicles were a prudent measure. But luck was often an unexpected ally. In the days after my departure as ambassador, my successor, David Sproule, had a rocket land just outside his driveway, badly injuring an Afghan guard.

It was often those who had done the most for the country who were victims of tragedy. In 2005, I spoke at a funeral ceremony for a Canadian missionary and aid worker who had died in a plane crash flying from Termez to Tashkent. In 2010, our friend Nellika Little lost her father, one of the country's most dedicated champions, in an unexplained attack in Badakhshan.

But new heroes always were popping up. Khaled Hosseini, author of *The Kite Runner*, visited Kabul courtesy of UNHCR. Tom Freston, the founder of MTV and architect of Oprah's TV empire, rekindled links he'd formed when he'd visited Afghanistan as a youth. Jude Law, bitten by the peace bug, came to visit under the UN's Peace One Day program. Angelina Jolie fetched up in Kandahar.

At times, we really did seem to be enjoying a rough semblance of peace. There were many days when the population of Kabul or Herat or Kandahar simply erupted into celebration—for Eid, Muharram (the first month of the Islamic calendar) or Nowruz. It was as if the nation were temporarily transported back in time to the days before the Soviets and the Taliban.

When I think back over all I'd experienced in the country since 2003, it becomes clear how far the city and the country have come. Imported power now hurdles the Hindu Kush. The lights now come on—albeit not everywhere, and not for the entire day. (The first power to light our home from the grid was apparently diverted our way in return for a modest bribe; a colleague later confessed there simply had been no other way to make it happen.) Living standards have risen. Roads have been paved where rutted tracks stood for years. Shops and bazaars across the city have grown out of all proportion. In the pulsing heart of the city, the warren of markets ringing Pol-i-Khishti Mosque, I've witnessed Kabul reclaiming its mercantile birthright. And I've done this not just as a diplomat but as a resident, shopper and tourist.

On Fridays, sometimes too early, a voice would rise over the slumbering streets in song. It was our mendicant *faqir*—part clown, part magician—giving his blessing to each house with a serenade. I would greet him, ask about his health and his family, then slip him a few score Afghanis in paper notes. This wandering minstrel would take his leave in a flourish of coloured ribbons and silk scarves.

His was the face of the Kabul that I lived and loved, and that so many of us have made it our mission to protect.

PART TWO
HANGING FIRE

If a great *padishah* like Sultan-Husayn, sitting in Temur Beg's stead, said merely to fortify
localities rather than to attack the enemy, what hope was left to the people?

—*The Baburnama*

CHAPTER SIX

TRAMPLED VINTAGE

How happy that time when, unbridled and unconstrained
We spent a few days in Gulkhana with persons of ill repute

—Hafez in *The Baburnama*

It's not something I could say openly at the time, but I'll say it now: Hamid Karzai's new Afghan cabinet made me nervous.

Sworn in on December 24, 2004—President Karzai's birthday, as it happens—his cabinet members were mostly top campaign backers and their allies being rewarded for their loyalty. The secrecy surrounding their selection was itself worrying: before announcing the new lineup, Karzai had been cloistered for long sessions with US ambassador Zalmay Khalilzad. UN special representative Lakhdar Brahimi and his deputy, Jean Arnault, had pushed hard for competent reformers. But ultimately, the imperative of political payback had driven Karzai's final decisions.

Karzai had decided early on that he would not be forming his own political party. Such parties were the *sine qua non* of political life in most places, but Afghanistan was not like most places. During Karzai's lifetime, he had witnessed Afghan parties rip the country apart, including the Communist PDPA, which acted as the Soviets' puppets after seizing power in 1978. Islamist parties, such as Sayyaf's Ittehad-i Islami, likewise had become key players in Afghanistan's various civil wars. To many Afghans, parties were spent shell casings from old conflicts. Karzai wanted to transcend the old partisan model of politics.

In 2004, this strategy had seemed to work. The wings of the old warlord class, from which the Islamist party bosses had sprung, were clipped, and Karzai's rivals, such as Younis Qanuni (a Tajik) and Abdul Rashid Dostum (an Uzbek), were unable to use their political machines to break out of their narrow ethnic constituencies.

But the price Karzai paid for his party-free approach was that he was constantly beholden to a constellation of parochial supporters with different agendas. These included jihadi leaders who had backed his campaign—Pir Gilani, Hazrat Mojadeddi and Sayyaf—who each got two ministries. Some of their own nominees were decent choices; others proved disastrous.

The influence of the old Northern Alliance declined—but only slightly. Out of cabinet were the former Alliance leader Fahim; Ahmad Shah Massoud protege Qanuni; Sayed Mustafa Kazemi (who would be killed by a suicide bomber in 2007); and Mohammad Mohaqiq, the Hazara leader. But Abdullah Abdullah, one of the Northern Alliance's few English-speakers, remained foreign minister, with General Bismullah Khan and Amrullah Saleh retaining key positions as chief of the general staff and intelligence chief, respectively. One of the younger brothers of Massoud, Ahmad Zia Massoud, who had been ambassador to Russia before the election, became first vice-president in succession to Fahim. Karim Khalili, a mujahidin veteran from Wardak province, remained as second vice-president—even though most Hazaras had voted for Mohaqiq.

The least that could be said for this group was that it was diverse. Despite winning primarily on the strength of the Pashtun vote, Karzai, to his credit, was keeping northerners who had battled the Taliban—many of them ethnic Tajiks, Uzbeks and Hazaras—close to him.

Another group of political actors whom Karzai was keen to promote and cultivate were multilingual, westernized, suit-and-tie intellectuals who had been part of the Afghan exile community during the Soviet and Taliban years. This "Rome group," as it came to be called, included the American-educated scholar Hedayat Amin Arsala, the

French-educated Zalmai Rassoul, the German-educated Mohammad Amin Farhang and man of letters Sayed Maktoum Raheen. All these men remained in cabinet, while the American-educated military officer Rahim Wardak was promoted to minister of defence.

This would be the last cabinet that Karzai would be able to form without parliamentary scrutiny. As a result, several major portfolios would now languish without strong leadership. A case in point was the thorny energy file. As noted in Chapter 4, in keeping with the deal done to secure his bloodless departure from Herat's governorship in September 2004, Ismail Khan had become minister of energy and water in the new cabinet. His appointment had the strong support of Khalilzad, though Ismail Khan himself had coveted the Interior Ministry. With Kabul and other Afghan cities mostly cold and dark for another winter, critics argued that the Energy Ministry file should be in the hands of an experienced technocrat, not an ex-warlord with a major political axe to grind. The counter-argument was that it behooved the country to have this ruthless power broker physically removed from his seat of power in Herat. As always, political decisions in Afghanistan involved choosing the lesser evil, which was anyway rarely subject to broad agreement.

Management of counter-narcotics also suffered. After endless discussion, responsibility for this critical issue was removed from the country's high-level National Security Council and downgraded to the level of ordinary ministry. Habibullah Qaderi, the new minister, was a straight-shooter from a respected Kandahari family but also an outsider to Kabul's power politics. His ministry lacked the clout to compel action from governors or other ministries. To make matters worse, several ministers, as well as generals at interior and defence, had intimate ties to major trafficking networks, which they barely sought to disguise.

All of which to say, Afghanistan's reform drive, which began with much fanfare at the 2001 Bonn conference, was running out of gas. A symptom of this unfortunate trend was the departure of Ashraf Ghani from the Finance Ministry.

Ghani had sufficient stature to later be spoken of as a possible successor to former UN secretary-general Kofi Annan. His departure not only dealt a blow to the Afghan Finance Ministry but endangered the country's relationship with its donors. One of the first actions of Karzai's new finance minister (Anwar ul-Haq Ahady, an Afghan-American political scientist, who will be discussed later) was to launch a review of the well-regarded National Solidarity Programme, an effective and widely lauded 2003 initiative aimed at permitting Afghanistan to manage its own rural development projects. Major donors, including the World Bank, the International Monetary Fund, and the Canadian and UK governments, were unimpressed.

———

It proved to be a harsh winter, with most of the snow coming late, in February and March. On February 5, we were at Kabul Airport waiting to fly to a heavy-weapons cantonment ceremony—a major focus of my work during that period. Our flight had been postponed by a heavy snowfall. The dozen or so ISAF flags were snapping in the wind, with the hills surrounding Kabul blotted out by the storm.

A Canadian friend I knew from Russia called from Herat, where he had been waiting for his own flight to Kabul. A former air traffic controller, he had gone up to the tower at Herat's airport to ask about the weather in the capital. Now he wanted the lowdown from me. "A bad snowstorm," I told him. "Kabul Airport may be closed for hours, even days." He rang off. A few hours later, Kam Air 737 from Herat slammed into a mountain east of Kabul, killing all 104 people on board—the deadliest air disaster in the country's history. Having found Kabul Airport paralyzed by what turned out to be the city's worst snowstorm of the decade, the pilot had been heading north to Bagram. We all lost friends and colleagues. But my Canadian caller had decided not to board.

The Taliban's senior military commander made a point of saying for once that his men weren't responsible for the aircraft's destruction and even expressed regret at the tragedy—a rare gesture of humanity from an enemy that normally placed no value on innocent human life.

The tragedy came at a time when the world's military footprint in Afghanistan was changing. With over 20,000 troops, Operation Enduring Freedom (the official name used for the US military campaign in Afghanistan) now operated over one dozen Provincial Reconstruction Teams (PRTs) in the west, south and east of the country. ISAF had completed its expansion to Afghanistan's north, where it now had five PRTs.

Kabul itself was still on edge. On the night of March 7, 2004, Steve McQueen, a British microfinance expert then advising Rural Rehabilitation and Development Minister Haneef Atmar, emerged from the Elbow Room, an ex-pat nightspot next to the Foreign Ministry. Minutes later, the vehicle he was driving was forced to stop by two others—one in front, one behind—on Qala-ye Faitullah Road. McQueen was shot dead at close range. The attack bore all the hallmarks of a targeted killing. The official version later blamed the hit on the same criminal kingpin responsible for the kidnapping of UN staff the previous autumn, a man who may have wanted a foreign hostage as leverage to spring his mates. When they went to kidnap McQueen, he had apparently reached behind the passenger seat. Fearing he was going for a weapon, his assailants shot first.

The episode horrified everyone. McQueen had been on the verge of heading back to the United Kingdom. His fiancée, pregnant with their first child, worked in Khalilzad's office. An economics whiz, McQueen also had been involved in a complex audit of AREA, an NGO managed over the years by many Afghans who now held positions of power. Adding another layer of murkiness to the episode, McQueen recently had been detained and interrogated by the National Directorate of Security, Afghanistan's domestic intelligence agency, during which time some claimed he had witnessed a violent episode he was not meant to see. The killing might have emerged from one of several directions, in other words. In my remarks at his memorial service, I paid tribute to his many outstanding contributions to Afghanistan. His tragic death was a stark reminder of the dark eddies of conspiracy still swirling around Kabul's heart.

———•———

There were glimmers of hope too. Prince Mostapha Zahir, the favourite grandson of King Zahir Shah, had joined the government as director general of the new Environmental Protection Agency. For years as a young prince, he had helped manage his grandfather's court-in-exile in Rome. Until 2004, he had served as ambassador of Afghanistan to Italy. A graduate of Queen's University in Kingston, Ontario, he, and his father also, had lived part of the former king's dream of life in Canada. Now forty, Mostapha Zahir was hungry to take on a challenge in the land of his birth. The royal family long had been a champion of hunting and the preservation of Afghan wildlife and natural environment. For Mostapha Zahir, a child of privilege and exile in equal measure, stewardship of the environment was a natural fit.

———•———

Then there was Sima Samar, chair of the Afghan Independent Human Rights Commission (AIHRC), who already possessed the confidence of a trailblazer and a survivor. In 1978, her husband was arrested and subsequently disappeared. In 1982, at the age of twenty-five, the Helmand province native became the first woman from Afghanistan's Hazara minority to obtain a medical degree from Kabul University. After violence and persecution forced her family into Pakistan, she established her own medical organization in Quetta dedicated to the treatment of women and girls. All in all, she spent seventeen years in the Pakistani city, coming and going to Afghanistan when it was safe, and eventually built over a hundred schools. In 2002, she returned to Afghanistan for good, first as deputy chair of the interim government and then as minister for women's affairs.

Samar had seen it all since 2001—the false starts, the hopes gone sour, the warlord comeback, the first executions, the clamour over civilian casualties—yet she remained an idealist. She once gave me a set of placemats with "No Peace without Justice" embroidered on them. A few years ago, she came close to replacing Louise Arbour as UN high commissioner for human rights. More recently, she became an honorary officer of the Order of Canada.

"No doubt there has been a lot of improvement [in Afghanistan]," she told me during an interview at an AIHRC office in the Karte Se neighbourhood of Kabul. She ticked off access to education and health care as major accomplishments ("though much less than what the government says," she adds). She was also bullish on freedom of expression and the blossoming of the Afghan media. On this file too, though, she added a caveat: a lot of the media was still controlled by warlords. ("Each one of them has his own TV station!")

She adds women's rights to the list, highlighting the number of women (27 percent) elected to Afghanistan's parliament. "Imagine somebody like me talking against everybody—against the president, against [then interior minister Haneef] Atmar, against the members of the parliament. But I'm still alive. So these are the things that are happening in Afghanistan."

Nevertheless, she was pessimistic about the chances for peace: "The president keeps saying that we should have a loya jirga to reconcile the Taliban. [That is] not going to solve the problem. First of all, with [the] Taliban, we do not know with whom we should talk. If we speak of Quetta Shura [the Pakistan-based Taliban leadership council], who [are they]? How many people do they have? Which parts of the country do they control? Is it really only [the] Taliban in Helmand [province] and those areas? Or is it the Hezb-i Islami and Jamiat-i Islami [militias]—the Taliban's brothers? There is a lack of clarity."

Without basic human security, corruption was inevitable, she added: "Anybody [regardless of position]—he doesn't feel secure, he thinks that he will lose his job, so he has to collect as much money as he can [in the meantime]." She cited the case of Zarar Ahmed Moqbel, ousted from the Interior Ministry for gross corruption. But there were many other examples; the Afghan government was full of foxes guarding chicken coops.

Regarding her own battle for human rights, Samar described her work as a series of small campaigns, not all of which become news in the Western media. One of her missions, for instance, had been to make Afghanistan's penal code for juveniles consistent with its human rights obligations. There was also her battle against efforts to encode retrograde attitudes toward women into Afghan law, attitudes she described as "stupid and crazy."

Some of Samar's critiques of Karzai's Afghanistan were quite shocking. On paper, she said, everyone had far more human rights now than under the Taliban, yet criminals who broke the law were rarely caught. Under the Taliban, there was "more security than now," she declared. "We have a court for counter-narcotics," she added, "which was not existing at all under the Taliban. It was not a crime. Now it is a crime, we have a court, but people are caught with 125 kilograms of heroin and they are released."

She also cited the example of Basir Salangi, chief of police in Kabul when twenty families in the city's Sherpur district were evicted from their homes so that senior Afghan officials could build private residences. "I think he [Salangi] has three palaces there." On such issues, Samar remained a kind of national conscience for Afghanistan.

———

Improbable as it may now seem, Afghanistan actually had a proud place in the post–World War II history of global human rights. Together with Egypt, Iran, Iraq, Pakistan, Syria and Turkey, it had been one of seven majority-Muslim countries to vote in favour of the Universal Declaration of Human Rights at the Palais de Chaillot in Paris on December 10, 1948. Afghanistan also acceded to the UN Convention on the Prevention and Punishment of the Crime of Genocide in 1956. In the 1980s and 1990s, even as the country plunged into civil war, Afghanistan signed on to more instruments, including the International Convention on the Elimination of All Forms of Racial Discrimination, the Convention against Torture, and the Convention on the Rights of the Child. Under the circumstances gripping Afghanistan during this period, these were mere symbolic gestures, of course. But at the very least, they showed the world that Afghanistan aspired to the lofty principles contained in these instruments, thereby suggesting that the gap separating them from Afghan reality was not unbridgeable.

Nor were the concepts of due process and rule of law foreign to Afghanistan. Long before it began to sign on to human rights instruments, Afghanistan was a centre for Islamic jurisprudence. As early as the eighth century, Abu Hanifa, founder of the most influential and commercially minded school of sharia, was born into a Kabul merchant's family. More recently, under the emirate of Habibullah Khan in the early twentieth century, Afghan judges were renowned for their incorruptibility. The country enacted its first written constitution in 1924.

But as Cicero put it, *Inter arma enim silent leges*—"At times of war, laws fall mute." During most of the two decades preceding 9/11, the country was effectively lawless. Since the Taliban's ouster, Afghans have been trying to reclaim their judicial traditions, but progress has been painfully slow.

When I visited Abdul Salam Azimi in the office of chief justice of the Supreme Court of Afghanistan, his walls were lined with collections of *fiqh*—books of Islamic jurisprudence compiled from his time at Al-Azhar University in Cairo, then as a professor in Kabul and at the University of Arizona. Before becoming Afghanistan's chief justice in 2006, he helped write the country's constitution (based mostly on the 1964 version) and served as Karzai's principal advisor on legal issues. Here was a serious and educated legal mind dedicated to building a just and humane legal system—but there were few men like him to do the front-line work of actually hearing cases.

Of all the sectors requiring reform after 2001, Azimi told me, justice had got off to the slowest start. By early 2005, senior prosecutors were still making as little as $50 per month, padding their income with bribes on all sides. The amiable attorney general, a Northern Alliance functionary named Abdul Mahmood Daqiq, presided over a shambolic bureaucracy that mixed cronyism and incompetence in equal measure. Religious extremism was also an issue. One particularly conservative chief justice, an elderly cleric named Fazl Hadi Shinwari who had once sided with the Taliban, was making noises about cutting media freedoms, while also moving to restore a Saudi-style department for the promotion of virtue and prevention of vice. (Meanwhile, his own two sons were reputed to be influence peddlers.)

The Ministry of Justice under Sardar Danesh had wholeheartedly embraced reform, but his office lacked the resources to make much of a difference. Moreover, the prisons for which the Justice Ministry was now ostensibly responsible were powder kegs. In 2002, they had been virtually empty. Now, they were full with the political opponents of the country's various governors, as well as violent criminals and Taliban. With illiterate staff and minimalist infrastructure—Afghan prisons often were just metal freight containers sunk into the earth, with padlocked doors—the country's detention and correctional facilities were hardly worthy of the modern Western-style justice system the country was supposed to be building.

In January 2005, Sima Samar's human rights commission published *A Call for Justice: A National Consultation on Past Human Rights Violations in Afghanistan*, a document offering recommendations for addressing the country's legacy of violence and persecution. Based on eight months of consultations with thousands of Afghans during 2004, the report called for the expulsion of past human rights abusers from positions of power in Afghanistan and the creation of an investigating body to prosecute war crimes and crimes against humanity. Samar and her colleagues drew on the examples of South Africa and Cambodia to argue that human rights victims needed an opportunity to tell their stories and pursue justice.

To hammer out an agenda for implementing these principles, interested donors led by the Netherlands, Britain and Canada met with an Afghan delegation, which included Samar, in The Hague on June 6 and 7, 2005. But the resulting action plan was short on specifics, and its provisions would prove notoriously difficult to translate into tangible initiatives. As a result, Afghanistan has never witnessed anything like South Africa's Truth and Reconciliation Commission.

But the pressure for action continued. In the spring of 2005, the Afghanistan Justice Project issued a hard-hitting report, entitled *Casting Shadows*, chronicling major abuses from 1978 to 2001. Human Rights Watch published a report called *Blood-Stained Hands*, just as the UN High Commissioner for Human Rights put the finishing touches on her own report—an attempt to inventory all categories of abuse since 1978. There was little prospect of confronting the perpetrators of these abuses. Still, for the first time, their crimes had been systematically catalogued. Some fraction of truth was being salvaged, even if reconciliation was nowhere in sight. In Afghanistan, that's progress.

The United States military is rightly given credit for ejecting the Taliban from power in October and November 2001. But it's important to remember that, as already discussed, much of the actual combat was done by a confederation of nine Afghan militias, loosely organized under the Northern Alliance banner, mostly led by men whom the Taliban had beaten back in 1996 and whom had been fighting to reclaim power ever since.

The militia commanders were well-known figures in Afghanistan and in many cases were infamous. Paid and supplied by CIA officers and US Special Forces units that had been mobilized in the days after 9/11, they advanced into Afghan provinces they had not held in years. With the Taliban reeling in the face of punishing US air power, Northern Alliance commanders and their subordinates moved into their old offices and started to call the shots for the first time in fifteen years.

The Bonn Agreement of December 2001, which essentially recreated the Afghan state, was designed to rehabilitate the country in the wake of Taliban rule. But the other, less widely acknowledged, function of the agreement was to impose some measure of control and accountability on the Northern Alliance leaders who suddenly were controlling the levers of power. Moreover, the United States and many Afghans knew that it was necessary to include exiled Afghan groups from Iran, Pakistan, Europe and North America. These various factions had failed in their last effort to put together a functioning country in the early 1990s. Old animosities still flourished.

Unfortunately, prospects for accountability slipped as the most aggressive militia leaders rushed to exploit their window of opportunity—the short period between the creation of the new Afghan state and national elections. And naturally, they had very little enthusiasm for investigative bodies snooping around the country, looking into 1980s- and 1990s-era human rights abuses.

One bright spot, as mentioned, was disarmament. After a slow start in 2003, heavy-weapons cantonment was mostly complete by 2005. Most of the nation's tanks, artillery, multiple rocket launchers, anti-aircraft guns and other heavy weapons were either in government hands or dysfunctional. (The last province to disarm was, not surprisingly, Panjshir, in the country's rugged northeast—the centre of resistance to both Soviet occupation and Taliban rule.) Afghan militia units also were disbanded, with commanders being co-opted by the prospect of influence in the new army and police forces, helping to consolidate power in the official Ministry of Defence.

Northern Alliance veterans still dominated the country's military establishment. But in December 2004, Mohammad Fahim was suc-

ceeded as defence minister by Abdul Rahim Wardak, a Pashtun and former Soviet-era mujahidin leader. General Bismullah Khan, an ethnic
Tajik, meanwhile, became chief of the general staff. Such partnerships
lay at the foundation of the new Afghan state.

President Karzai was deeply involved in both heavy-weapons
cantonment and the process formally known as Disarmament,
Demobilization and Reintegration (DDR), hosting at least eight major
meetings on the subject and encouraging Japan to fund the project.
Then finance minister Ashraf Ghani also was involved, as was I—
alongside the ambassador of Japan and UNAMA. In late 2004, Ghani
cut state salaries for militias, both to encourage the centralization of
force within the Afghan military and to cut down on the deliberate
inflation of budgets through the use of ghost combatants.

On July 7, 2005, President Karzai attended a ceremony to mark the
completion of DDR at the new West Point–style officers' academy constructed in the old Soviet-built air force facility at Kabul International
Airport. It was clear to everyone present that DDR had been a necessary program. But by that time, it also had the air of being yesterday's
news: in mid-2005, everyone already knew that the principal security
concern was cross-border infiltration and the drug industry. The army
still numbered only 40,000; the police remained unreformed. Despite
having taken 35,000 small arms off the streets and putting over 10,000
heavy weapons in cantonment, Afghanistan was just starting to come
to terms with its new security challenges.

"Has demilitarization had any enduring success?" I put this question
to Masoom Stanekzai, long-time presidential advisor and deputy chair
of the demobilization commission. In the early years of the transition,
Stanekzai was communications minister, delivering the reforms that
made telecom the most successful sector of the Afghan economy, with
11 million wireless subscribers (by 2010). But he was one of the reformers to leave cabinet with Ghani at the end of 2004. With fears growing

of a resurgent Taliban, men such as Stanekzai were under pressure to neutralize the jihadis in the same way they'd helped rein in the militias.

"Without DDR and heavy-weapons cantonment, without destroying ammunition and decommissioning old militia units, we could not have a national army today of this capacity—able to respond effectively to the kind of attack that took place last Monday," he told me, referring to four suicide attackers from North Waziristan who had briefly occupied a commercial office in Pashtunistan Square in Kabul a few days earlier. "I think you can see a tangible result in some areas," Stanekzai concluded.

He was proud of the program to secure the country's heavy weapons. In the first years after Bonn, he remembered, "we witnessed heavy fighting between the big warlords. They were using all kinds of weapons. [DDR helped to reduce] the power bases of the very strong people in five or six different regions." This allowed "central government to extend its authority gradually into the provinces, and into the districts."

The problem was that DDR had been too modest in scope. "We targeted commanders for DDR too narrowly," Stanekzai told me. "We forgot about the other commanders." There were hundreds, from various phases of the conflict, who had not been part of the standing militia forces of 2001. "They were heavily armed," Stanekzai added. "They were part of the whole campaign—whether with one group or another—and we forgot about that." The insiders had received incentives to cooperate—study trips, training, small business packages, government positions—and so they "came to the conclusion that, yes, there was something for them; and then they started to cooperate." But outsiders were ignored, even commanders who had turned in the most weapons of all. An unknown number from among these militia veterans had found their way into the insurgency. "I think we had a double standard," Stanekzai admitted. "The program was not designed to be flexible."

By 2005, when the Taliban insurgency began heating up, Afghanistan's leaders began to realize all this. But by this point, the political momentum for demilitarization had been spent.

The larger problem, according to Stanekzai, lies with foreign attitudes: there is still an unspoken understanding that it is somehow acceptable for neighbouring countries to arm and train their chosen allies in Afghanistan. Unfortunately, Karzai was giving mixed messages about how these proxy forces should be treated. By nodding and winking to the old jihadi establishment, which the president had courted as part of his power base, the government itself was still indirectly supporting illegal armed groups.

To counter these influences, Stanekzai told me, the government would have to deliver physical protection and material benefits at the local level, in villages and districts. Specifically, it had to deal with the mass of youth in the countryside that both the anti-Soviet mujahidin and the Taliban had exploited. Moreover, the country would have to enforce established codes of conduct at the village level: "If somebody is killing someone, using a gun, and he is brought to justice, nobody will do it again. Afghanistan has a culture and accepted norms—even women use guns for hunting. . . . But you cannot kill somebody, because the relatives will come after you. For that reason, people are extremely careful not to use guns to kill innocent people."

As Afghanistan moved toward another election campaign in 2005, this time for the lower house of parliament and the first-ever elected provincial council, on September 18, it was clear security would be a tougher challenge than it had been for the presidential race. On May 7, a suicide attacker detonated inside a Kabul Internet café. Later the same month, the rumoured desecration of the Koran by US forces at Guantanamo Bay led to demonstrations in several cities. Criminal kidnappings and gang-related violence were on the upswing as well. In the countryside, attacks by the Taliban-led insurgency were far outpacing those of previous years.

On June 1, 2005, the amiable new police chief of Kabul, Major General Akram Khakrezwal, was killed by a remotely detonated IED while visiting a mosque in his native Kandahar. He had been a fierce opponent of the Taliban but also a pillar of the Alikozai, a key Durrani tribal grouping in southern Afghanistan. Later in July, a major road accident involving a coalition truck whose brakes failed led to an angry standoff with US forces in west Kabul, followed by a riot that swept through the city, targeting compounds where foreigners lived. The violence was mostly contained; casualties in the end were light. But the situation in Kabul was shown to be on a hair-trigger.

The situation in the provinces was volatile in part because former warlords were being installed in regional governments. In June, on the basis of a deal brokered mostly by Zalmay Khalilzad, Gul Agha Sherzoi became governor of Nangarhar province. Former Kabul governor Sayed Hussain Anwari went to Herat, and Haji Din Mohammad, scion of Jalalabad's most influential family, whose two brothers had been killed since 2001, came to Kabul. With the appointment of Ustad Mohammad Atta in Balkh, each one of the major provinces (outside the south) was now in the hands of a figure from the mujahidin past. But with the exception of Atta, none was serving in his home region, in keeping with the precedent set when Ismail Khan was removed from Herat and brought to Kabul in 2004. These figures were not being brought to justice for their past actions, but at the very least, they were being detached from their power bases, making them somewhat less of a threat to the central government.

Meanwhile, relations between Afghanistan and Pakistan were swinging back and forth between suspicion and cooperation. Thanks to the strong relation between Ghani and Pakistani prime minister Shaukat Aziz, trade between the two countries was increasing, a fact that helped soothe various bilateral irritants. Karzai was an official guest of Islamabad for Pakistan Day in March 2005, a visit that may in retrospect have been a high point in the countries' post-Taliban relationship.

In May 2005, Karzai went to Washington to formalize a memorandum of understanding between Afghanistan and the United States. In a passage that no doubt raised eyebrows in other nations, the document stated that "the United States and Afghanistan plan to work together to develop appropriate arrangements and agreements to implement their strategic partnership." To Teheran and Islamabad—even to Moscow, Tashkent and Beijing—this was code for permanent military bases. It went well beyond the Bonn Agreement and the language establishing UN and ISAF mandates in successive Security Council resolutions. It was Khalilzad's last bequest to his native country before leaving his post as US ambassador in June. By July 19, the United Kingdom had negotiated a similar declaration of their "enduring relationship" with Afghanistan. By mid-2006, the EU and China signed on to similar bilateral agreements. So did Iran and Pakistan.

But these two latter agreements could not paper over the conflicts between Afghanistan and its neighbours. Karzai had made his first official visit to Teheran in January, finding ample common ground with the relatively moderate Mohammad Khatami, then the country's president. He later sent his chief of staff, Umar Daudzai, as Afghanistan's ambassador. But the election of the viciously anti-Israeli and anti-American Mahmoud Ahmadinejad to Iran's presidency in August 2006 would stretch bilateral relations to their breaking point.

Relations with Pakistan followed a similar course. In June 2005, dismayed by Kabul's carping about Pakistan's inaction against the Taliban, President Pervez Musharraf made a speech in Australia placing blame for the worsening violence on Afghan shoulders. He continued to deny the existence of the Taliban's leadership council (including the Quetta Shura) and the presence of Mullah Omar or any of his lieutenants on Pakistani soil.

This did not prevent Pakistani prime minister Shaukat Aziz from making a two-day visit to Kabul in July, together with a delegation of ministers, during which he confirmed Pakistan would make up to $100 million available to support development and reconstruction in Afghanistan. Then, in September, as part of the diplomatic see-saw, Musharraf proposed that the border between the two countries be fenced or even mined, to erase any remaining doubts about the role of cross-border infiltration in Afghanistan's conflict.

In fact, Musharraf had larger problems to deal with: the strategic balance in South Asia was shifting. In July 2005, President Bush signed a civilian nuclear cooperation agreement with India, a move that excited jealousy and heightened anxieties in Islamabad. As always, Pakistan looked to Afghanistan as a source of strategic depth in its rivalry with its larger neighbour.

In September, at the UN General Assembly, Bush met with Musharraf and Karzai together, extracting as firm an undertaking as he could from the former to ensure security conditions were conducive to the holding of elections in September. At a meeting on election preparations in Kabul held around the same time, I warned the Pakistani representative that the international community would not stand idly by when all evidence pointed to Afghan insurgents being trained, controlled, financed and supplied from Pakistani territory. He was furious, but several colleagues from other NATO countries chimed in with support. (Later, the poor man had the temerity to have his government complain to Ottawa about my comments, which only drew more attention to his government's disingenuous stance.)

By summer, the parliamentary race had moved into high gear. The walls of buildings across Kabul and other major cities were plastered with posters of candidates—elders and young upstarts, men and women alike. There was a mad scramble to prevent those with active armed groups still under their command from qualifying as candidates. In the end, only thirty-four people were removed from the ballot, out of at least a hundred who deserved close scrutiny. But the pressure resulting from this single criterion for candidacy was enough to trigger the collection of over 14,000 light weapons. It was the first success for the program to disband illegal armed groups, known as DIAG, the successor to DDR.

With 2,379 male candidates and 328 women divided among thirty-four provinces, some of the ballot papers ended up becoming small books. This led to confusion in Kabul and other places. Even larger numbers of candidates contested the provincial-council elections. At the height of the process, the Joint Electoral Management Body had nearly 180,000 local staff working for it. This complexity drove costs well over $170 million. On election day, September 18, turnout was lower among the 12 million registered voters than it had been for the presidential elections. But at 51.5 percent, it was still respectable. Jihadi political heavyweights such as Kazemi, Mohaqiq and Sayyaf in Kabul, Burhanuddin Rabbani in Badakhshan province, and Hazrat Ali in Nangarhar were returned easily. Provincial councils turned up a mix of old-timers and newcomers. Controversies over complaints, mostly involving disqualifications for failure to disarm, raged for weeks, placing the Canadian head of the Electoral Complaints Commission under terrible strain. At one point, crowds outside his office chanted, "Death to Grant Kippen." But all disputes were fairly resolved, and the results were widely accepted.

With the last major milestone of the Bonn process completed, Jean Arnault, now UNAMA's head, turned his attention to the post-Bonn framework for continuing partnership. There was broad agreement that the US-led military effort in the country must continue, even deepen. But with the conflict in Iraq getting worse, few combat-ready units were on offer, and fewer still with the capability to train Afghan forces. Although a few development programs had excelled, government institutions remained weak.

How could this be remedied? In 2004, Afghanistan had presented a blueprint for development called *Securing Afghanistan's Future*, but with Ghani's departure, the impetus behind it had been lost. An Interim Afghanistan National Development Strategy, including an anti-poverty plan required by the World Bank, was in the works. However, its adoption wouldn't guarantee continued support from the international community, much less that this support would be delivered coherently or effectively. The risk of donor fatigue was real. With Iraq generating new divisions and controversy every week, a rush for the exits seemed possible.

Arnault's elegant solution was an Afghanistan Compact, a five-page political declaration to be issued by the Afghan government together with donors, detailing commitments to security, governance, development, aid effectiveness and counter-narcotics, backed by concrete benchmarks for success. It was an attempt to enlarge the Bonn framework, which had focused almost exclusively on political legitimacy, to include the broader goals of stability and national development. Would anyone buy it?

I met regularly with other national representatives, starting in the summer of 2005, then continuing all autumn. At first these sessions brought together selected donors, then all of those represented in Kabul. There were a few fiery debates, with the United States at one point unwilling to support the creation of an Afghan army exceeding 70,000 troops by 2011. Aid experts doubted whether it was realistic to bring electricity to 25 percent of rural households or build functional justice institutions at the provincial level. Few of these objectives were yet backed by firm plans or programs, let alone funding. But all were desperately needed. It was at least an outline of what would be required to make the country's economy, government and infrastructure viable.

———

After the parliamentary elections, I left my position as ambassador of Canada, after twenty-six months on the job, as part of the normal rotation that comes with life in the diplomatic corps. By this time, 2,300 Canadian troops were on their way to take the lead in Kandahar province. A new phase was beginning for Canada in Afghanistan.

I had a decision to make. NATO secretary-general Jaap de Hoop Scheffer had asked me to be his senior civilian representative in Kabul. At the same time, colleagues in UNAMA, backed by Under-Secretary-General for Peacekeeping Jean-Marie Guéhenno in New York, wanted me to replace Filippo Grandi, the Italian who had replaced Arnault as deputy special representative of the secretary-general.

Both roles were important. NATO was becoming, by its sheer scale, the most influential international player in Afghanistan. It had Kabul and the north under its command; expansion to the rest of the country was due in 2006. But we already knew military action inside Afghanistan would not be enough. Taliban and al Qaeda leaders were across the border, out of NATO's reach. Persuading Pakistan to do the right thing was a *political* task.

In the end, political leadership would have to come from national capitals. And the political umbrella under which we all worked inside Afghanistan would remain UNAMA. Ultimately, this is why I decided to take the UNAMA job.

Not that I was naive about the UN's shortcomings. With offices in only ten of thirty-four provinces, its mission was still small. Joint planning and execution among UN agencies, funds and programs was spotty at best. Worst of all, UN diplomats were unwilling to confront Pakistan over its blind-eye approach to jihadis and cross-border interference. Even with fresh insurgent campaigns being launched from Pakistani soil, New York was unwilling to confront the problem. After all, Islamabad was a top troop contributor to UN peacekeeping.

The pressure to take the NATO job had been heavy. The idea of working even more closely with the military professionals I had already seen in action was tempting. We needed more unity of effort in the Provincial Reconstruction Teams and elsewhere. But I was a diplomat—a political animal. Only within a UN framework did we stand a chance of getting the politics of peace right for Afghanistan. UNAMA already had the most talented team of political officers in the country. We would press forward with political prerequisites for stability, from elections to reconciliation, while championing larger investments in institution building.

There were risks. New York might fail to come through with additional resources; some there even thought UNAMA should scale down. My own career might suffer as I took leave without pay from the Canadian Foreign Service, but without any real interest in a UN career after Kabul. Moreover, the regional dimension was fraught with risk and complexity: generations of UN envoys had been gored on its many horns. Still, UNAMA was the best place for me to continue contributing. I would start in December.

In the meantime, my wife-to-be, Hedvig, and I travelled in early October 2005 to Islamabad, then north to Skardu and Shigar in Pakistan's north, on the way to the base camp for K2, the world's second-highest mountain peak. On the day of the devastating Kashmir earthquake, October 8, we were in a beautiful Kashmiri maharaja's palace lovingly restored by the Aga Khan Trust for Culture. Pervez Musharraf's brother had been staying there just before us. The old building had rattled and swayed, remaining wholly intact. Elsewhere in our area, roads were washed away and landslides had buried parts of villages. But as we would later learn, the local damage was nothing compared with the devastation farther south.

We travelled onward to Gilgit, a transit point for Himalayan mountain climbers, and then into the picturesque Hunza Valley. We then passed over the Khunjerab Pass from Sost into China's Xinjiang region, staying successively in Tashkurgan, Kashgar and Urumqi, where the Silk Road came to life before our eyes.

In late November I was back in Kabul, in my new capacity as deputy special representative of the secretary-general, drafting and redrafting the Afghanistan Compact's dense language, seeking clarity and consensus. It would be the centrepiece of a conference in London that would renew the international commitment to Afghanistan for another five years.

By December, the political renaissance ordained by the 2003 Bonn Agreement had been implemented almost in full. The new 250-member lower house of the National Assembly, the Wolesi Jirga, or People's Chamber, was inaugurated on December 19, 2005, again with speeches by Zahir Shah and Karzai. US vice-president Dick Cheney represented the Bush administration.

The new Afghan state now had its skeletal structure, complete with a veneer of political legitimacy. But with the exception of disarmament, nothing had yet been done to challenge the local power of commanders in most villages and districts. In fact, the military campaign of 2001, the two loya jirgas and the elections themselves had in some ways reinforced their influence and impunity. To make all these national projects work, Hamid Karzai and his men had to cut deals with the people who held power on the ground. As the Afghanistan Compact itself would later say, "The transition to peace and stability [was] not yet assured."

In fact, security was slipping, even in Kabul. In August, the Taliban claimed credit when a Spanish helicopter crashed near Herat, killing seventeen. In November, suicide attacks were launched against German ISAF soldiers. In December, there were attacks at the Friday Mosque in Herat, followed by suicide attacks elsewhere in the city. It was a sign of the brutal campaign to come.

The UN mapping report chronicling past atrocities was not yet published. In fact, the only substantial action to legally address past Afghan human rights abuses was taking place in foreign jurisdictions. In London, a commander by the name of Faryadi Sarwar Zardad was arrested for war crimes on July 14, 2003. He was convicted on July 18, 2005, for his sadistic acts, including torture and summary executions, which he had committed in the early 1990s while running a checkpoint between Kabul and Jalalabad. (Abdullah Shah, convicted in Kabul in October 2002 and later executed, had been his subordinate.) Several persons suspected of war crimes at earlier stages of the conflict were indicted in the Netherlands. In Afghanistan itself, Assadullah Sarwary, intelligence chief and deputy prime minister under the pro-Soviet administrations of the late 1970s and 1980s, was tried in late 2005 for incidents of torture and mass murder that took place under his watch. He was sentenced to death in March 2006 in Afghanistan's first indigenous war crimes trial. A report from the United Nations High Commissioner for Human Rights found numerous procedural short-comings: "Detained without charge since 1992, [Sarwary] had no legal representation, and standards of evidence, as well as other due process safeguards, were ignored."

Massacre sites in Kabul and elsewhere began to be uncovered. Witnesses came forward, often pointing fingers; statements were taken. But commanders often acted quickly to bury the evidence. In some cases, mass graves were destroyed on the spot. NGO workers and eyewitnesses were threatened. Transitional justice had become a tug-of-war, recalling the anything-goes thuggery of the 1990s. In one of my first speeches as deputy head of the UN mission, I addressed a workshop on transitional justice bringing together activists from across the country. After consultations in many provinces, they con-cluded that there could be no substitute for real criminal-justice prosecutions.

A case study in the manner by which *realpolitik* has trumped accountability is the Islamist militia Hezb-i Islami, which was Afghanistan's most potent military force throughout the anti-Soviet jihad and ensuing civil war, until it was displaced from Kabul by the Taliban in 1996. Gulbuddin Hekmatyar, the group's leader, with a reputation for brutality, spent most of the Taliban years in Iranian exile. In 2002, Tehran made a show of extraditing him but sent him to Pakistan, where he was welcomed in radical circles with open arms. Though Hezb-i Islami was largely excluded from government positions in the early years of Afghanistan's post-Taliban regime, it received several ministries at the 2002 emergency loya jirga. In the years since, Hezb-i Islami reportedly has joined forces with al Qaeda and the Taliban. In 2003, the United States government identified Hekmatyar as a "Specially Designated Global Terrorist." Yet several major segments of Hezb-i Islami had been reconciled in 2004—even though Hekmatyar himself remained at large, just like Osama bin Laden and Mullah Omar.

The situation in Afghanistan's southern Helmand province, the centre of the nation's drug trade, also put on display the frustrating moral complexities of Afghan *realpolitik*. In the summer of 2005, the gubernatorial incumbent was Mullah Sher Mohammad Akhundzada, a scion of the province's most famous jihadi family. They had ruled the province with an iron fist in the early 1990s. Since their return in 2001, they had meted out summary justice to many of their rivals, who had sided with the Taliban in the interim. By sharing power with notorious commanders from the other main tribes, Sher Mohammad had kept stability in Helmand. But he and his ilk also had presided over the most spectacular drug bonanza in Afghan history.

For London, which then had the NATO lead on counter-narcotics, this made Sher Mohammad an unacceptable bedfellow. And it made his removal a condition of its deployment as it moved to take over responsibility for Helmand in 2005. Karzai complied, but it was a decision he later would come to regret. Sher Mohammad's removal was just the opening that the Taliban, now returning in numbers to neighbouring Oruzgan, to the northeast, were awaiting.

What was worse, as Sher Mohammad returned to Kabul in December to take up a seat in the new upper house, he ordered his followers not to hinder the Taliban resurgence. For him, this was a good business decision: the financial needs of the insurgents would take opium cultivation to new heights in Helmand, visiting a new form of revenge on the British.

The story of Sher Mohammad is just one example of one politician, in one region. But it lies at the intersection of many factors that make Afghanistan complicated and violent: drugs, warlords, power politics and a culture of payback and vengeance. After more than two years in this country, I was coming to realize how difficult it would be to prepare the ground for peace.

CHAPTER SEVEN

NEW COLONIALISTS

October.
The hungry province grows restive.
The Imperial army must visit the Frontier.

—Christopher Logue, *War Music*

I n the end, there was just enough space. True, it was a tight squeeze to shoehorn the Sultan of Oman's emissaries into the last free corner of the London Conference room. But the happy truth was that diplomats from around the world *wanted* in on the project to rebuild Afghanistan. Whatever the yawning divides over Iraq, the world community nevertheless turned out in force on January 31, 2006, to place its seal of approval on the Afghanistan Compact, a document that a few of us had laboured long and hard to draft. Fifty-one countries took part alongside ten international organizations, from the Aga Khan Foundation to the World Bank, with fifteen more states observing.

British prime minister Tony Blair opened the proceedings, with UN secretary-general Kofi Annan and Afghan president Hamid Karzai following as co-chairs. Karzai was visibly pleased: the updated benchmarks contained in the new document would come with more aid for his country—though no blank cheques.

The venue was Lancaster House, the massive pile started in 1825 for Field Marshal Prince Frederick, the "Grand Old Duke of York," commander-in-chief of the British Army at the time. It had seen two G7 summits—the last one joined by Mikhail Gorbachev in 1991, shortly before his fall from power. It had also been the venue for the 1979 negotiations that led to Zimbabwe's independence.

The compact focused in large part on restoring Afghanistan's national institutions, which had been decimated since the 1970s. It featured ambitious goals, everything from reform of land registration to major investments in irrigation. Some tracked existing UN Millennium Development Goals; others were unique to Afghanistan.

The main vehicle for this work would be the Afghanistan National Development Strategy, essentially a poverty-reduction plan. After a period of countrywide consultations, it would be used to map out plans for each sector of the national development. These would then be costed for inclusion in the national budget.

The conference was an enormous success, with attendees pledging $10.5 billion. Even so, diplomats went home without having discussed several key issues. The compact lacked detail on police reform, for instance—a major problem area in Afghanistan to this day. It was also silent on watershed management. (Irrigation is critical to improving Afghan agriculture, but rights to the principal rivers draining Afghanistan also are claimed by downstream nations, including Iran, Pakistan and the former Soviet republics.) Some of the provisions included in the compact would later be criticized as unrealistic. The National Drug Control Strategy and the Action Plan for Peace, Justice and Reconciliation, to cite two obvious examples, were honoured more in the breach than in the observance. Nevertheless, the compact accomplished its main goal: establishing the institutional bureaucratic framework that defines a normal, functioning country. In the years to come, it would be replicated under UN auspices in Haiti, Iraq and Sudan, each of which has received some version of the compact.

As the London Conference was under way, the Western military structure in Afghanistan was in flux. The NATO-led International Security Assistance Force (ISAF), whose presence was technically distinct from the US contingent known as Operation Enduring Freedom, was preparing to take command of forces in the south of Afghanistan by summer and throughout the country by fall. Meanwhile, US force strength was scheduled to remain level, or possibly even decline, depending on troop needs in Iraq. The United Kingdom, Canada, the Netherlands and other troop-contributing nations would pick up some of the slack. But the overall trend was worrying: US commitments were not rising to match the compact's ambitions. As the year wore on, it would become obvious that there simply were not enough troops in Afghanistan to stabilize the country.

Like the Bonn Agreement four years earlier, the compact was not a peace deal, though it did seek to demilitarize Afghanistan through regional cooperation and confidence building. This meant that the agreement contained no explicit discussion of the Taliban, which at the time many still imagined to be a spent force. The subject of insurgent sanctuaries in Pakistan also wasn't mentioned, an omission that later would be regretted, first and foremost by the Afghans themselves.

With the Bonn agenda completed, there was a changing of the guard at UNAMA. In the months leading up to the London Conference, Kofi Annan's team in New York had planned to wind down their mission in Kabul (something I obviously did not know about when I took the job). To manage the task, New York chose Tom Koenigs, a former German Green Party politician who had donated his private fortune to the Viet Cong in 1973. He'd served as deputy head of the UN mission in Kosovo, then as head of the mission in Guatemala.

Koenigs proved to be an independent thinker. After studying the situation at UNAMA, he came to realize that shutting the mission's doors would be a bad idea. On the contrary, the London Conference had created a new warrant for UN leadership. A board, co-chaired by the Afghan government and UNAMA, would coordinate aid budgets. UNAMA would strengthen its human rights–monitoring capacity but also offer technical support through UN agencies, funds and programs where appropriate.

This was good news for Afghanistan. For those of us at UNAMA who had helped craft the compact, it was good news for the partnership we had forged over five years.

———

In retrospect, it is clear that the London Conference took place in an atmosphere of unwarranted optimism. Despite brave assurances from Afghan and Western leaders alike, security was not adequate. On the contrary, a reinvigorated Taliban was preparing its first major offensive since it was run out of Kabul in 2001. Their target was Kandahar, the Taliban's traditional base, where they (wrongly) expected that Canadian and other NATO forces would have no stomach for a real fight. The Taliban had been preparing the ground for this step for four years, gradually pushing into the same valleys in the east and southeast that the mujahidin had once used during the anti-Soviet jihad.

During this period, there were a handful of scattered military confrontations across Afghanistan. Two and a half years before, for instance, in July 2003, US and Italian forces mounted Operation Haven Denial against what were then called "Taliban remnants" in parts of Paktika and Khost provinces, in eastern Afghanistan, near the Pakistan border. (This was near the site of Anaconda, a 2002 operation in which US-led forces had attempted to trap remaining Taliban and al Qaeda fighters before their escape into Pakistan.) A few months later, in November 2003, elements of the US 22nd Infantry Regiment and the 10th Mountain Division undertook Operation Mountain Resolve in the high country of Nuristan and Kunar provinces, farther up along Afghanistan's border toward the northeast. In that battle, one insurgent commander was reportedly killed, but most of the others skipped back to safety across the border. A year and a half later, on June 28, 2005, a four-man SEAL team was attacked at high altitude in the mountains east of Asadabad, the capital of Kunar province. A total of three US Navy SEALs were killed, as were sixteen more Nightwalkers and aircrew when a rescue helicopter was shot down.

Taliban terrorists were most active in the south of Afghanistan, where they observed no red lines. On March 24, 2003, for instance, Mullah Dadullah Lang, the Taliban's senior military commander until his death in 2007 at the hands of US and British Special Forces, executed Red Cross delegate Ricardo Munguía in the Shah Wali Kot district of Kandahar. Yet such outrages did not receive the international attention they deserved. From late 2002 onward, the world's attention was focused mostly on the conflict in Iraq.

In the years between 2003 and 2006, insurgent combatants continued to funnel into Afghanistan from the southeast. Despite setbacks, the Taliban managed to establish an infiltration "jet stream," a line of small strongholds running from northwestern Pakistan into Afghanistan that deposited groups of fighters into the valleys of Helmand and Kandahar. The removal of two notoriously ruthless governors—Sher Mohammad in Helmand and Jan Mohammad in Oruzgan—had cleared formidable obstacles from their path. The fighting capacity of British, Canadian and Dutch troops was still unproven; most had not yet deployed. The stage was set for a major Taliban surge.

By 2005, there were already signs that the Taliban were confident enough to take the offensive. In the last week of May 2005, Mullah Abdullah Fayaz, a powerful cleric leading the Kandahar Ulema Shura, or Council of Islamic Scholars, delivered a withering denunciation of Taliban brutality. On May 31, a few days later, he was gunned down by two assassins on his way home from prayers. At his funeral the next day, a huge bomb tore through the mosque, killing twenty people, among them Major General Akram Khakrezwal, the influential Alikozai tribal leader whom Karzai had made police chief for Kabul. Dozens more mullahs would be killed over the next eighteen months, crippling the power of government to gain new allies within Afghanistan's powerful religious institutions in the south.

Afghans grasped the meaning of these setbacks faster than foreigners. In late spring 2005, Defence Minister Abdul Rahim Wardak acknowledged that the insurgency was more robust than anticipated, and that previous upbeat reports had been "wrong." In a July 2 meeting,

Karzai signalled deep concern for Kandahar's northern districts, now under vigorous Taliban pressure. Amrullah Saleh, the youthful head of Karzai's National Directorate of Security, declared that the country was experiencing a "creeping invasion" of Taliban operatives from Pakistan.

In the same July 2 meeting, Karzai discussed a recent broadcast from the newly established Khyber television service, now transmitting from Pakistan to both sides of the border. Their newscast was one long advertisement for the Taliban. Even Pakistan's intelligence service seemed to be openly cozying up to the Taliban: around this time, we received reports that Pakistani intelligence (ISI) agents were inviting Afghan governors to Dubai to meet a notorious Taliban sympathizer.

In describing the threat, Karzai disliked the term "insurgency," which implied a level of grassroots support that the Taliban still lacked. They were using bombs and attacking schools, tactics that ordinary Afghans found just as loathsome as we did. Nevertheless, these random attacks put the new government on the defensive. Property prices in Kabul, always a leading indicator of the country's situation, were tumbling.

In August 2005, I bid adieu to the Canadian troops, who were leaving Kabul and redeploying to their new (more dangerous) mission in Kandahar. It was moving to stand before them on the parade ground at Camp Julien, which had been the principal base for the Canadian contingent of ISAF since 2003. The soldiers who served in the capital had protected Kabul's population and secured huge caches of weapon. They richly deserved the city's gratitude.

Later that month, my colleagues and I went to Kandahar to see Canada assume responsibility for the Provincial Reconstruction Team (PRT). The US task force commander for Afghanistan, Major General Jason Kamiya, accompanied me. Canada's move into Kandahar freed up the American contingent that had been operating in the area. Washington was delighted to see an ally filling a key slot, as the Iraq campaign continued to place huge demands on US military resources.

My speech that day was an appeal for moral clarity. It would take real bravery to stand tall alongside the people of Kandahar against Taliban violence, I said. But stand tall we would. The outgoing contingent—US Army Task Force Bayonet—had done an exceptional job under hard circumstances. But the Canadians would face even greater challenges. Their move into Kandahar coincided exactly with the gathering Taliban offensive.

The insurgents were not even pretending to be a pole of attraction for ordinary Afghan villagers. But by wrecking the state-building effort, they hoped to create a vacuum that one day, when international will flagged, they would fill.

Karzai and the people around him therefore knew that the best bulwark against Taliban influence was a strong state. Amrullah Saleh, the country's security and intelligence chief, for instance, was a firm believer in the rural-focused National Solidarity Programme (NSP), which according to World Bank estimates delivered dramatically positive results, anchoring stability at village level. Saleh's analysis showed that districts where such programs had been implemented were much more likely to withstand Taliban pressure. (Unfortunately, even as the Taliban threat was rising, the NSP was being cut, a casualty of post-election turf battles.)

The enemy was also adept at tapping into grievances that sprung from amid Afghanistan's complex tribal structure. Some tribal leaders, for instance, nursed grudges against Karzai's Popalzai clan, and also begrudged the Barakzai clan of Nangarhar governor (and formerly Kandahar governor) Gul Agha Sherzoi, both of whom had been part of the governing clique that had called the country's shots since 2001.

Among Afghanistan's shadowy drug barons, the Taliban had powerful allies. Some were still based in the eastern Afghan city of Jalalabad, at the junction of the Kabul and Kunar rivers, where the industry took off in the late 1980s. Others preferred the relative anonymity of Kabul, Quetta or Dubai. But ever since the Taliban got their start in the 1990s,

Kandahar, farther west, had been the country's drug capital, fed by a true horn of plenty—the fertile, well-irrigated rhombus of farmland Lashkar Gah in neighbouring Helmand province.

In September 2005, a counter-narcotics jirga took place in Kandahar. Six hundred elders from across the province gathered under a white tent next to the governor's office. They were magnificent to behold, a sea of white robes, snowy beards and bobbing turbans ranging in colour from flaxen white to raven black. Almost all tribes and all districts were represented. Only a few had boycotted. Several opium kingpins sat in the front row, shifting uncomfortably when a statement displeased them, yet unable to change the tenor of the debate. Others preferred to monitor events through their placemen, who were well known. It was not quite democracy, but the community had come out in force to send a message of solidarity with the new governor, Asadullah Khalid.

The drug industry was becoming entrenched. The village of Baramcha, on Helmand's southern border with Pakistani Baluchistan, was a bustling narco-bazaar. Helmand itself was considered a sort of opium Klondike for ambitious Afghan criminals. There had been talk of an eradication program, but by mid-August 2005, only 5,000 hectares had been eradicated across the entire country, an amount corresponding to less than 10 percent of the total growing area for this national crop.

By the time we arrived at the jirga, elders had been making speeches for two days. Governor Khalid called opium a "blot" on Afghanistan's reputation. Haneef Atmar, the minister of rural rehabilitation and development, declared that honest and unified government would be impossible if farmers didn't step back from drugs. British ambassador Rosalind Marsden and I argued that if Nangarhar province in the east could end opium cultivation, as it had that year, then so could Kandahar and Helmand in the west.

In the end, the jirga's pronouncement went against poppy. The elders understood that embracing opium meant embracing the war that came in its wake. But there was a condition: they needed seeds, fertilizer and other inputs for legitimate crops to replace drugs. I recall one senior Alikozai tribesman from Kandahar's Arghandab district declaring to me forthrightly, "If aid was forthcoming we would not grow poppy."

Indeed, Arghandab stayed drug-free in the period following the jirga. Cultivation fell sharply all across Kandahar—but it kept growing in Helmand. The problem was that support for legitimate, less profitable forms of agriculture remained weak.

———

As summer 2005 turned into fall, the Taliban's three main war councils (shuras), all based in Pakistan, were on the warpath. The largest, in the city of Quetta, about 160 kilometres south of Kandahar, although nominally under the control of Mullah Omar, was dominated by Mullah Dadullah Lang and Mullah Abdul Ghani Berader, veterans of the Taliban's brutal reign in the central Afghan highland region of Hazarajat. Together, they would lead the fight in southern Afghanistan for the next three years, backed by training and logistics cells scattered across the lawless northeastern fringes of Pakistan's Baluchistan province.

The Miram Shah Shura—based northeast of Quetta, in mountainous North Waziristan, within Pakistan's violent and largely autonomous Federally Administered Tribal Areas (FATA)—was a platform for Jalaluddin Haqqani, his hotheaded sons and their al Qaeda allies.

The Peshawar Shura, based even farther north, included representatives from both Quetta and the Taliban-allied Haqqani network. But Gulbuddin Hekmatyar and his lieutenants were its animating spirit. It relied for its recruits on the Darul-Uloom madrassa near the city of Attock, in Pakistan's Punjab province. (Peshawar had traditionally been a staging centre for Pakistani meddling in Afghanistan, but over time it lost ground to Quetta; the experience of 1994–96 had taught the Taliban and their Pakistani ISI patrons to make the Afghan south, the centre of gravity of the Pashtun tribes, their natural focus.)

Each shura was headed by a local legend. Hekmatyar and Haqqani had been lions of the anti-Soviet jihad. Dadullah and Berader had been among the Taliban's most terrifying field commanders. But the golden thread linking them all was the Pakistani ISI, which was using Taliban proxies to orchestrate a new push for influence in Afghanistan in 2005.

The Taliban playbook was taken from their successful campaign of the mid-1990s, in which they had subdued almost every Afghan province. They also drew inspiration from the anti-Soviet jihad of 1979–89 (in which the mujahidin had been allies, not enemies, of America). But their concept of operations had even deeper origins—in General Vo Nguyen Giap's adaptation of Mao's guerrilla principles to Indochina, as described in his Vietnam War–era bestseller, *Military Art of People's War*. Within the Taliban inner circle, Giap was a hero. His reliance on ambush and manoeuvre, booby traps and intimidation was easily translated into the Afghan vernacular of war.

The new wave of suicide attacks was coming mainly from North Waziristan, where a series of truces negotiated by the Pakistan Army with local groups had given militants the run of the place. Like South Waziristan, it was teeming with Taliban logistics-and-training centres. These arrangements were seen by Taliban leaders as starting points for the fully fledged Afghan state they hoped soon to be running, a state that might even include parts of Pakistan. At the very least, they expected to be negotiating their place in a post-Karzai landscape once the state institutions created at Bonn failed. In the meantime, their short-term military objective for 2006 was the same one they had seized so suddenly in 1994: Kandahar city.

This was about much more than revenge for the Taliban's rout in 2001. They were fighting for an "Islamic Emirate of Afghanistan," a land that would be ruled with an iron fist under sharia. Ironically, this Taliban campaign would have been stillborn without the active support of the ISI, an intelligence service promoting the interests of a Pakistani nation that these same jihadis decried as un-Islamic.

Most of Pakistan's senior officers were raised during the era of the anti-Soviet jihad, and they still believed that support for the Taliban, and the policy of creating strategic depth in Central Asia, was the only effective means to counter Indian influence: only by making Afghanistan a kind of vassal state could Pakistan be certain its western flank would never be turned. Taliban rule, it was imagined, would thereby buttress Pakistan's own unity while ridding Afghanistan of Indian influence—the invisible hand they saw forever poised to pry Pakistan apart. Through Giap and his ilk, the Taliban spoke the language of anti-colonialism. Yet the Taliban were, and remain, a very real neo-colonial force themselves, proxies of a power with regional ambitions centred in Pakistan.

Pakistani backing for the Taliban came from a variety of directions. Pakistani madrassas and religious parties provided funds and facilities. Pakistani drug traffickers and other merchants involved in the war economy lent helping hands. Military advice, cash and sometimes guns flowed through official channels. Serving officers, from the ISI and other Pakistani military commands, could not always be easily distinguished from Taliban commanders and their hired guns.

Their orders inside Afghanistan were to hit US, ISAF and Afghan government objectives, in that precise order. Since schools, clinics and roads were growing proof of the government's competence, they were legitimate targets too. If civilians got in the way, such "collateral damage" could be justified. The main thing was to sow fear, knock the government off balance, then blame foreigners for the loss of innocent life.

There was some friction, however. Taliban commanders bridled at the hauteur and pettiness of their Pakistani masters. But they were powerless to slip the ISI yoke. Those who stepped out of line were threatened or imprisoned; unauthorized contacts or operations could lead to reprisals against family or home villages.

Without ISI patronage, the Taliban campaign would have quickly faltered. Retired general Muhammad Aziz Khan, instrumental in Pervez Musharraf's coup in 1998, was revered by the Taliban, as was former lieutenant general Hamid Gul, a militant firebrand who had led the ISI during the difficult period after 1989, when US support shrunk following the end of the Cold War.

The Pakistani officers who had served with the Taliban on Afghanistan's battlefields were emulating the British frontier officers of previous generations—hand-picked by viceroys from Lawrence to Curzon to further their empire's interest. A select few were flamboyant figures, such as Colonel Imam (aka Punjabi Brigadier Amir Sultan Tarar), who had been Pakistan's consul general in Herat in 1994 and remained a principal liaison with Mullah Omar. With his long beard and fluent Pashto, Imam was nevertheless something of a laughing-stock among more discreet ISI and military intelligence officers, most of whom simply got the grim work done without becoming caricatures.

According to the best-informed observers, a half dozen or so Pakistani colonels and brigadiers, all active during the Taliban's years in power, were now back in the saddle, coaxing the coals of insurgency back into flame. They were joined by trainers, tacticians and specialists from across the armed forces, as well as by bomb makers and other irregular assets on which Islamabad traditionally had relied in its mischief making in Kashmir and elsewhere. It was a light structure, working to a proven formula. But behind this group stood the "deep state"—Taliban-friendly allies in politics, business and media. Some in this group justified their involvement on grounds of patriotism backed by providence, holding their cross-border campaign to be ordained by the Holy Koran.

By 2006, these Pakistani facilitators had restored an astonishing degree of regimentation to Taliban ranks. When pressured by Washington to arrest Taliban operatives, the ISI picked up innocent Afghan refugees. New commanders or fighters who failed to follow orders were shipped off to Kabul, where they were exposed to the vicissitudes of the Bagram detention centre or an unreformed justice system under the Northern Alliance. Or they were simply branded al Qaeda, then handed over to US authorities.

Almost all Taliban leaders named on the Consolidated List of the UN's Al-Qaeda and Taliban Sanctions Committee were now living in Pakistan. A few had been killed or carried off to Guantanamo. A few more had been rehabilitated, including Abdul Wahed in Helmand, an archrival of Sher Mohammad. But well over a hundred active, listed jihadis were living in Pakistan's cities and towns, with most supporting the revived campaign.

Not that the life of these Pakistani-enabled Taliban operatives for the most part was anything but nasty, brutish and short. In 2005, at least 2,000 insurgents were killed in Afghanistan. In 2006, the Taliban death toll doubled. Field commanders who dared step foot on Afghan soil lived in fear for their lives. Even those who hid in Pakistan were not entirely safe from US drones.

Ordinary Afghans were terrified of the Taliban, but especially of the prospect of suicide bombings, a tactic that by this time was common in Iraq, Israel, and Sri Lanka but had not yet gained wide acceptance in the rest of South and Central Asia. But this was changing. In January 2006, Taliban spokesman Mohammad Hanif said 250 more *fedayeen* were trained and ready to carry out their bloody missions. Thanks to the globalization of jihad via the Internet, the nihilistic violence of Iraq's civil war was migrating to the Hindu Kush.

On January 15, 2006, just two weeks before the London Conference, a vehicle loaded with explosives detonated alongside a convoy carrying Canadians in Kandahar. Glyn Berry, the accomplished diplomat who was political director of Kandahar's PRT, was killed, along with two Afghan civilians. Ten others were wounded, including three Canadian soldiers, despite the heavy armour designed to shield them from such blasts. After sizing up the new Canadian equipment, the Taliban had simply started building bigger bombs, whose size quickly drew comparisons to those fielded in Iraq. The IED war was only beginning.

On February 15, 2006, President Karzai began a two-day visit to Pakistan, where he publicly asked President Musharraf to do more to stem cross-border attacks. In private, the Afghan side had presented a list of suspected Taliban leaders in Pakistan implicated in the suicide campaign. A heated argument ensued, with Musharraf focusing much of his ire on Afghan security and intelligence chief Amrullah Saleh. Afghan foreign minister Abdullah and others also quarrelled fiercely with their hosts. Everyone was frustrated with Pakistan's see-no-evil approach.

On February 28, 2006, I was back in Kandahar to observe the transfer of command to Canadian brigadier general David Fraser. I had attended such ceremonies before. But this time I was representing the United Nations, which provided ISAF with their mandate. United States Army lieutenant general Karl Eikenberry, who later would become US ambassador to Afghanistan, was officiating. Fraser put on the bravest of faces, emphasizing the difficulty of the mission but also speaking to its multinational character and the willingness of Canadians to support their allies in this critical combat theatre.

Well trained and well led, the new Canadian battle group would go on to distinguish itself in the years that followed. But apart from a couple of Afghan National Army *kandaks* (light infantry battalions) and a stay-behind company of US infantry, the Canadians had little in the way of ground support. The British 16th Air Assault Brigade would not reach full strength in neighbouring Helmand for months, with Dutch forces in Oruzgan to follow.

Now the situation in southwestern Afghanistan was only getting hotter. In the first two months of 2006, there had already been eleven suicide bombings in Afghanistan, mostly in Kandahar—compared with seventeen across the whole country in all of 2005. By the time the full British force arrived, its six platoon houses were pinned down, unable to manoeuvre. British and Canadian resupply lines were constrained by a limited number of helicopters. Dutch forces in Oruzgan, meanwhile, were reluctant even to engage with the enemy. All in all, there were still only three battalions of international forces in southern Afghanistan, an area almost as large as England and Scotland combined. Afghanistan's agricultural heartland was vulnerable, public opinion teetering, and the Taliban knew it.

If the military situation was bad, governance was worse. Sher Mohammad's replacement in Helmand, the amiable engineer Mohammad Daoud, was an English-speaking moderate beloved by all but respected by few. In the hard-knock school of Helmand, he would have difficulty coming to grips with the chaos around him. With the province lurching into full-blown insurgency, there simply was no firm hand on the tiller. This was the problem with the educated "reformers" so beloved by Western diplomats and journalists: they were often unable to get the jobs done in tough places like Helmand.

For better or worse, the real power brokers who had checked Taliban power since 2001 were on their way out. As a consequence, Oruzgan and northern Helmand saw a heavy influx of new fighters in early 2006. The towns of Sangin and Gereshk, on the Helmand River, and Maiwand in Kandahar—from which it was a short jump to the Panjwayi district, called the birthplace of the Taliban because it is home to so many of its senior leaders—were filling up with fresh militant cadres.

Panjwayi is just thirty-five kilometres west of Kandahar city. The Canadians concluded that the city was at risk of assault by the Taliban (who'd been pushed north of the Arghandab River by Panjwayi elders wishing to avoid battles on their land). In Zhari, north of Panjwayi and west of Kandahar city, the Taliban were defeated by Canadians in four successive skirmishes around the town of Pashmul. But the victorious Canadian battle group was too thin to remain deployed in the area, or in most of the other areas where it had routed Taliban soldiers. This was a common story throughout Afghanistan during this period. There were just too few soldiers to go around.

As well as anchoring the defence of Kandahar, Canadian forces supported US, UK, Dutch and Danish forces operating in neighbouring provinces. Operation Mountain Thrust, as this combined effort was called, covered parts of Kandahar, Helmand, Oruzgan, Zabul and, farther east, Paktika. In the Helmand town of Gereshk alone, the Canadians were called upon to push the Taliban back three times.

I returned to Kandahar in early April 2006, my fifth visit in the space of less than a year. Despite the passage of only a few months since my last trip, I could see that the floodwaters of insurgency had risen markedly. Yet violence wasn't the only thing on the minds of the locals. "The actual problem is the government itself," said Hayatullah Rafiqi, the respected head of Kandahar province's education department. Without qualified people, institutions could not be built. The police and courts were perceived as predatory institutions, mechanisms for extracting bribes, not enforcing justice. Unemployment was high. Alcohol use, a taboo in many traditional parts of Afghanistan, was growing. All this was giving the Taliban their opening.

In many cases, the level of competence of Afghan officials was truly appalling. Kandahar's first post-Taliban governor, for instance, had been Gul Agha Sherzoi, "an illiterate man who could not even write his own name," as one hostile elder put it. This was an exaggeration but perhaps not a great one. The greater knock on Sherzoi (now governor of Nangarhar) was his reputed link to the opium trade. Nevertheless, he's skipped from one powerful position to another thanks to his close alliance with Hamid Karzai—a bond strong enough to survive a fist fight between Sherzoi and Ahmad Wali Karzai, the president's brother. Kandahar's elders had one message: Bring back strong Afghan institutions led by qualified officials.

Kandahar was just one province. But because of its size, Taliban roots, drug connections and agricultural richness, it was Afghanistan's strategic centre of gravity, at least for a plurality of its population, which was Pashtun. If Kandahar was in danger, the entire country was in peril. Issues such as the Durand Line and land disputes could be solved over time. But uncontrolled insurgency in the country's heart was a problem of another order. When shots were fired outside the president's own Kandahari village of Bala Karz, no one could feel safe.

———

My UNAMA boss, Tom Koenigs, and I visited Islamabad in April 2006. After a short glide over the jagged funnel of Khyber, we landed amid a warm zephyr at Chaklala Airport in Islamabad—home to Pakistan's strategic nuclear command. Our meetings with ministers and ambassadors revealed two broad preoccupations.

First, the Pakistani government vociferously continued to deny that support for the Taliban was coming from anyone in Pakistan other than rogue elements. In the same breath, it took great pains to emphasize the sacrifices of the forces it had deployed along the border. Though cynical, this self-serving narrative still had traction in Islamabad. Indeed, some of the people we spoke to actually believed it.

Second, for diplomatic reasons, the US embassy and UK high commission were pressuring Afghan leaders, from Karzai to Afghan peace commission head Hazrat Sebghatullah Mojadeddi to then Kandahar governor Asadullah Khalid, *not* to finger Pakistan for its insurgency-related miseries. This campaign was proving to be notably unsuccessful, as withering denunciations were hurled down the mountain passes from Kabul almost every day. From a certain angle, it looked like a slow-motion farce, with Musharraf playing the role of Walter Mitty. But too many people were dying for anyone to laugh.

Ahmed Rashid, perhaps the most famous Pakistan expert living, adamantly told me that Pakistan's army was covertly supporting the Taliban. He had personally confronted Musharraf earlier in the year, in fact. According to Rashid's information, Pakistan's objective was either to appoint governors in Afghanistan's south or to partition the country outright. In other words: naked, neo-colonial aggression.

Musharraf himself was unleashing the heaviest salvoes in the barrage of denials. We met him in his full general's regalia—he retained the title of chief of the army staff—in his official residence, the Aiwan-e-Sadr, on Islamabad's Constitution Avenue. He presented us with a history lesson, which lapsed into an impassioned monologue.

His story began in 1979, when over 30,000 mujahidin were sent north and west into Afghanistan to fight the Soviets. Not one of these mercenaries, Musharraf said, had been on his own. The entire web of operations had been controlled "from here." Together with indigenous Afghan forces, they ultimately had forced a Soviet withdrawal. But the mujahidin force also had left its mark on Pakistan in the form of a new "Kalashnikov culture." Millions of Afghan refugees had remained in camps on the Pakistan side of the border, breeding grounds for extremism that Pakistan was not able to control.

The next chapter in his story began in 1989, when, with the Cold War ending, the United States had dropped its support for Pakistan's interventionist policy in Afghanistan. The breakup of the Soviet Union also had brought Chechens and Uzbeks to Pakistan's borderlands and into Afghanistan itself. Some of the Arabs imported to join the anti-Soviet jihad, meanwhile, had splintered off into al Qaeda. In the 1990s, amid all these developments, Musharraf told me, Pakistan bravely did its best to end the warlord-led butchery in Afghanistan. (He passed over his country's support for Hekmatyar, Haqqani and the other Taliban-friendly militia leaders, which we didn't bother bringing up.)

The September 11 attacks, he continued, had come as a shock to a country already reeling under these pressures. Musharraf had championed a policy of confronting the hard core of terrorism with military force, while using economic growth to overcome the broader phenomenon of extremism. He called it "enlightened moderation." In his telling, this policy had achieved spectacular economic growth, which was helping on many fronts. Pakistan had supported the Bonn Agreement, then the Afghanistan Compact, pledging $250 million for Afghan reconstruction. Al Qaeda itself had been reduced to fighting in "penny packets," even if it retained links to the Taliban in Afghanistan.

It was a tour de force of self-serving chutzpah, a victim's narrative from a military officer who still had not gotten beyond the outdated notion that India was the region's greatest military threat. Like a jilted lover, he complained that Pakistan had been a major US proxy in a decisive Cold War theatre but then was unceremoniously dropped. He was portraying Pakistan as a passive victim hard hit by the downward spiral of violence in Afghanistan.

Perhaps many of the people who heard this spiel from the Pakistani president accepted it. But I had already been in the region too long. Since I'd begun work in Afghanistan, I'd been briefed by legions of military and intelligence analysts, including a healthy number of candid ISI officers, active and retired. I also had spoken to a few ex-Taliban leaders who told me stories about their days as playthings for the ISI.

I could not name names to Musharraf, of course. But I didn't have to. Pakistan's president, of all people, knew the truth perfectly well. How could he not?

Picking the most obvious hole in Musharraf's narrative, I asked him about Taliban sanctuaries in Pakistan, noting that I had seen their handiwork first-hand in Kandahar. The question hit a nerve. It was all a fraud, Musharraf told us. He said he could discern the hand of (who else?) India in fabricating documentary evidence purporting to prove Pakistan's complicity.

The meeting ended with more denials. All of the intelligence that we presented to him was "rubbish," and it was the Afghans who should "get their own house in order." The Taliban had some backing from religious parties and "rogue elements" in the ISI, he was prepared to admit—but that was all.

This was the brick wall we were up against in Pakistan. And with Musharraf in power, I didn't see any prospect of things changing any time soon. In my notes at the time, I made a very personal list of the five reasons why Pakistan was continuing its proxy war.

First, it was determined to retain influence built up since 1979, culminating in the period of Taliban rule from 1994 to 2001, when Pakistan had treated Afghanistan in many respects as a fifth province. Second, it sought unfettered access to Central Asia for commerce, as well as strategic depth against India. Third, it was uncomfortable with India's new post-2001 prominence in Afghanistan, which extended from building the new Afghan parliament to erecting cold-storage facilities south of Kandahar city. Pakistan did not have the strength to confront India directly but instead engaged in a two-front proxy war, with Kashmir and Afghanistan being the two theatres. Fourth, it saw Afghanistan as a pawn in its ongoing rivalry with Iran, whose ports competed with Karachi and Gwadar as inland gateways. Fifth, many in Pakistan were livid at the international attention and aid lavished on Afghanistan, which was perceived to be in some vague sense coming at Pakistan's expense.

Pakistan's ultimate ambition was to have events follow the same pattern as in 1989, when the Soviets withdrew from Afghanistan and Pakistan asserted control through its Taliban proxies. When Mullah Omar had the crucial meetings to launch his movement in Kandahar, ISI convoys were already at the gates of the city, orchestrating their success. As they advanced toward Herat in 1995, then later toward Kabul in 1996, the hapless but ever-enthusiastic "Colonel Imam" and other ISI officers were at their side. When Taliban prime minister Mullah Rabbani established his home in Kabul, it was right next to Pakistan's embassy. The ambassador's residence was itself the property of Abdul Rasul Sayyaf, the Islamist warlord and early ally of Osama bin Laden, both in the 1980s and then again when bin Laden returned to the country after his time in Sudan. The telephone lines for Kandahar and Kabul after 1996 had been linked to domestic exchanges in Quetta and Peshawar. It was an open secret that Afghanistan under the Taliban had resembled an imperfect Pakistani protectorate. Some version of these events, people in Pakistan believed, would happen again once the US and NATO forces packed up and left. As Musharraf and the ISI saw things, history simply was repeating itself.

On May 4, 2006, British lieutenant general David Richards assumed command of ISAF in succession to Italian lieutenant general Mauro del Vecchio. His task would be to complete ISAF's expansion to the south and the east, where the US Combined Forces Command (CFC) under Eikenberry still had the lead. Richards led an impressive military command team in the form of the headquarters of the NATO Allied Rapid Reaction Corps (ARRC). But he concluded that without more substantial political leadership to drive improvements in reconstruction, administration and services, there was little prospect of reversing the slide in security.

Informed by much the same intelligence about Pakistan that I have described in this chapter, Eikenberry initiated an analytical effort to "profile the enemy"—to describe the facilities, command structures and personalities attached to the three shuras in Pakistan. In late 2006 and 2007, this led to a revised US assessment of not only the Taliban generally but also the more specific roles played by Hekmatyar's forces and the Haqqani Tribal Organization.

On July 31, 2006, I joined Richards, Eikenberry and Afghan defence minister Wardak for the formal transfer of command from CFC to ISAF in the southern region. By this time, the new team in the south was starting to look impressive. The Afghan National Army, complemented by incoming British and Dutch forces, was becoming more capable. The Canadians, meanwhile, were developing into a battle-hardened force. Starting on July 8, elements of their battle group operating in northern Kandahar were involved in a week of fighting in Zhari district, north of the Arghandab River. On July 13, they relieved British forces in the Helmand town of Sangin.

Stung by criticism of its capacity at the local level, the Afghan government had begun to hold provincial security-assessment meetings, where governors would describe obstacles to security and reconstruction in their provinces. Under the impetus of Richards and our UNAMA team, these meetings grew into the Policy Action Group (PAG), the first joint forum in which local and international players met at a senior level to analyze the nature of the growing insurgency. We developed key objectives and resolved to meet weekly. Unfortunately, progress was uneven. And the reason was the same one we'd always confronted: nothing we said or did could control what was happening on the Pakistani side of the border.

Koenigs and I returned to Islamabad in late August 2006, spending two hours with Major General Shujaat, deputy director general (analysis) of ISI. His dubious script echoed what we'd already heard from Musharraf: "There is a perception that the ISI is still sponsoring the Taliban," he told us, labelling this charge "ridiculous." Pakistan had pursued a hands-off policy for four years. We have "disassociated ourselves," he added. Pakistan, he told us, was taking a "black-and-white" approach to anyone on the UN sanctions list. And so on.

As proof, he offered that his men recently had shut down a medical facility in Quetta that stood accused of treating injured al Qaeda operatives. This last claim was true, for all we knew; Pakistan often made symbolic moves against the Taliban to present the appearance of acting responsibly. (Following the August 2006 discovery of a Pakistani-linked al Qaeda plot to blow up jetliners departing from Heathrow Airport, for instance, the ISI was quick to take credit for the early warning.) But these were merely token moves. The real ISI policy had changed little since 2001.

Over the summer and fall, Musharraf took his propaganda campaign on the road, even appearing on Jon Stewart's comedy show during a trip to the United States. In the memoir he published during this period, *In the Line of Fire*, he side-stepped Pakistan's relationship with the Taliban entirely. For local consumption, meanwhile, he played up the Indian threat, accusing Delhi of stirring up a Baluch insurgency in Pakistan's largest province. He even claimed that India was assisting the Taliban. Many Pakistanis no doubt believed these conspiracy theories, as anti-Indian paranoia had remained a common feature of Pakistani life since the country's creation.

In late July, Operation Mountain Thrust was continuing in southern Afghanistan. Its new centrepiece, Operation Medusa, would clear a cluster of Taliban fighters out of the lush orchards along the Arghandab River in and around the key Panjwayi district. The Canadian battle group, backed by US infantry, led the attack, with supporting elements from British and Dutch units. On September 2, the Canadians surrounded another large group of Taliban, destroying it from afar with artillery and air strikes. The next day, Charles Company of the 1st Battalion, Royal Canadian Regiment, crossed the Arghandab to attack the village of Pashmul (again). They lost four soldiers in two engagements but eventually pushed the Taliban back, inflicting punishing losses—over 500 killed, more than 150 captured. Hundreds more Taliban fled westward, many to Gulistan in Farah province, south of Herat, where they torched the district administration building on September 14.

Together with recent US engagements in Kunar, at the eastern end of the country, it was the largest sustained allied engagement with Taliban forces since 2001, and the most serious battle that NATO forces had fought on the ground in their near-sixty-year history. All in all, in 2006, 130 US and NATO soldiers were killed in hostile actions, mostly from small-arms fire. This was up from 74 in 2005 (in fact, the number had been just 50 in that year, if one excluded losses from the aforementioned SEAL team incident and a helicopter shot down in Zabul). In 2007, the figure would rise to 184, with most of the casualties now being caused by IEDs (improvised explosive devices), mines and suicide attacks.

Taliban soldiers were battlefield zealots. In the Panjwayi and Zhari districts of Kandahar, where more of the summer combat took place, they had stood their ground in the face of far superior military power, and paid for it. Out of a force of 2,000 Taliban fighters, nearly half had been killed or injured. But their passion for martyrdom was not limitless, and over time the Taliban began to avoid concentrating their forces. Instead, their main effort moved westward into Helmand, as well as northwest into Farah, and featured an increased reliance on IEDs.

During all this, Pakistan could have helped NATO by cutting Taliban supply lines and preventing the arrival of reinforcements from jihadi training camps. Instead, it gave the Taliban one less thing to worry about by renewing its ceasefire agreements with the Islamic Emirate of Afghanistan, as the loosely organized Taliban confederacy in Pakistan's Waziristan border region called itself.

The Pakistani government portrayed these agreements, concluded on September 5 and 6, as traditional peace deals guaranteed by tribal elders. But they appeared much more like a gesture of appeasement. With these measures, on the same day that NATO troops were flushing Taliban fighters out of Pashmul, Ali Muhammad Jan Orakzai, former XI Corps Commander and the governor of Pakistan's North West Frontier province, was in effect giving the Haqqani network the green light to scale up its campaign of suicide attacks.

On September 28, 2006, Koenigs and I visited Quetta for the day.

To our surprise, the local police chief was refreshingly candid. He sheepishly acknowledged that the city and province were packed with Taliban operatives over whom he had "no power." His authority, he confessed, applied only to a small percentage of Baluchistan territory. Baluchistan's governor, Owais Ghani, meanwhile, gave us Musharraf's party line. The Taliban must be elsewhere, he told us—probably in Afghanistan. This was not his concern. Besides, he could not resist stressing, their cause was just.

On precisely the same day, Musharraf was in Washington, dining at the White House with President George W. Bush, Vice-President Dick Cheney, Secretary of State Condoleezza Rice—and Hamid Karzai. The Afghan president avoided eye contact with Musharraf and at first declined even to shake hands. As the night went on, however, Karzai decided to engage his Pakistani counterpart. He put a new idea on the table that evening: Afghanistan and Pakistan should jointly hold a peace jirga with tribal leaders from both sides of the border to define ways to restore trust and improve security. Afghanistan would host the first session. Musharraf reluctantly signalled his acceptance. But of course, he would drag his heels before such a meeting actually took place. The show of cooperation with Karzai was kabuki for the Americans' benefit.

In late 2006, the multilateral Policy Action Group overseeing Afghanistan's southern region travelled to Kandahar under Hamid Karzai's leadership. Governor Asadullah Khalid hosted the delegation, joined by governors of neighbouring provinces. While in Kandahar, Karzai met and prayed with elders and visited several important shrines. He spoke to students at Ahmad Shah Baba High School, invoking national heroes like the first Afghan amir, Dost Mohammad Khan, and urging the youth of Kandahar to cherish their stories. Then he turned to his main theme, defiance of terrorism. "Being martyred for the sake of learning is better than being illiterate and slaves," he told the students.

The president urged Afghan parents to send their children to school, and children themselves not to be frightened: "We can tolerate when our children are killed on their way to school, but we cannot accept slavery and illiteracy." He then unleashed this barb, for the benefit of the diplomats and politicians in attendance: "The government of Pakistan wants our children to serve as doormen at their hotels in Karachi instead of becoming doctors and engineers." Afghanistan's neo-colonial plight had never been put more bluntly.

"Pakistan is fearful of a stable and prosperous Afghanistan," he added, "even though I have repeatedly assured [Pervez] Musharraf that stability and prosperity in Afghanistan is in the best interest of his country. After the collapse of the Soviet Union, the world left Afghanistan at the mercy of its neighbours. . . . Pakistan, in particular, destroyed our system and our national institutions. Afghans and Pashtuns are still being killed on both sides of the border, and I tell Pakistan to cease hostilities and animosity against Afghans and Pashtuns."

The president also had a warning: "Pakistan wants to rule a land where great empires of Genghis Khan, Alexander the Great, Britain and [the] Soviet Union have been brought to their knees. Great empires have not been able to occupy this land; how can Pakistan dream of doing so?"

Addressing the elders, the president said that "reconstruction projects can only be implemented when there is security. It is not only the government's duty to protect Afghanistan's security; it is the people's duty too. People have a duty to defend their houses, roads, schools and clinics, and to collaborate with the security institutions in ensuring a safe environment for the implementation of reconstruction projects."

He was ashamed of the depths to which Afghan pride had sunk: "Regrettably, those who build roads, power stations, clinics, and schools for the Afghan people are being killed. The Afghan nation defended their country during the Soviet invasion of Afghanistan and defeated the world's then biggest colonial power. Today, a Canadian girl defends Panjwayi and loses her life for the sake of your security."

Karzai was referring to Captain Nichola Goddard of the 1st

Regiment, Royal Canadian Horse Artillery, killed on reconnaissance in Panjwayi when her armoured car was hit with two Taliban rocket-propelled grenades. For Afghanistan's traditional patriarchs, the idea that they required protection from female foreigners serving in combat was a bitter pill to swallow.

———

Although the battle against the Taliban had become my number-one concern, other critical issues were also competing for UNAMA's resources. One was police reform. In the spring, Koenigs had put his foot down over the new police chief for Kabul, the successor to General Mohammad Akram Khakrezwal, who'd been killed the previous year in a Kandahar suicide bombing. Karzai's nominee was a Soviet-era officer suspected of torturing witnesses. Karzai yielded but was incensed that his hands were being tied by outsiders. Still, in subsequent meetings to place qualified police officers who had passed an exam as well as UNAMA vetting, Karzai appeared composed and cooperative. And together, we were able to fill the lists of senior officer appointees across the country.

Yet even when Karzai acted responsibly, we often still received pushback from the power brokers surrounding him, including at the Ministry of Interior. Some officials wanted to control trafficking routes. Others wanted a say in supplying contracts or patronage for hand-picked private security companies. Scandal, conspiracy and manipulation seemed to lurk behind every corner. It was a difficult reality to convey to outsiders.

At the end of 2006, as Kofi Annan was leaving his post as UN secretary-general, I helped prepare UNAMA's biannual report to the UN Security Council. For the first time since these reports had been written, we highlighted Taliban command and training centres in the Pakistani borderlands from Quetta to Peshawar. Yet in the final version of the report approved by New York, these references were removed. Pakistan was a major contributor to UN peacekeeping, the justification went, and so it would not pay to rock the boat. The "plausible deniability" of Islamabad's neo-colonial policy remained intact.

All in all, it had been a terrible year for the international effort in Afghanistan. The sense of hope, and even complacency, in evidence at the London Conference in January had yielded to growing violence. Karzai and Musharraf now were engaged in a public war of words. The US strategy for resolving this feud was to have the two countries hash out their differences together at polite White House discussions and in tribal gatherings. Neither approach was working.

The only consolation was that we were showing the enemy that he was not invincible. On December 24, 2006, Mullah Akhtar Mohammad Usmani, the Taliban's Helmand shadow governor, was killed in an air strike, creating a new job opening at the Taliban council of war in Quetta.

Many more job openings would be created in the years following. If Pakistan wasn't going to fight the Taliban, the United States and NATO would have to do the job instead.

CHAPTER EIGHT

WESTERN APPROACHES

Herat, a large town with a very strong shahristan, a citadel and a suburb.
It has running waters. Its cathedral mosque is
the most frequented in all Khorasan.

—Hudud al-Alam

No single observer could bear witness to all of the traumas that Afghanistan has suffered in recent years. By closely studying a geographically representative handful of the country's myriad regions, a clear picture can now start to be drawn of Afghanistan's overall state. Many of my travels were in the western provinces of Nimruz, Farah and Herat, on the border with Iran, which is where I begin this chapter.

Farah had once been a rich province, with wide irrigated valleys of wheat, orchards and pasture for animals. But three decades of neglect had left it a virtual wasteland. The ancient system of underground water channels had silted up. The anti-Soviet jihad had been fought here, especially in the vicinity of the strategic airport at Shindand, just to the north in Herat, blasting much of the province into rubble. No Afghan government had bothered to rebuild.

Farah's link with the Afghan population centres of the east was the country's ring road, and it was a mess. Despite ongoing work to repave it, and the deployment of a US-led Provincial Reconstruction Team, little progress had been made. By early 2007, many Pashtuns in Farah were embittered toward the Karzai government and the provincial governor, the son of a tribal elder once convicted for heroin possession in the United States. After 2001, plum jobs had gone predominantly to those, like Karzai, who traced their ancestry to the country's Durrani tribes. The Taliban were tapping into a reservoir of ill will.

In the province of Herat, to the north of Farah along the Iranian border, a complex contest for power had broken out following Ismail Khan's ouster from the governorship in 2004. His allies were now pitted against assimilated Farsi-speaking Pashtun tribal leaders and Shia community leaders, led by, respectively, Maulavi Khodaidad, a prominent cleric and judge, who served as one of Karzai's local lieutenants; and governor Sayed Hussain Anwari, himself a Shia but also a former agriculture minister and governor of Kabul province.

The influence of Iran's Shiite theocracy was strong in this part of the country, and not just among Afghan's Shiites (who, though an overall minority within Sunni-majority Afghanistan, had a strong presence in Herat). The diminutive Ismail Khan, with his white beard and turban, had deepened his flirtation with Iran even after 2001 (though he himself was Sunni), flouting Afghan convention by maintaining a household in Mashhad, the capital of Iran's Khorasan province. Shia influence had grown throughout Ismail Khan's time as governor: Hezb-i Wahdat, a Soviet-vintage outfit based around Afghanistan's largely Shiite Hazara ethnic minority, had been the only political party permitted to open an office in Herat until the very eve of Ismail Khan's 2004 ouster.

In the mujahidin government of the early and mid-1990s, Ismail Khan had never been a towering figure. The man's military record certainly wasn't particularly impressive. His attempts to block the Taliban advance on northwestern Afghanistan in 1995 had been risible, and Herat ended up falling a full year before Kabul. In an attempted comeback, Ismail Khan's most effective lieutenant was killed. In another, a betrayal caused his force to be badly mauled in Badghis province, east of Herat. As mentioned, Ismail Khan himself spent nearly three years as a Taliban prisoner.

Yet like so many of the country's warlords, the man had a talent for bouncing back. And his enemies had a habit of perishing at convenient times. By the time he was muscled out of Herat, he had made himself a necessary evil. And his departure caused the province to tip into anarchy during the years that followed.

Businesspeople were fearful. Rival groups, fearing reprisals, rearmed for their own protection. Two-bit jihadis quickly developed into public menaces. Ghulam Yahya Siyaushani, a self-styled Robin Hood from a small village in the Gozara region, who had briefly been Herat's mayor in 2001, then head of public works under Ismail Khan, began to agitate against foreigners. He evaded Afghan and Italian efforts to corner him, launching a regular campaign of rocket attacks against UN offices. Khwaja Issa, another member of the anti-Ismail coalition in 2004, blossomed into a full-fledged rebel. The most dangerous was Fazel Ahmad, a notorious figure linked to the group that had torched Herat's UN buildings in 2004. In early 2006, gangs linked to Fazel Ahmad incited attacks on Shia processions at the Shiites' annual Ashura mourning ceremonies, resulting in dozens of casualties. By the beginning of 2007, Herat's body politic was a bloodied mess, and highly vulnerable to encroachment by the Taliban, who by this time had penetrated into neighbouring Farah.

Then, in April 2007, things got worse. During a battle against Taliban fighters in Herat's Zerkoh Valley region, US Special Forces called in air support from bombers and an AC-130 gunship. Masses of Taliban fighters were killed. But so too were several dozen civilians, including women and children. The episode disgusted many locals and even prompted one power broker, Nangilai Khan, to switch allegiances to the Taliban.

This was in just one of the country's many regions. Yet what happened here symbolized so much of what was going wrong across the country: corrupt or indifferent governance, local squabbling, Taliban infiltration, battlefield mistakes. It wasn't hard to see why so many were tempted to throw their hands up in despair.

The miseries of Farah and Herat would only complicate efforts to stabilize the south, which is where much of my attention was focused. By early 2007, the Taliban had carved out commanding positions in Kandahar, Helmand and surrounding provinces, as well as in ancient Zabulistan, to the east, comprising the tiny provinces south of Kabul, on the Pakistan border. One of my challenges was to describe this new reality accurately, even though it might dampen the generally upbeat military reports that were being circulated at the time and thereby promote skepticism of the mission among the international leaders whose support we needed.

Our analysis was used selectively by all parties. Afghan officials downplayed their own shortcomings, emphasizing passages in our reports that focused on Pakistan's Taliban sanctuaries. Their Pakistani counterparts, meanwhile, played the opposite game. The truth was that there was plenty of blame to go around. On both sides of the border, police generally were on the take, predatory or both. They made their own arrangements with drug networks or insurgents just to survive.

Shortly after New Year's Day 2007, we gathered in the residence of my boss, UNAMA chief Tom Koenigs, which was affectionately known as Palace Number Seven, to review the counter-insurgency campaign so far. Six or seven Afghan ministers were present, as well as ambassadors from the main countries with troops in Afghanistan and the top ISAF military brass. I urged those present to embrace fully the principles of counter-insurgency that our Afghan partners had articulated: civilian casualties had to be avoided, and the lies of the Taliban and their Pakistani allies had to be exposed.

Unfortunately, nothing we decided in that room could change the fact that Pakistan was doing little or nothing to control the Taliban menace, and that there simply were not enough Western troops in the country to secure all of the provinces under threat.

A week later, on January 8, I decided the time had come to be clearer in public about these issues. In a press conference at UNAMA's headquarters, looking ahead to our activities in 2007, I raised the issue of the international sanctions prescribed by United Nations Security Council Resolution 1267, which targeted a long list of Taliban and al Qaeda leaders.

When one reporter asked me about the Taliban presence in Pakistan, I appealed to common sense. "When someone makes a statement that Mullah Omar is living outside Kandahar and has never set foot in Pakistan since 1995, this is not a true statement," I said, directly addressing Pervez Musharraf's disingenuous talking points without naming the man. "It does not help us focus on reality and build trust. When someone says that there is a [grassroots] uprising of Pashtun people against the government in Kabul, this is not true. . . . The truth is that these networks are operating in both Afghanistan and Pakistan, that the leaders spend time in both countries and that law enforcement and even military action is required wherever they are located."

For insiders in Kabul, everything I said was well known, even banal. But for these things to be said from a podium marked with the UN logo—that was something new. The last journalist pressed me on what Pakistani actions would be required to bring peace. "In our view," I concluded, "there is more work to be done in and around Quetta."

While my candour was well received by my Afghan and international colleagues, it didn't go over so well in New York, where incoming secretary-general Ban Ki-moon—on one of his first days in office—was taken to task by Pakistan's ambassador. In Islamabad, it provoked a furious response. On January 9, the day after my press conference, the Pakistani Foreign Ministry in Islamabad issued the following statement: "The suggestion that some of the 142 Taliban on the 1267 Sanctions Committee may be in Pakistan is an unsubstantiated assertion that demonstrates ignorance of ground realities in Afghanistan and insensitivity to Pakistan's efforts to counter militancy and terrorism."

It went on: "Actions taken by Pakistan have led to the arrest of several leading Taliban figures. One may ask how many Taliban on the list have been apprehended by the Afghan and multinational forces especially when the statement implies their presence inside Afghanistan. Pakistan is not solely responsible for taking action against militants and terrorists. To capture undesirable elements and prevent them from entering into Pakistan is the responsibility of the forces operating on the Afghan side. . . . The UNAMA officials would be well advised to restrict themselves to their mandate and refrain from questioning the intentions and sincerity of Pakistan, which has done more than any other country in the international efforts against terrorism."

Validation of UNAMA's position came swiftly, and from an authoritative quarter. In an annual threat assessment dated January 11, 2007, outgoing US director of national intelligence John Negroponte concluded: "Many of our most important interests intersect in Pakistan, where the Taliban and al-Qa'ida maintain critical sanctuaries. . . . Pakistan is our partner in the war on terror and has captured several al-Qa'ida leaders. However, it is also a major source of Islamic extremism. . . . Eliminating the safe haven that the Taliban and other extremists have found in Pakistan's tribal areas is not sufficient to end the insurgency in Afghanistan, but it is necessary." This was the first US acknowledgment from a senior level that Afghanistan's deepening insecurity had its roots on the Pakistani side of the border.

The assessment went on to mention al Qaeda's "leaders' secure hideout in Pakistan." This language elicited another frenzied denial from Islamabad. It must have appeared to some in Pakistan's Foreign Ministry and army that our two January 2007 statements had been coordinated. In fact, we had drawn our conclusions independently from the bloody evidence of 2006. It had been obvious for more than a year that escalating violence was being fuelled from Pakistan.

—————

Over that winter, I happened to be ploughing through Tolstoy's *War and Peace*. Having served for six years as a diplomat in Moscow, I was somewhat embarrassed to be doing my remedial reading in Kabul, far from any battlefield graced by Bolonsky or Kutuzov. But Afghanistan proved to be the perfect backdrop to this literary epic, with its sweeping, cinematic take on Napoleon's incipient invasion of Russia. That conflict, I reminded myself, also featured a confident Western power ultimately bogged down amid extreme brutality in unfamiliar terrain.

Sure enough, Afghanistan's fighting season began early in 2007, long before the snows had fully melted. On February 1, a large Taliban force overran the town of Musa Qala, in the north of Helmand, executing several pro-government elders in the process. Over the next ten months, Musa Qala would become a major hub for Taliban fighters, bomb makers and opium traders. It became one of the first Afghan district centres under full enemy control post-9/11.

It was impossible to say who was now calling the shots in Helmand, jihadis or drug barons. Since the arrest of Haji Bashir Noorzai, the most powerful member of Kandahar's leading drug-trafficking family under the Taliban, pre-eminence in the southern drug trade had passed to Haji Juma Khan, a Baluch tribal elder with assets in Kandahar and Kabul, who now preferred to operate from Quetta and Dubai. As poppy cultivation vaulted skyward in 2007, Haji Juma Khan was backing anyone who could move his product across southern Afghanistan and on through the red desert to Baramcha, the narco-bazaar on the Helmand–Baluchistan border, as well as other infiltration points into Pakistan.

Pakistan may have been supplying the Taliban with leadership and training, but it was opium that was bankrolling the insurgency. And those whom the drug dealers couldn't bribe, they would kill. Neither the Afghan government nor ISAF could offer ordinary Afghans protection from the bands of thugs stalking the land, some under Taliban commander Mullah Dadullah Lang, others in fee to Juma Khan's drug cartel. With the fall of Musa Qala, the Taliban had almost total control of a wide swathe of Helmand. Karzai wanted ISAF to take the region back. But Western commanders simply didn't have the forces to do the job.

On March 5, 2007, south of Lashkar Gah, Helmand's capital, the Taliban kidnapped Italian journalist Daniele Mastrogiacomo with his Afghan driver, Sayed Agha, and well-known Afghan correspondent Ajmal Naqshbandi, who had been acting as interpreter. When Agha was beheaded, Mastrogiacomo was shown on a video pleading abjectly for his life. On March 20, he was freed from one of the Taliban strongholds along the Helmand River in return for the release of five of their commanders. It was a show of profound weakness on the part of the Afghan government and its international partners. As for Ajmal Naqshbandi, he was killed on April 8. It would now be open season for copy-cat kidnappers eager to exact their own ransoms or to sell prisoners to the Taliban.

But with growing frequency, ISAF got their man. Mullah Dadullah Lang, a notoriously brutal Taliban commander in southern Afghanistan, had called the shots throughout the Mastrogiacomo episode. The released commanders were his associates, including a brother. Buoyed by such success, this wraithlike presence overplayed his hand. He was detected moving through open ground on May 12. Thanks to the handiwork of the British Special Boat Service (SBS), operating together with US Special Forces, Dadullah was killed, his body later washing up in an irrigation canal. (It was publicly displayed to quash Taliban claims he had escaped.)

Sadly, however, there were always more jihadis ready to fill the leadership void: at the Taliban's Quetta Shura, Mullah Abdul Ghani Berader was swiftly named Dadullah's successor.

In Pakistan, meanwhile, Musharraf was having his own problems. On March 9, the president suspended Chief Justice Iftikhar Muhammad Chaudhry, citing dubious corruption charges against the jurist. The president's real motivations, insiders knew, were connected to Chaudhry's interest in government human rights abuses. It was also believed that Chaudhry wanted Musharraf to step down as chief of the army staff prior to embarking on a new term as president—a nod to separation of powers that Musharraf was not prepared to give.

Within days, lawyers across the country took to the streets to protest the bullying of their chief justice. Chaudhry became a folk hero, feted by crowds at every stage of his journey down the Grand Trunk Road to a dinner in his honour in Lahore on May 5. For the first time since Musharraf had become president in spring of 2001, a grassroots movement was imposing real limits on his power.

With his Pakistani counterpart weakened, Karzai seemed to become more careful with his rhetoric, lest he push Pakistan too far. Still, tensions along the border continued to build, often flaring into violence. In a major incident in May 2007, uniformed Afghan and Pakistani security forces each crossed over into one another's territory—the Jaji district of Paktia in Afghanistan, and Kurram Agency of Pakistan's FATA—backed by artillery barrages.

During this period, the security situation across Afghanistan varied widely from province to province and even from district to district, a situation that persists to this day. This was especially true of the four provinces to the east of Kabul: Kunar, Laghman, Nangarhar and Nuristan. These valleys of the Kabul and Kunar rivers had been crucibles for ancient civilizations going back to the Greco-Bactrian Kingdom of the pre-Christian era. The Mughals had treated the area as a duchy of their own empire. In some mountainous areas, communities didn't adopt Islam until the late nineteenth century, when Amir Abdurrahman imposed it at musket point.

Nangarhar, in particular, was a case study in Afghanistan's complex demography. It is home to roughly 1.5 million Afghans, most of them from three Pashtun tribes—Shinwar, Mohmand and Khogyani. The first two are Ghilje Pashtuns, while the Khogyani are Panjpay Durranis. Nangarhar also is home to various minorities, including the Pashayi, who speak their own Indo-Iranian language, as well as smaller tribal groupings. This diversity is reflected in Nangarhar's politics. In the 2005 elections, eight out of fourteen members elected from the province to the national Wolesi Jirga were from the Mohmand tribe, three were Shinwari, one Khogyani and two Pashayi. In the first provincial council elections, seven members were Mohmand, four Shinwari, three Khogyani and three Pashayi.

At about 30 percent, Nangarhar's adult literacy rate is relatively high by Afghan standards. The province has long been a hotbed of political activity, with up to forty parties active in recent election campaigns. Unfortunately, the most influential remain jihadi outfits such as Hezb-i Islami. Since 2001, local politics has been dominated by a bewildering assortment of feuding strongmen and sheriffs—a mélange that became a special object of my study while in Afghanistan but which is too complex to describe in detail here. Suffice it to say that (as of this writing) Nangarhar has had eight police chiefs (of widely varying degrees of competence and honesty) since 2001.

Up to 2005, Nangarhar had produced up to one-quarter of Afghanistan's opium. It also had become a major hub for trafficking and heroin production. Most of the old guard of families who began cultivation in Afghanistan in the 1980s had come from Jalalabad, Nangarhar's capital, and neighbouring districts. But aggressive eradication and political pressure by Governor Gul Agha Sherzoi gradually reduced cultivation, confining it to mountainous districts such as Achin, Pachir wa Agam and Khogyani. The old families adapted by exporting their activities to the drug frontier in Helmand and beyond.

In 2006, Nangarhar became a staging ground for terrorism as well. When radical Hezb-i Islami leader Mohammad Younis Khalis died on July 16, 2006, he was succeeded by his even more radical son, Anwar ul-Haq Mujahed, who launched the insurgents' Tora Bora Front, which would pour fighters, bomb makers and propaganda from Peshawar and Waziristan into Nangarhar's Khogyani district.

At 9 a.m. on September 10, 2006, two remotely controlled Pakistani anti-tank mines detonated under a convoy on the main road near

Khwaraan village in Khogyani. Five people were killed, including Khogyani administrator Abdul Jabar, as well as his district chiefs of police and intelligence, one driver and one bodyguard. With one strike, the local leadership was decapitated. Tensions rose throughout Nangarhar.

The attack had followed a crackdown by the governor and border-guard chief, Haji Zahir Qadir, the headstrong son of former Northern Alliance leader and Nangarhar governor Abdul Qadir, in the province's southern districts. In a bid to prevent the Tora Bora Front from gaining traction, Zahir's men had arrested two former criminals in Sherzad district. Senior Khogyani power brokers had also been sent packing from the provincial government, including Dr. Mohammad Asef Qazizada, a former deputy governor and 2004-era Karzai campaign manager. Zabeth Zaher, a former provincial director of finance, had been captured by US ISAF forces on suspicion of conspiring with insurgents, along with former Khogyani district governor Malik Omar. Governor Sherzoi and his border-guard chief were cleaning house, in other words.

Any of the parties marginalized by these moves could, jointly or separately, have ordered the September 10 attack. It was sophisticated, involving an IED sourced outside the country. It also coincided with the torching of a nearby girls' school—a Taliban hallmark.

In subsequent months, six more US soldiers were killed in IED attacks, stoking further tensions. On March 4, 2007, in Nangarhar's relatively peaceful Shinwar district, F Platoon of the US Marine Corps Special Operations Company was attacked as their convoy drove down a road. Believing themselves to be experiencing a large-scale ambush, they opened fire on dozens of passersby. Nineteen civilians were killed, another fifty wounded, in one of the worst civilian-casualty incidents to date. The outcry was deafening, and understandable. The plight of these innocent families touched us all. President Karzai visited Shinwar to pay respects. (A Marine court later investigated the incident but declined to press criminal charges.)

In another incident, in Deh Bala district of Nangarhar, air strikes were called against a large gathering of what were believed to be militants. In fact, it was a wedding. Forty-seven civilians were killed, including the bride.

Then, on June 11, 2007, the Toor Ghar police post came under fire in the Grabawa area of Khogyani. When police called for backup, a firefight erupted in the ensuing confusion between them and the ISAF and Afghan National Army forces that had responded. Air strikes on the police post in the early morning of June 12 killed eight police, injuring five. It was a tragic case of mistaken identity.

All of these incidents roiled the otherwise calm waters of what had been, until 2006, a relatively peaceful Nangarhar. But remarkably, none of them pushed any major segment of the population into a posture of rebellion. Outside a few valleys in Nuristan and Kunar, there was no grassroots indigenous insurgency in eastern Afghanistan. In this sense, the situation in the province was unlike that of Herat, Kandahar, Helmand and other border provinces. Despite major incidents involving civilian casualties and friendly fire, the main security challenge in the province was confined to Khogyani district.

When border-guard chief Haji Zahir was transferred to Takhar in far northern Afghanistan (where he was later implicated in a major drug seizure), Governor Sherzoi took the opportunity to consolidate his authority, cut poppy production and impose rough justice on the province. As US troop levels increased throughout 2007, the governor reached out to tribal elders, who helped him form a united front against the Taliban menace. Gradually, the area began to stabilize.

It was an example of what could be done when the crucial security pieces—a strong-minded Afghan governor, an adequate number of Western troops and buy-in from tribal leaders—combined in the same area. Unfortunately, in most parts of Afghanistan, some or all of these elements were still missing.

Even before 2001, the Taliban presence in Nangarhar had been weak. But in neighbouring Kunar, to the north, it had been almost non-existent. And once the Taliban regime fell following 9/11, Kunar's few high-profile jihadis either fled or ended up in Guantanamo.

When the Taliban insurgency started up in 2006, it at first had virtually no old guard in Kunar on which to build. Instead, much of the province remained a corrupt (but relatively peaceful) fiefdom for timber smugglers. With the arrival of Assadullah Wafa as governor, the province began to make headway toward more competent, well-ordered government.

Nevertheless, Kunar eventually would get caught up in the wave of Pakistani-backed insurgent violence that swept over virtually all Afghan border regions in 2006 and 2007. Anwar ul-Haq Mujahed, the leader of the Taliban's Tora Bora Front, began to organize attacks in the area. And the Taliban shura for the eastern zone, with its network of staging areas extending from Peshawar to Bajaur, had decided to prioritize Kunar and, immediately to the north, Nuristan.

These strengthened Taliban contingents met little in the way of Western military opposition. Having concentrated on the Taliban heartland to the southwest, the commanders of Operation Enduring Freedom, the US military campaign in Afghanistan, had sent only a few thousand troops to the country's eastern provinces. At one point, a single brigade—the US 3rd Brigade Combat Team of 10th Mountain Division, led by Colonel John Nicholson—covered no fewer than eighteen provinces. As for the crucial cluster of Nangarhar, Nuristan, Kunar and Laghman, grouped between Kabul and the Pakistan border to the east, it had once been secured by a single US battalion.

As a forerunner of the sort of counter-insurgency campaign that America would come to develop in the latter part of the decade, Nicholson tried to drive a wedge between the Taliban and the local population. Where necessary, his troops established a permanent presence in platoon houses, together with Afghan army and police units, sometimes in remote areas. They would then ensure that civilian partners were engaged—government and private sector alike—to transform the environment in ways that elicited a deeper loyalty from communities. One battalion pushed into the Pech Valley in Kunar. Another was installed, at heavy cost, in Kamdesh, in Nuristan province. These units came under regular attack and often relied for their survival on called-in air and artillery strikes. But the strategy showed signs of success.

In June 2007, the 173rd Airborne Brigade Combat Team under Colonel Chip Preysler, augmented by two additional battalions, took up where Nicholson's team had left off. As Task Force Bayonet, Preysler's force focused on building up the capacity of Afghan national security institutions—army, police and border police—as well as on road building. By the end of their tour, they had tripled the capacity of the Afghan National Police in the four eastern provinces. By living closer to the population and achieving the right ratio of forces to inhabitants, US units had found a way to win credibility with local communities. At Kabul's Counterinsurgency Academy, the experiences of Nicholson, Preysler and the other commanders of Regional Command East were held up as models to be studied by Afghans and their Western allies alike.

In spite of the worsening security situation in parts of the south, the national mood still generally was optimistic during this period. Aside from the Taliban, Afghanistan's old-style warlords gradually were giving up their independent fiefdoms and coming under government control. (According to one official government list, the number of such rogue commanders declined from 936 in 2005 to just 265 in April 2007.) There also was a movement afoot to expand the country's successful National Solidarity Programme, which had played a key role in developing rural regions, into new areas such as small-scale water projects and microfinance. There were plans to develop Afghanistan's mining industry, and to bring some measure of Western-style urban planning to Kabul and other large cities.

In May, Education Minister Haneef Atmar launched a five-year strategic framework for reform of the education sector. Enrolment had already shot above 6 million children. Now the focus would be on improving the national curriculum, as well as on training teachers. The response to Atmar's vision was positive. Britain, Canada and the European Commission all expanded their aid commitment.

Coordination between Afghan leaders and Western officials was facilitated with the launch of the Joint Coordination and Monitoring Board (JCMB), as authorized by the Afghanistan Compact. It had first met in the Sedarat Compound area of Afghanistan on April 30, 2006, bringing together seven Afghan ministers (the country's Oversight Committee) with twenty-one international members. The co-chairs were the senior economic advisor to the president, Ishaq Naderi, and my boss at UNAMA, Tom Koenigs.

The new mechanism was warmly welcomed. But it proved difficult to limit membership, especially on the international side. There was a pro forma quality to the first meetings, with an excessive focus on compact benchmarks rather than policy issues of substance. The next meetings took place on July 30 and November 12, 2006, in Kabul, the latter in the presence of the visiting United Nations Security Council delegation. The meeting marked the first time that the important subject of police reform was discussed at the forum. Several more meetings were held in 2007 in Berlin, New York and elsewhere.

A worrying trend began to plague these meetings. Though aid for Afghanistan was increasing, less of it was being directed through the country's government, whose new projects—with scattered exceptions, such as education—failed to attract fresh donations. The reason for this was that most Western countries wanted to spend their money where their own troops were deployed. For Britain and Canada, this meant Helmand and Kandahar. For the United States, it was in the east. This trend created new headaches, largely in the form of embittered, cash-starved Afghan cabinet ministers. By weakening the reform impulse in his government back in 2005, Karzai had himself set the stage for this pattern of want.

In June 2007, at Kabul's Serena Hotel, His Highness the Aga Khan hosted the Conference on the Enabling Environment for Private Initiative. He acknowledged the importance of laying firm foundations for a new state. But civil society and the private sector were, he felt, at least as important. "Too often, the various actors go about their business without enough reference to one another," he said, concisely capturing my own impressions of what I'd witnessed in Afghanistan. "The result often reminds me of an orchestra made up of talented and dedicated artists—but playing from different scores. The result is not harmony but cacophony."

He concluded: "Extreme forms of fragmentation have been a barrier to progress in Afghanistan." But the will and resourcefulness of individuals would permit us to overcome our challenges. In closing, he quoted an *ayat* from the Holy Koran, the motto for the Afghanistan National Development Strategy: "Verily, God does not change a people's condition unless they change that which is in themselves."

It was a brilliant event. The organizers even had the foresight to ensure Pakistani prime minister Shaukat Aziz was present to close the conference the next day. Though immediate follow-up was disappointing, an agenda was launched that has focused international attention on the role and success of the Afghan private sector ever since.

A second conference in July 2007—convened by Italy on July 2 and 3 in Rome—addressed the issue of criminal justice. After the Transitional Justice Action Plan was created at The Hague in 2005, implementation of its provisions had slowed to a crawl. In early 2007, the lower house of the Afghan parliament had passed a resolution granting an amnesty to those suspected of crimes on all sides of previous conflicts. Though of dubious legal force, the resolution had dealt a serious blow to efforts to curb impunity in Afghanistan.

The conference was attended by President Hamid Karzai and Chief Justice Abdul Salam Azimi, as well as UN secretary-general Ban Ki-moon and NATO secretary-general Jaap de Hoop Scheffer. New funding was announced for a wide variety of projects, particularly by the United States. But the key strategic result was an agreement to enhance support for the sector through an Afghan-led National Justice Programme. For the first time, this initiative would serve to unite donor efforts under a single programming framework.

Immediately thereafter, Azimi began to review the professional qualifications of the country's approximately 1,500 judges. More than 100 would be dismissed. He also compiled the ambitious National Strategy for Anti-Corruption, which was presented in 2008. It recommended an action plan, including the establishment of a high office for anti-corruption.

Azimi also improved the quality of training for new judges. Dissatisfied with an Italian-funded National Legal Training Centre aimed at all justice professionals, Azimi struck out on his own, establishing the court's own training programs. He developed the curriculum himself and was delighted when 50 of the 250 participants accepted in its first year of operation were women.

But progress was slow. Judges now had vehicles, and some had renovated courts, but their salaries were a pittance, their education in new statutes incomplete, administration lacking. Most still operated out of mud-walled facilities, with unscrupulous regional power brokers only too eager to undo judgments when they went against them. Many judges were unwilling to live in the province or district of assignment out of fear for their lives.

As the Rome conference ended in July 2007, world attention shifted to Pakistan. Gun battles were raging around Islamabad's infamous Lal Masjid, or Red Mosque, a major centre for Taliban training and indoctrination. After stating publicly that he knew the mosque's leaders harboured terrorists, including those responsible for the bombing of Islamabad's Marriott Hotel earlier in 2007, Pervez Musharraf sent in his troops on July 8. An untold number of Red Mosque occupants— thought to be at least several hundred—were killed.

Within days, the Taliban in Waziristan and elsewhere, swearing vengeance on Musharraf, declared jihad against Pakistan's army and state. In the surreal world of South Asian jihad, Pakistan's government somehow had become both a supporter and a target of the Taliban.

—·—

Just over two weeks after the Lal Masjid was stormed, on July 23, Afghanistan lost one of its titans. Zahir Shah had been a symbol of continuity in statehood reaching back to Babur and beyond. But the former king had also been a national champion of resistance to Soviet occupation, Taliban repression and Pakistani interference.

We had not seen much of him over the last eighteen months of his life. He had been treated in Delhi and Abu Dhabi for pneumonia and various heart problems. But the outpouring of public tributes on his passing was unparalleled. There was a full week of mourning after his death. His funeral bier was carried on a gun carriage from the Arg, across the Kabul River, by Eid Gah Mosque, where *fateyah* was said for his soul, and on to the hilltop where his father and wife already lay under the dome of the bombed-out family mausoleum.

As President Karzai, his government, Mostapha Zahir and we in the diplomatic corps walked behind the procession, Abdurrahman's Kabul seemed to spring back to life, if just for a day. The goodwill of the old king would be missed, I knew.

It was against this backdrop that hundreds of Afghan and Pakistani officials and tribal elders met at the loya jirga tent on the grounds of the Soviet-built Polytechnical University—where Karzai had been confirmed as president and the new constitution adopted—to chart a path forward toward ending the conflict in both countries. Many, including me, had doubted that this meeting, first discussed in Washington, would ever take place. Yet here we were.

The speeches in plenary and working groups were refreshingly frank; Pakistani officials were powerless to silence those who cited the presence of Taliban sanctuaries on their side of the border. But the agenda set by the meeting was vague. There would be a joint approach to fighting the Taliban, it was announced, and plans for another meeting in Islamabad. But with Pakistan teetering on the brink of another crisis, there was no political appetite to confront substantive issues such as whether the Pakistani army would clean house in the tribal regions or shut down the shuras. The unspoken conclusion among insiders was that Pakistan's support for the Taliban would continue, business as usual. Musharraf acknowledged as much in his final address to the plenary, on its last day, when he admitted that some Taliban leaders were present on Pakistani soil. Several observers said he was drunk. He was certainly unrepentant. Everyone knew that he had come only under duress.

Even as Karzai and his ministers did their best to deal with Pakistan, they had more mundane domestic problems to worry about, such as rebuilding Afghanistan's bureaucracy. Throughout 2006 and 2007, there had been growing criticism of the quality of Afghan administrators at the local level—in provinces and districts, cities and towns across the country. Since 2001, there had been no major program to train these people or even a systematic approach for hiring and promoting them based on competence and merit.

On August 30, 2007, the president sought to turn the tables on all those who had criticized him for his inattention to subnational governance. He removed responsibility for governors and their underlings from the Interior Ministry, a move that affected up to 10,000 staff in total, and transferred it to a new entity called the Independent Directorate of Local Governance (IDLG), which would report directly to him.

The drastic move had been championed by his chief of staff, Umar Daudzai, and by US ambassador Bill Wood. The first director of the new body was Jilani Popal, who had been Ashraf Ghani's deputy for customs at finance. Within less than a month, the IDLG produced a strategic framework for subnational governance in Afghanistan—a landmark in the country's nation building.

A whirlwind of activity, Karzai was active on yet another file during this period: multilateral trade and regional cooperation. On October 20, 2007, foreign ministers of the Economic Cooperation Organization (ECO)—comprising Afghanistan, Azerbaijan, Iran, Kazakhstan, Kyrgyzstan, Pakistan, Tajikistan, Turkey, Turkmenistan and Uzbekistan—met in Herat at a shiny new hotel that had been completed for the occasion. It was the largest multilateral meeting to take place in Afghanistan since 2001. Speaking to the assembled representatives, Karzai called for less red tape and faster transit times to ports. Afghanistan had $4 billion in annual trade with its ECO partners. It wanted to spur more regional cooperation to "show the right face of Islam to the world."

Turkish foreign minister Ali Baba Jan paid tribute to ECO achievements, including those in Afghanistan. Pakistani foreign minister Khurshid Kasuri warned ECO not be discouraged by "temporary setbacks," while showcasing its facilities at the Gwadar deep-sea port in Baluchistan. Iranian foreign minister Manouchehr Mottaki spoke passionately of the culture of the region shared by Afghanistan and Iran, which he referred to by its historic name of Khorasan. He also enumerated the many scholars and cultural contributions to Islam that had emerged from the Afghan-Iranian borderlands in Herat.

The dinner that evening was in the Ikhtiyaruddin, the Herat citadel that had been rebuilt by UNESCO. It was a magnificent sight, with torches burning on both upper and lower levels—a rear-view archeological mirror peering far back into Afghanistan's past.

Against a discouraging backdrop of military uncertainty, these initiatives—on justice, governance, regional trade and the continuing threat of Pakistani meddling—gave us in UNAMA and all the Afghan and international partners with whom we worked a sense of forward movement. But we were haunted by a recurring question: Would Afghanistan survive, with its new institutions, to see such an ambitious agenda implemented?

On September 9, UNAMA released an incisive report on suicide attacks in Afghanistan. The word "Pakistan" appeared in it dozens of times, including in such lines as "The tribal areas of Pakistan remain an important source of human and material assistance for suicide attacks in Afghanistan," and "In recent years, it has become increasingly clear that FATA (along with Baluchistan) is not only a Taliban and al-Qaeda sanctuary, but also the base for Taliban decision making and its logistical apparatus." Naturally, the report was rubbished by Islamabad. And our headquarters ordered it removed from all UN websites (though, thankfully, it can still be found on the wider Internet).

By late 2007, our mission was estimating that 8,000 people had been killed in insurgency-related violence across the country over the previous year. Seventy-eight districts, representing over a fifth of the country, were too insecure to allow UN programs to operate. The insurgency was spreading. From Farah and Ghor in the west, it was moving northward into Herat and Badghis. From Zabul and Oruzgan in the south, it was extending its reach north into the central provinces of Ghazni and Wardak—to the western gates of Kabul itself.

The conflict was bloody on both sides. On November 6, 2007, in a Pashtun-dominated district of Baghlan province, a suicide bombing at a sugar factory and ensuing gunfire killed nearly one hundred victims, among them seven visiting members of the lower house of the Afghan parliament. It was the largest single loss of Afghan civilian lives since 2001. The Taliban were also feeling the heat, however. Through our extensive network of local contacts, UNAMA began to be approached by Taliban commanders eager to save their skins. They had seen hundreds of colleagues killed and were ready to negotiate a way out. In every case, they were directed to Afghan officials. A few were reconciled. Most were not.

Over the late summer and fall, Helmand had remained a major focus of attention for Karzai's government, ISAF, the United States and Britain alike. After strenuous debate, a decision was taken to launch an operation to end Taliban domination in the Helmand Valley region, centred around the village of Musa Qala. The operation took place from December 7 to 10, with the US 1st Battalion 508th Parachute Infantry Regiment in the lead, backed by Afghan and UK forces. After the Taliban had been routed, Mullah Abdul Salaam, a former Taliban commander won over to the government side, was named *uluswal*, or district administrator. With this critical region in government hands, we could all breathe a little easier heading into the new year.

Changes were at hand within the UN mission too. In the autumn of 2007, several senior policy makers in London and Washington started to engineer the recruitment of Paddy Ashdown to be the next special representative of the secretary-general. But when Karzai met Ashdown in Kuwait, the chemistry was wrong. Ashdown, an experienced former British politician and diplomat, had made downbeat public statements on Afghanistan, including: "We have lost, I think, and success is now unlikely." Karzai and many others weren't impressed, as they made very clear at the time. Ashdown's name eventually would be withdrawn from consideration for the job.

News of one consequence of this episode reached me on a beach on December 26, 2007—Boxing Day. After an exhausting year, Hedvig and I had retreated to a vacation spot far from Kabul. At the town of Thandwe in Myanmar, the Bay of Bengal shimmered in the tropical heat, almost burning with turquoise phosphorescence. A hotel staff member interrupted my serenity with an important message. It was from my special assistant, Jo Nickolls, a talented British officer who had worked in Iraq and Sudan, who told me about the breakdown over Ashdown's known appointment and a growing rift between Karzai and the West.

Karzai's rejection of Ashdown was just one sign of that estrangement; the Afghan president increasingly was heard to remark that Western leaders were naive about the larger issue of Pakistan. The West, meanwhile, had come to see Karzai as a failing, indecisive manager, out of touch with the depredations that police and others were visiting on the population in his name.

View of Kabul, including the Pol-i-Khishti Mosque and Sar-e Chowk.

© KATE BROOKS

The Emperor's Tomb, Babur's Garden, with a new neighbourhood of mud-brick houses behind, Kabul. COURTESY CHRIS ALEXANDER

Then–interim leader Hamid Karzai visits Bamiyan, Afghanistan, in 2002. © KATE BROOKS

Karzai meets with tribal elders from the southern province of Paktia in a bid to resolve a clan dispute between two rival ethnic Pashtun clans, Kabul, February 13, 2002. © KATE BROOKS

Karzai stands between Foreign Minister Abdullah Abdullah (*right*) and Defence Minister Mohammad Qasim Fahim (*left*) at a burial, Kabul, February 16, 2002. © KATE BROOKS

Camp Julien, Kabul, the main base for the Canadian contingent of the International Security Assistance Force (ISAF). The site closed in 2005.
COURTESY CHRIS ALEXANDER

Canadian Ambassador to Afghanistan Chris Alexander presents his credentials to President Hamid Karzai at the Arg Palace, September 2003.
COURTESY CHRIS ALEXANDER

President Hamid Karzai (next to King Zahir Shah [*left*] and his chief of protocol) signs into law the new Afghan constitution following approval of the document by the loya jirga, Kabul, January 26, 2004. © KATE BROOKS

UN Deputy Special Representative of the Secretary-General Chris Alexander (*left*), Richard Holbrooke (*top*), then president of the Asia Society, and others seated on Ismail Khan's former heavy weaponry, now at a cantonment site, Herat, spring 2006. COURTESY CHRIS ALEXANDER

Alexander in a bazaar near the Kabul River on a typical market day, Kabul, 2007. COURTESY CHRIS ALEXANDER

Alexander and others under fire at the Islamic Revolution Day parade, Kabul, April 28, 2008. COURTESY CHRIS ALEXANDER

Canadian soldiers of the Royal 22nd Regiment on patrol in Kandahar in southern Afghanistan, searching a barn in the Panjwayi district, 2011. © BAZ RATNER/REUTERS

The day of departure—Alexander and his wife, Hedvig Christine, leave Kabul for the 4,000-kilometre drive to Moscow, accompanied by a security convoy, February 18, 2009. COURTESY CHRIS ALEXANDER

The Seduction of Yusuf, illustrated by Kamaleddin Behzad for the poet Sadi's *Bustan*. Herat, 1488. National Egyptian Library, Cairo. Fol. 52v.

Departing on holiday in mid-December, I had asked Mervyn Patterson, one of our senior political officers, who hailed from Northern Ireland, to use our UNAMA helicopter to visit Lashkar Gah, the capital of Helmand, to take the temperature there after the Musa Qala operation. We needed to hear from the governor, know how the police were doing, interview the Provincial Reconstruction Team. Patterson had invited his friend, Deputy EU Special Representative Michael Semple, to join him.

In their meeting with Assadullah Wafa on December 23, the governor had suddenly ordered the arrest of their Afghan staff. Semple was accused of supporting the Taliban.

It was a spurious accusation. But as so often happens, it had been kindled by a grain of truth. Semple had been pursuing a plan, hatched with just a few senior members of the Afghan government, to set up camps to rehabilitate Taliban forces who turned their coats. Upon learning of the plan's existence, Karzai and others around him had felt blindsided. For the Afghans it appeared to confirm all their worst fears about foreigners overstepping their authority. It also tapped into deep-seated Afghan anxieties about British motives in Afghanistan, still keenly felt almost a century after the last Anglo-Afghan war had ended.

Despite strong protests, Semple and Patterson were ordered to leave the country. Their Afghan colleagues were kept in detention for weeks. By the time the message reached me on the beach on December 26, we were powerless to intervene to change this result.

The dust from this incident would not settle for months. Semple's initiative may have gone off half-cocked, but the Afghan president had crossed some new lines of his own, undermining his most crucial relationships in enduring ways. It was the worst crisis of confidence to hit Afghanistan's relations with its international partners since 2001. The outlook for 2008 was bleak indeed.

CHAPTER NINE

INNER LIGHT

My name is Ahmed and my homeland is Turkestan.

—Yassawi creed

At the beginning of 2008, Afghanistan was a very different place from the one it had been seven years earlier. Echoes of celebration could be heard emanating from Kabul's wedding halls in the night. Barber shops and other communal meeting places were packed with audiences watching the latest Bollywood hit on rabbit-eared TVs. Television news was saucy and hard-hitting. All across the mass media, sacred cows were being butchered.

I regarded all of these as important steps in Afghanistan's rehabilitation. It is one thing for foreigners to build roads and schools. But without a proud and vibrant culture for Afghans to call their own, the crucial ingredient of self-respect is absent.

Islam, of course, is a dominant part of Afghan culture. On this front, I was struck by the unity of the *ulema*, the senior Islamic clerics. More than sixty of them would meet every month in the National Ulema Shura, a major consultative body that Hamid Karzai had re-established early in his presidency. It was his principal sounding board on religious issues; members were drawn from across the country, roughly two from each province.

Despite countless losses from among their number in Kandahar and elsewhere, these clerics remained fiercely loyal to the state and its new constitution. While denouncing civilian casualties on all sides, a move that sometimes involved criticizing NATO, they also explicitly denounced the Taliban message as un-Islamic. Whatever the state of the counter-insurgency, the country's religious leaders were proving a major bulwark against extremist propaganda.

They were an impressive group, and I had the opportunity to meet many of them, including one memorable figure in particular. At the opening of jirgas—the inauguration of parliament—a blind, compact man with black beard, white skullcap and dark sunglasses invariably would first take the microphone, making great rooms resonate with a powerful, clear nasal voice. *"Bismillah-i rahman-i rahim . . ."*—"In the name of Allah, the compassionate, the merciful . . ."

The man behind the voice was Qari Barakatullah Salim, one of the most eminent masters of Koranic recitation in the Islamic world. Born in Askamena, in eastern Nangarhar province, he had become *hafiz*—the honorific title of those who have learned the entire Koran by heart—by the age of nine.

As a boy, he had been educated in Cairo, learning Koranic recitation in all seven of its classical forms. He had come first in twelve international competitions, a record for one of his generation. He also published poetry in Pashto under the title *Ishq-e Nalem*, or "Failed Love." His opening prayers from Islam's holy book had become a kind of invocation for a country trying to retrieve its identity and confidence. This musical voice, simultaneously new and ancient, was the one I identified most closely with the new Afghanistan.

Yet he was far from alone in leading the effort to revitalize Afghanistan's ancient culture and sense of collective self-respect. In this chapter, I take readers to different parts of the country, and briefly profile some of the people, Afghans and foreigners alike, trying to perform that essential task.

The night watchman at Kabul's Christian Cemetery had not heard of any of the famous explorers whose remains he guarded. In fact, he seemed quite detached from his low-paying job. The small graveyard—a walled parallelogram—lay beneath Bibi Mahru, a low hill at the junction of several postwar neighbourhoods, near the Sherpur cantonment, built by British and Indian troops during the Second Anglo-Afghan War. A sop to British entreaties, the cemetery had also once contained Kabul's first prison outside the royal palaces.

It was Abdurrahman, the legendary amir who presided over Afghanistan in the late nineteenth century, who had allocated this plot for non-Muslim burials. Deputy Officiating Surgeon General Joshua Henry Porter was here, having succumbed to pneumonia in Sherpur in 1880. Brevet Major John Cook VC (5th Gurkhas) died in 1879 in the battle to seize Takht-i-Shah, the highest point on the ridgeline that overlooks Bala Hissar, as it was then described. Monuments to eight more fallen soldiers from the nineteenth century had been repaired by the first British units who happened upon the cemetery in 2001.

Now they were surrounded by the names of hundreds of fallen ISAF members (if not their remains, which had been flown home for burial), mostly those who had served in Kabul. There were five tablets of British names on the wall, one still on the ground, bearing more than two hundred names in all. Over twenty-five German names were inscribed. There were sixty-two Spaniards who had perished in a plane crash in 2003, as well as twenty-five killed in later incidents. The names of seven Canadian soldiers killed in the first three years were here, and those of thirty-six others who fell in 2006. There was another tablet with French, Italian, Romanian, Spanish, German and American names. It was today a multinational mausoleum.

I observed this moving sight on a warm, sunny, snowless January day. The shouts of children playing on the slope above already had the shrillness of spring. But my eyes were riveted on these newly engraved memorials, whose ironic juxtaposition with nineteenth-century graves called out to the historian in me.

The British had fallen in the nineteenth century in pursuit of their Forward Policy, designed to protect India from Afghanistan and the Russians who lay beyond it. This policy had been followed by "masterful inactivity" and the "closed door," but in reality the Raj had never forsaken its focus on influence at Kabul. Since 2001, on the other hand, soldiers from Britain and other Western countries had died defending Afghanistan against neo-imperialist forces based in Pakistan. It was an odd inversion of geopolitical roles. Yet some things hadn't changed. Now, as in the days of the East India Company, opium was a driving economic force in the region. Today, as then, not every subsidy was having the desired effect.

Many of those buried in the cemetery were aid workers and international emissaries who lived and died during the Cold War. Lyubov Mikhailovna Kudriavtseva—*"grazhdanka CCCP,"* a "citizen of the USSR"—had fallen on June 3, 1946, age twenty-three, her lovely tombstone now permanently wreathed in red poppies. Charles Clarke of the International Civil Aviation Organization died in 1955. Frederick Newgard, an American engineer, passed away at Kandahar in 1946. George H. Harding of Ohio, an engineering consultant, died in 1962. Robert Walter Logan of Australia died in 1965. Anastasia Vasilievna Samoilova, of Mezina in what is now the Czech Republic, died in 1946.

The Hippy Trail also had its victims. There were the Henleys, presumably British, killed on June 30, 1969, in a "motor accident on the Salang pass"; Serge Guy Letessier of Le Mans, France, who died at Farahrod on August 13, 1969; Germain Tanguay and Gregoire Laflamme of Quebec, who died in 1972. The lack of organizational affiliation or other detail on the tombstones suggested that these people had come to Afghanistan for no other purpose than to experience its beauty.

But soldiers still had pride of place. Charles Hinstin, of French resistance fame, *"commandeur de la Légion d'honneur,"* died in 1962. A monument to the memory of reporter and cameraman Andy Skrzypkowiak and "all Polish freedom fighters fallen in Afghanistan during the war with the Soviet Union, 1979–1989" had been placed in 2008 by Polish foreign minister Radoslaw Sikorski. French foreign minister Bernard Kouchner had also left a tablet in 2008, "*en hommage aux victimes de l'engagement humanitaire en Afghanistan.*" There was also a small memorial to Lieutenant Colonel Carmine Calo of the Italian army, killed by the Taliban while serving as a military advisor to the UN Special Mission to Afghanistan, on August 22, 1998.

Then there were the post-9/11 NGO workers who had been in Afghanistan at the same time as my colleagues and I. United Nations High Commissioner for Refugees protection officer Bettina Goislard had been killed in Ghazni in 2003; Raffaele Favero (Raphiulla Khan), "*morto a Kandahar nella terra che amava e che noi tutti abbiamo amato*"; Gayle Tamsyn Williams, killed by the Taliban in 2008; Reverend Father Aloysius Fonseca S.J., "taken by God on 8th February 2004 whilst on a mission to serve the people of Afghanistan"; Tim Rogers, Leo Ryan and Zachiolla, "who gave their lives helping Afghanistan hold the democratic elections of 9 October 2004 & thereby promote an era of peace for the Afghan people."

They were a mixed bag of humanity—all well-meaning but each dealt an unexpected blow. Cold War competition and post-9/11 reconstruction had drawn most to these latitudes. Their resting place was well tended— far better than many of the Muslim cemeteries that dot Kabul. The Taliban never got around to destroying it, perhaps because the location was discreet, hidden by wooden gates opening onto a dog's leg in the road.

After several hours of searching, I found the two names I had been seeking. Both were explorers who'd lain here for decades. One was Henning Haslund-Christensen, who had worked under the great Swedish explorer and travel writer Sven Hedin before dying in 1948. According to his biography, Haslund-Christensen "though born in Denmark had the soul of a Mongol nomad."

The second tombstone sat above a true giant. Marc Aurel Stein, born in Budapest in 1862, had also taken Hedin as his inspiration. His tombstone boldly announced: "Scholar, explorer, author. By his arduous journeys in India, Chinese Turkistan, Persia and Iraq he enlarged the bounds of knowledge."

Stein also had been a "Great Gamer"—best known for his discoveries of Buddhist treasures at the Chinese oasis of Dunhuang, on the Silk Road, as well as for retracing Alexander's probable path from what is now Kunar province in Afghanistan, through Mohmand Agency in Pakistan, to the Indus.

Although a plaque had been added in Hungarian by the country of his birth, Stein had spent much of his career in the Archaeological Survey of India. But he had been vexed by his inability to secure entry to Afghanistan. The French had stolen a march by securing a monopoly on archaeology from King Amanullah's government in 1922. When Stein finally arrived, with American assistance, he took a chill in the National Museum, then died within days in the old US Legation on October 26, 1943. As with all the other names, this beautiful corner of Kabul would become his final destination.

By 2008, Kabul had become a mishmash of shoddy housing studded with new office towers. Billboards advertising modern electronics obscured rusting murals of wilting poppies with broken syringes from bygone government counter-narcotics campaigns. "Alhaj Ghulam Tarakhel Pump Station" competed for public attention with "Dunya Private Hospital." Burkas could be seen pinned alongside T-shirts on clotheslines strung from crumbling *khrushchovki*—the Soviet-backed multi-storey apartments that were still favoured addresses in Kabul.

During this particular weekday stroll, the shops were full. A shipment of Aria oil filters lumbered past on a truck, passing Hazara men hauling carts of butane to hillside kitchens. Every city block was a riot of construction, mostly involving the questionable materials and unregulated techniques typical of all Third World real estate booms. Whatever the sufferings of Afghanistan, people in this city were making a tidy fortune off the needs of the soldiers, aid workers and entrepreneurs who'd flocked to its capital.

As new buildings went up, ancient ones were crumbling, including some real treasures. Over thirty years of war, every major archaeological site had been looted, some literally stripped bare. Ai Khanoum, the magnificent Greek city on the Oxus River (now known as the Amu), rediscovered by King Zahir Shah on a hunting trip to northern Afghanistan and excavated by the French in the 1960s, had surrendered every significant brick. Surkh Kotal, a Kushan fire temple in Baghlan, had also been picked over. The valleys of Jam and Bamiyan were now dotted with holes sunk by locals to fish out the pottery and sculpture of Buddhist and Ghorid kingdoms for cash.

Antiquities had been commoditized. Most museums in the national network had been looted or had seen their collections pulverized into shards. Most of the purloined largesse flowed to dealers in Pakistan. The more rarefied pickings, including those taken from museums, popped up at the homes of private collectors in Peshawar, Islamabad, Rawalpindi and further afield. There was no more graphic evidence of the indignities to which Afghanistan had been subjected, particularly under the Taliban, who had dedicated themselves to erasing every shred of the country's pre-Islamic history. The videos of their commanders hammering sculptures into dust in Darulaman Palace must rank among the vilest acts of cultural vandalism known to modern history.

In the Kabul Art Gallery, paintings in which human or animal life was depicted (anathema to the Islamist dogmas embraced by the Taliban) were destroyed. Buddhist stupas were blown. The culmination of this bacchanalia of ignorance was the edict to destroy the giant Buddhas of Bamiyan on February 26, 2001, an event that put the Taliban into international headlines half a year before the greater barbarism of 9/11. Following that act, some Taliban commanders reacted with disbelief at what their movement had become.

As a long-serving minister of information and culture in Afghanistan's government, Maktoum Raheen is well apprised of all these losses. On one of my trips back, we met for lunch at his ministry, an office tower near Zarnegar Park, near Abdurrahman's tomb. We were joined by Aga Khan Development Network representative Aly Mawji and Canadian filmmaker Teri McLuhan (who was then working on her 2010 documentary, *The Frontier Gandhi*, about British-era Pashtun spiritual leader Khan Abdul Ghaffar Khan). With its modular furniture and Scandinavian lighting, this room's decor seemed frozen in Afghanistan's "decade of democracy"—the years from Zahir Shah's democratic constitution in 1964 until his overthrow in the 1973 coup.

What was the situation like in 2001, after the Taliban had decamped? I asked. "Everything was gone," Raheen said. "The Taliban used this ministry more as a centre to *prevent* cultural activities." They were determined to make Afghans and the world forget that this had been a crossroads of civilizations.

After taking office, Raheen had difficulty accomplishing even the smallest tasks, such as providing a proper burial to the country's passing icons. "Do you remember Rahim Bakhsh?" he asked me, referring to a famous Hindustani classical musician and singer, very popular in the 1980s and 1990s, who had died in 2002 while in Pakistani exile. "Mahmud Khan Achakzai"—a major Pashtun tribal leader resident in Pakistan—"had sent the body to Kandahar with great honour and dignity. . . . The body reached Kabul. But the family was in very bad financial shape. I went to President Karzai and personally borrowed $1,000 [for last rites]." It was the least they could do.

Raheen's first major priority had been to reopen the press-and-information centre—a gathering place for journalists, artists, writers and cultural activists. (He succeeded, but with tragic results: the facility became the target for a suicide bomber in 2008.) He was also working on tougher measures to end looting of archaeological sites.

Here was a professor of Persian literature—full to bursting with knowledge of Attar, Sanai and Rumi, the renowned Sufi poets. But

Raheen's greatest pride was a political achievement—the passage of a liberal media law by the Wolesi Jirga in 2008. Now over fifty television stations, a hundred radio stations and hundreds of print publications in Pashto, Dari and Uzbek were creating a lively media environment— and safeguarding Afghan culture at the same time.

Afghanistan's many recent conflicts have produced a worldwide Afghan diaspora—talented (and in some cases wealthy) men and women who've fled their beloved homeland for safety and opportunity. But some of them come back, such as Zolaykha Sherzad, a graduate of New York City's Fashion Institute of Technology.

Sherzad was born into a well-connected Kabul family in the days when Zahir Shah was king. Among her first memories was the 1973 coup led by His Majesty's cousin, Mohammad Daoud Khan. In the same year, her father left Afghanistan to avoid military service. Her parents divorced, and she and her siblings moved in with their paternal grandparents.

Five years later, on April 27, 1978, Daoud's presidential reign itself ended instantly and brutally at the hands of Afghan Communists. Rumours had spread that the military was on the move. Sherzad's school sent children and teachers home. Many men had already been taken for interrogation. A curfew was enforced. At 3 a.m., Zolaykha Sherzad saw security forces arrive outside her home, with two buses already filled with her relatives.

The whole lot of them were driven out of town—and toward Pol-i-Charkhi prison, east of Kabul. Sherzad remembers the points of the soldiers' bayoneted rifles dancing in the air as the truck bumped along the road. At the prison, where they were unloaded, gunfire could be heard, and it was whispered that Daoud was already dead. "We did not know what would happen," she remembers. "Would they kill us? We heard torture at night. We saw signs of it on the floor—bloodstains.

"At first we were locked up. Then later we could move up and down corridors. Children were the messengers [between cells]. My grandmother used to write notes with matchsticks. When we came out into the courtyard to wash, we saw the guard towers and concrete walls. Eventually, the [Red Cross] found us—*voilà!* We were released." In 1978 and 1979, some 27,000 political prisoners were executed at Pol-i-Charkhi prison, but Sherzad and her family were not among them.

From then on, exile became a fact of life. "We were flown, all in the same aircraft, to Tehran. There was a big hotel—modern in contrast with Kabul," she remembered. But Iran itself was becoming unstable. The country's Islamic Revolution was only months away, and everyone in her family was deciding where to flee. Eventually, they ended up in Switzerland, where Sherzad lived until 1994.

But there was no storybook ending. For some members of the family, it was more like a sprawling five-act opera. Years of exile beckoned for many—in America, Europe or Pakistan. Others would face the painful exertions of jihad and civil war. Whole generations of Afghans, including Sherzad's, found themselves beset by a downward spiral of tragedy, dislocation and despair. Many felt helpless. All too often, lives were brutally cut short. Once-vital institutions, indeed entire fields of culture, were wiped out. The iconic Afghan singer Ahmad Zahir, a family friend who was the country's John Lennon and Elvis Presley wrapped into one, was simply lured out of Kabul on June 14, 1979, his thirty-third birthday, then shot in the head. His daughter was born the same day.

By the time planes hit the Twin Towers in 2001, Zolaykha Sherzad was working as a fashion designer in New York. As for many Afghan residents in the United States, it was almost as if this young woman was enduring a curse: after she'd already lived through coups and revolutions in two Middle Eastern countries, the mass-murdering handiwork of jihad had followed her all the way to her adopted home in peaceful America.

After American troops ousted the Taliban from power in Kabul, she decided to return to her childhood hometown to help rebuild it. "I found a workshop of artisans, run by Mercy Corps," she said, referring to an NGO with a long and distinguished record in Afghanistan. "I saw people creating economic [and] artistic development, and a heal-ing process." Sherzad became an art teacher, showing Afghan students how to be creative with the few household items at their disposal. She started her own workshop, and then a business called Zarif Design (*zarif* is Dari for "precious"), using traditional Afghan fabrics to pro-duce modern hand-embroidered designs fusing Eastern and Western fashion styles. The idea was a hit. In time, Zarif's jackets and dresses began selling in Tokyo, Paris and New York.

But Sherzad well knows what is happening beyond the relative safety of Kabul. And her childhood experiences teach her that the country can fall apart in an instant. "I am restraining myself in terms of planning," she told me. "My best employees want to leave for Iran or Turkey. I can't do this work if the Afghans don't believe in the future."

On the other side of Asmayi—the mountain otherwise known as TV hill, which divides Afghan's capital in half—Kabul University was bone dry under its canopy of pines. The trees constitute the city's largest sur-viving copse, safeguarded from foragers and woodcutters even during times of war. After being founded in 1931 by King Mohammad Nadir Shah, the university was moved to its current picturesque site shortly thereafter by Prime Minister Mohammad Hashim Khan. Over the years, the United States, the USSR, France and Germany all supported various faculties in the merry-go-round of aid and scholarships that drove the university's Cold War expansion.

One of the university's hubs of intellectual activity was the Center for Policy and Human Development (CPHD), a joint initiative of the United Nations Development Programme and former Kabul University chancellor (and national finance minister) Ashraf Ghani. The CPHD was headed up by Khwaga Kakar, whose father, Hassan Kakar, perhaps the most famous Afghan historian alive today, was arrested on campus by the Soviet-backed regime in 1981. (He spent six years in jail for alleged sedition, but the government was never able to prove his involvement in the resistance.) Khwaga finished ninth grade at Zarghuna High School in Kabul before fleeing to Pakistan in 1988, during which time she spent a year living as a nomad.

Khwaga hated Pakistan, she told me. It was conservative and restrictive, especially for women. Peshawar in the late 1980s was a far cry from the teenage life she remembered in Kabul, full of Michael Jackson and Madonna videos. Eventually, she wound up in the United States, teaching Pashto language at the University of Nebraska, of all places. Khwaga made her first trip back to Afghanistan in 2003, to collect some materials for her course work.

It was an uneasy homecoming. Kabul was a changed city, grown more conservative and fearful thanks to the lingering Taliban influence. It was a dirtier city too; garbage was everywhere. Khwaga returned to Kabul for good in 2005, to work for the Asian Development Bank on anti-corruption.

As we reached the end of the *allée* on which her centre and the chancellor's office faced each other, we encountered a garden next to the fine arts faculty graced by a 2009 statue dedicated to youth and peace. Nearby was the faculty of sharia, as well as the building site for the university's Afghan Studies Center, the creation of Nancy Dupree, an octogenarian American woman who has devoted her life to preserving Afghan culture. Farther down, on the right, past a computer-sciences centre, was a large, well-built academic building "gifted by the people of Pakistan."

When the UN's first Human Development Report for Afghanistan was issued in 2004, there was no university department qualified to assist in the development process. Khwaga's CPHD was created to help rectify that situation. Yet now, just four years after opening its doors, the centre was slated to close, a victim of the vicissitudes of donor funding. Just as it was during the Cold War, academic programs rose and fell according to the funding whims of foreign powers. The same pattern could be seen in the university's language-training courses, with Chinese, Turkish, Persian and Russian all jostling for supremacy.

One day in 2006, this Kulturkampf flared into conflict when pro-Iranian students proposed the Persian word *daneshgah* to replace the Pashto *pohantun* as the official translation for "university" on campus. The dispute was purely symbolic. Yet some students started carrying knives in their book bags for self-defence. Even the campus's Alokozai tea shop had to close. Women, in particular, felt uncomfortable, unsure of whose social and dress conventions they were supposed to be following. Even at the heart of the country's best university, two of Afghanistan's greatest problems—the scourge of militant Islam and the game of identity politics—lay just below the surface.

Across town, at Bagh-e Bala park in the Karte Parwan neighbourhood of Kabul—the city's gateway to the north and the hub for its Hindu and Sikh communities—the morning air was heavy with the dark smudge rising from many hearths, blending with the dust from demolition work. The area is home to the original British legation, the city's most venerable diplomatic mission, where we had met to launch heavy-weapons cantonment back in 2003. As viceroy of British India more than a century ago, George Curzon had insisted the legation be the most impressive in Asia. It now answered to the opposite description, neglected after partition, transferred to Pakistan after the Taliban took over, then lapsing into a hopeless ruin.

On the rise above it stood the neighbourhood's new centre of attention. Qala-e-Noburja, the Palace of Nine Towers, had been built by Amir Abdurrahman in the late nineteenth century, apparently for one of his wives. As recently as 2003, it had lain nearly abandoned, its nine towers reduced to just one and a half. But today, it houses the operations of Turquoise Mountain, an organization founded by globe-trotting British politician Rory Stewart to revitalize the country's architectural treasures and breathe new life into Afghanistan's traditional arts. From this base, Stewart's team have mobilized calligraphers in Herat and potters in Istalif, and even repaired Murad Khane, a historic precinct of Kabul's

Old City. Over the last six years, Turquoise Mountain has hosted exhibitions, readings, lectures and screenings that have made it Afghanistan's shadow culture ministry.

According to managing director Shoshana Coburn, a Williams College graduate who started life as an astrophysicist, Turquoise Mountain launched its operation with modest projects, including cleaning up garbage in Kabul's historic areas, some of which hadn't had regular sanitation services in generations. The group's head engineer "would just run down every morning to see what new building had collapsed," Coburn told me. "It was once every two or three days. These buildings had essentially been ignored. They just melt—the foundations fall apart."

Turquoise Mountain also established a training centre and clearinghouse for the city's artists. The mission was to preserve traditional techniques while raising the quality of the finished product. ("You cannot make chintzy things and sell them outside the country" was the prevailing message, Coburn told me.) After just a few years, Turquoise Mountain's artists began to find buyers, in the Gulf, Europe and elsewhere, who were commissioning screens for palaces, panels for hotels and ornamentation for mosques.

Few rival Afghan artists in monumental Islamic woodcarving. In calligraphy, they are competing with Saudi Arabia, Iran and Turkey. Their new jewellry is exquisite. "Part of the importance of the institute is that it holds the top end," Coburn said. "It brings through a generation of young people who seriously study the art and the history of this country. . . . Some of them will study abroad and sell abroad, and some of them will sell in the bazaar here."

———

Philippe Marquis was making tea. For another sun-kissed January day, the mild weather was continuing. In this quiet corner of Kabul's Shash Darak neighbourhood, the windows and doors of the Délégation archéologique Française en Afghanistan were mostly open. The rooms of the library were piled high with research materials. On a long wooden trestle table, French and Afghan workers were engaged in the painstaking task of reassembling fragments of shattered pottery into bowls. An air of quiet scholarly efficiency reigned.

DAFA, as the outfit is affectionately known among academics and NGO types, has been operating in Afghanistan longer than virtually any foreign organization. After inviting proposals from a number of nations—Britain being pointedly excluded, for historical reasons that readers will by now understand—Afghan king Amanullah Khan concluded a formal agreement with France to launch modern archaeological investigations in Afghanistan in 1923. DAFA's original founder, Alfred Foucher, had exclusive access to the country's many treasures. It was an antiquarian's bonanza.

Foucher himself was best known for originally proving classical Greek influence on Gandharan sculptural representations of Buddha. But DAFA researchers also made other major finds, such as the rediscovery in 1957 of the minaret of Jam (never lost to nomads and shepherds). In 1964, they began over a decade of work at Ai Khanoum, the only genuine Hellenistic city yet found in Central Asia. Under Soviet pressure during the occupation, DAFA closed its doors in 1982, reopening them two decades later with Marquis as the new director.

The office where we were drinking tea together was in Old Kabul—a guesthouse where DAFA members lived, worked and studied behind sturdy brick. In season, they embarked in Land Cruisers or Land Rovers for rural Logar, Wardak or Balkh to decipher the history of ancient civilizations that had inhabited the country's hillsides and valleys. The work could be dangerous, and not just because of the Taliban. In 2009, Marquis himself was buried up to his shoulders in the same avalanche that struck the Salang Pass, a route that Hedvig and I took on our way to Moscow. But the accident had done little to dim his enthusiasm for his work. He was particularly excited about Herat, where with US support the Ikhtiyaruddin citadel, originally built under Alexander the Great, was being further restored.

In parts of Old Kabul and other cities, unfortunately, it already was too late; the past was disappearing under a sea of concrete with every new half-baked building project. Already a road had been allowed to pass between the remaining minarets of Hussain Bayqara's madrassa in Herat, for instance, running over who knows what undiscovered treasures. It was not just funding that was lacking but staff with the right skills, and the political will to make preservation a priority. DAFA now operated on a combined budget of just half a million euros per year. Meanwhile, their main local partner, the National Institute of Archaeology under Abdul Nasea Firozi, had only about 30 staff, down from 120 before the conflict.

Afghanistan was still basically a rural society, where archaeology got off to a late start, Marquis told me. The countryside itself was mostly unspoiled, thus making the "archaeological potential" quite high. (By contrast, countries such as Iran, Egypt, Iraq, Syria and Turkey were already dense with excavated sites.) "In Afghanistan, everything has yet to be done," Marquis added. "Despite thirty years of war, where many things were destroyed, despite looting—in spite of everything, many things remain [in the ground]."

His research on Afghanistan's ancient civilizations, he believed, could have real-world modern-day implications. Many Afghans have a tendency to think, as he put it, "We were Muslims; we were always Muslims." By showing them that the country was home to many other faiths, historians could lead the way to a more pluralistic outlook. "The history of Afghanistan is one of a Zoroastrian country, a Buddhist country, a country with a Jewish community, one that probably had Christians," Marquis said. "This diversity is compelling. Archaeology can transmit many things."

At the time of my visit, DAFA was working on a major new discovery: the city of Cheshmeh-ye Shafa, twenty kilometres south of the ancient walled city of Balkh (itself once a great centre for Zoroastrianism). Marquis believed Cheshmeh-ye Shafa had been on a traditional road from Balkh to Bamiyan, and had been the defensive citadel for the rich, fertile lands extending from the hills to the Amu River.

As excited as he was about his new projects, Marquis also was conscious of how much had been lost in recent years. This included the Mir Zakah coin hoard—dating back more than 2,000 years and constituting perhaps the largest collection of ancient coins ever unearthed, with hundreds of thousands of specimens that together weighed up to three tons. In the civil war of the 1990s, many of these coins were dispersed by antiquities traffickers through the bazaar in Peshawar. Some turned up in Pakistan, some in Japan.

The illegal trade in antiquities mirrored the drug industry. Fed by international demand, it generated tens of millions of dollars per year, even though the diggers themselves earned little. Buyers in Europe had no idea that they were committing a criminal act. Each sculpture or bas-relief was for them simply another beautiful art piece, with a professionally invented provenance. It was another tragedy, one most Afghans did not even register. But each dirty deal struck at their very identity.

———

Kabul's most famous *librairiste* began peddling books at the age of fifteen. That was in 1969. He had taken school holidays in Pakistan and seen booksellers plying their wares by the seaside. Another childhood holiday took him to the Iranian port city of Bandar Abbas, then Teheran, where he lingered in the bazaars with that country's book merchants. By 1974, he'd started a shop at his current location in the Shahr-i-Nau neighbourhood of Kabul, a meeting spot for tourists, hippies, ex-pats and students from nearby Kabul University. He concentrated on books about Afghanistan, mixing old with new. The Daoud years of the mid-1970s had been good ones for his business. But the Communists who came in afterward were hardline censors. "It was a very dark time," Mohammed Shah remembered. In 1979, he was imprisoned for a year. After reopening his store, he was arrested again in 1981.

Things got only worse under the Taliban, many of whom were illiterate and distrusted any text that wasn't Islamic scripture. "They were not big readers," Shah told me. "We had limited customers—[a total of] around four hundred foreigners in Afghanistan. They were our customers. A few times some [of the Taliban] came to our shop and purchased guides."

Then came 9/11 and everything changed. With the Taliban gone, schools opened again. Kabul was flooded with Western newcomers, many of them eager to learn all they could about Afghanistan.

TV and radio stations began flourishing in Afghanistan as soon as the Taliban were gone—including a smash-hit *American Idol*-style TV show, *Afghan Star*, that almost single-handedly has brought about a kind of pop-culture awakening. The nation watched Rohullah Nikpai win the country's first Olympic medal at Beijing in tae kwon do. It followed the cricket team as it climbed the ranks of international competition. Information technology is now a fact of life for city dwellers. The most ambitious students are focused on careers in IT, telecom and English.

But even as many Afghans embraced the written word through text messaging and social networking, the state of real Afghan literature was slower to recover. True, there was an online surge in poetry and literature—in Dari, Pashto and even Uzbek. International conferences were held in Afghanistan to celebrate the intellectual legacies of the country's great writers, from Jamaluddin Afghani and Mahmud Tarzi to Nawai and Rumi. But Shah complained to me that not a single good book about Afghanistan had been written in the last two decades, with the possible exception of one by Dutch scholar Willem Vogelsang (a specialist on Central Asian history who published *The Afghans* in 2002).

He's a tough critic, in other words. I'm curious what he'll think of this book, which was partly inspired by the same conclusion—at least with regard to the decade since 2001.

———

His name was Jalal ud-Dīn Muhammad Balkhi. But to many, he is known simply as Rumi. Born to probable Persian heritage nine centuries ago in what is now the northern Afghan province of Balkh, Rumi ("the Roman," meaning the Eastern Roman Empire, then covering much of what is today Turkey) migrated west to Anatolia with his family, fleeing the Mongols. After encountering a wandering Sufi mystic from Tabriz, Rumi set a spiritual course that eventually would make him of one of Sufi Islam's great poets, mystics and intellectuals. Following his death in 1273, his shrine at Konya (in present-day Turkey) became a fail-safe magnet for pilgrims.

It was here that I stood with Masood Khalili, an Afghan poet and diplomat I introduced earlier in this book, as he ran through the first sixteen verses of Rumi's epic 50,000-line *Masnavi* before asking the shrine's master how he had done. It was an interesting spectacle to behold. Here was an Afghan reading to an Afghan—in Turkey, in Persian, with a Canadian looking on, dumbfounded.

Today, Rumi brings over $2 billion in annual revenue to Konya. Most pilgrims aren't even Muslims: they come from Japan, Italy, South Korea, France and Germany, not to mention Iran. Rumi was in recent years the bestselling poet in the United States. Afghans come too, claiming Rumi as one of their own. "He was an Afghan, from Afghanistan," Khalili emphasizes to me. "That is very important for us."

He explained to me Rumi's special gift. "An ordinary mullah . . . should talk through rules and scripture," he said. "It translates into order." But for a Sufi—or dervish—"there is something else, which no one can define. It is not scientific. All of a sudden you are beyond the rules [of Islam], even while you are accepting the rules totally."

Only one in a million could feel this "vibration," as Khalili described it. One never knew when or how it would arise. "It is not because of going to hajj. . . . It is not because of a religion, not because of Islam, Christianity. It's not because of even Hinduism . . . that vibration enters you, catches you, makes you something. Why? You don't know yourself what happened. . . . You can feel it. Others can see it."

Over a millennium, there have perhaps been only three or four hundred true Sufis, Khalili said. Abdullah Ansari, the patron saint of Herat, had been one; Data Ganj Bakhsh, the patron saint of Lahore, had been another. Rumi had been one of the strongest, "writing poetry like a volcano, on fire, without being scared for a moment."

After his mystical rapture, Rumi was never again seen praying, or even with the Koran. Instead, he dictated nearly 25,000 rhyming couplets of intense passion to his disciples. As Jami, one of the last great Sufi poets, said a century after Rumi's death: "Oh my goodness, he is not a prophet, but he has a book."

Rumi was rejected by the traditional clergy. "He stood alone," Khalili said. "Not on the ground but on the roof, with a drum, telling the world [there is] one God, and that is love." If the Koran had been the root of Islam, Rumi's *Masnavi* was its fruit.

Were there real Sufis in Afghanistan today? I asked. "There have been some," Khalili said. "Not many, but a few in the valleys of Badakhshan, in Yamgam, in Panjshir, in Gulbahar, in Herat. They were not that strong. But they had some sense of power greater than us, than ordinary people."

Sufism could never be a product of mere schooling or of acceptance in any particular orthodoxy, he added. Such mystics were absolutely different from the traditional *ulema*—opposites, even. Nor was it a force transmitted by heredity. It was absolutely individual.

Khalili's father, the eminent poet Khalilullah Khalili, wrote a book about Rumi called *From Balkh to Konya*. He once had come to Konya with King Zahir Shah himself, and had read Rumi's work aloud to His Majesty. The king had not sought to become a Sufi. But he had believed in a spiritual life and respected spiritualism in others.

It was the sort of tolerant spirit Rumi himself had championed. Nothing could do more to heal Afghanistan's fractured sense of self, I thought, than if the country could reclaim this tradition of love and pluralism created in the thirteenth century by this native son.

PART THREE
BOLDER STROKES

They that dig foundations deep,
Fit for realms to rise upon,
Little honour do they reap
Of their generation

—Rudyard Kipling, "The Pro-Consuls"

CHAPTER TEN

TALENT'S TABLE

The throne is threatened by three things. First, if the king is unjust;
next, if he promotes worthless men . . . ; third, if he . . .
is always trying to increase his income.

—Ferdowsi, *Shahnameh*

As storm clouds gathered over Afghanistan in early 2008, it became clear our counter-insurgency strategy was inadequate. The basic idea had been right. But we didn't have the resources to apply it across the country's many threatened regions. With the breakdown in trust between Karzai and his partners, injuries on the battlefield had been compounded by insults flying around the backrooms.

The situation was worst in the southern provinces of Helmand and Kandahar, where the government's writ no longer extended far beyond provincial capitals and adjacent districts. All in all, across Afghanistan, forty districts were now off limits to UN and development workers—10 percent of the country. Much of the violence was financed with narcotics. In 2007 there had been a bumper crop, a sea of poppies encompassing an area half the size of Rhode Island.

Using their opium proceeds, Taliban commanders were spreading their "rat lines" farther north. All the while, they sent fresh Afghan recruits in the opposite direction, across the Pakistan border and into Baluchistan for training. No provincial capital was yet in imminent danger, but the mere presence of Taliban units in far-flung provinces such as Badghis in the north and Wardak in the east was driving up tensions in Kabul, where a full Taliban restoration was no longer inconceivable.

ISAF commanders did their best to beat back the Taliban tide. But it was difficult to engage with an enemy that deliberately took cover in civilian areas. This tactic paid dividends in two ways: either ISAF would hold its fire and the Taliban would live to fight another day, or ISAF artillery and aircraft would let loose, and innocent bystanders would die at Western hands, thereby serving up a Taliban propaganda victory. (A typical Taliban tactic, for instance, was to open fire on an ISAF patrol from the roof of a mud building in which women and children were sheltering. If ISAF took the bait, the entire village was likely to turn against NATO, driving a fresh crop of recruits into the waiting arms of the Taliban.) In 2007, over 40 percent of the 1,500-plus civilians killed in the conflict had been killed by coalition air strikes, artillery or gunfire. The dangerous myth was taking root that ISAF was not really there to protect the population.

In Western capitals, much of the blame ended up being heaped on Hamid Karzai, who increasingly was spoken of as mercurial and irrational. These descriptions became self-fulfilling. Stung by the criticism, Karzai began to see enemies everywhere, even among the ranks of loyal Western supporters.

In January 2008, Karzai became particularly enraged by a *Times of London* editorial—published the same day news was leaked about Paddy Ashdown's imminent appointment as UN envoy to Afghanistan—that dismissed him as a powerless figurehead and "a lonely Pashtun in a government made up largely of Tajik veterans of the Northern Alliance."

The editorial writer's overall analysis was correct. The Afghan president did have limited control over security and budget matters. And he certainly had promoted a variety of unsavoury characters in order to placate factional interests. But to a reader sitting in Kabul in 2008, the *Times*' argument that Karzai was a plaything of the Tajiks seemed a gratuitous overstatement. The editorial implied that the Taliban, not the government, spoke for the country's Pashtuns, a falsehood many in Islamabad were only too eager to endorse.

By its content and its timing, this became the single most influential newspaper editorial regarding the Afghan mission since 2001. It almost certainly contributed to Karzai's decision to reject Ashdown's appointment. Generations after the Great Game, Afghans could still be roused to anger by the perceived arrogance of British leaders and intellectuals.

———

It was 6:30 p.m. on Monday, January 14, 2008. Norwegian foreign minister Jonas Gahr Støre had just finished meeting with Sima Samar, chair of the Afghan Independent Human Rights Commission, in the Kabul Serena Hotel, the city's only five-star establishment, midway between Zarnegar Park and the bazaars of the Old City. The pair heard gunfire, then an explosion. The hotel was under attack.

One gunman was killed at the entrance. A second detonated himself in the security screening area. A third was shot in the forecourt before reaching his target.

A fourth gunman alone managed to enter the building. After shooting several people in the lobby, he entered the fitness centre, where he dispatched several more. Horrible as it was, the toll could have been significantly higher: a large group hid in the adjacent women's change room, avoiding detection.

With the public areas of the hotel now deserted, the attacker suddenly paused in the midst of this spree. On the surveillance-video recordings, he can be seen displaying utter calm, awaiting further orders. He made several outgoing calls on a mobile phone, all to Pakistan. His goal, investigators later determined, was to arrange an escape.

At one point, he simply removed his explosive vest, dropped it behind a wall, then disappeared into the basement. Soon after, the hotel was stormed by security forces. They found the gunman—who may have had second thoughts about the merits of suicide—dressed in a cleaner's uniform.

In the weeks following the Serena Hotel attack, the episode was dissected in every possible way. Training, command and control all had been in North Waziristan, it was determined. The terrorist support team operating outside the hotel had been as large as, or larger than, the team inside. Two Afghan police officers had facilitated everything, even providing the four terrorists with uniforms to wear during their attack. In the aftermath, one had skipped back to Pakistan; the other had been cornered and killed in a house near Babur's Garden.

The Kabul hotel had been the scene of dramatic events in the past. On Valentine's Day 1979, most notably, US ambassador Adolph "Spike" Dubs, who'd been seized in his car on the way to work, was taken to one of the hotel's rooms, where he was killed when Afghan forces attacked. That Cold War incident had taken place in a Kabul whose urban fabric was still otherwise intact. Three decades later, the hotel represented one of the scarred city's few surviving symbols of progress.

The Serena attack was a watershed that saw the Pakistani-spawned terrorist menace come out of the villages and into the capital. It sowed panic among Afghan officials charged with protecting foreign visitors and missions. It was feared that foreign dignitaries would stay away from Kabul—a prelude to full-scale abandonment by the international community. Even those who stayed were less visible, buttoning themselves down behind double bulletproof doors and sheets of concrete.

It was not just Kabul. Kandahar had suffered multiple IED and suicide attacks since the start of 2008. On February 17, a month after the Serena incident, a jihadi detonated himself in the middle of a crowd that had gathered to bet on dog fights in Arghandab district, just north of Kandahar city. The intended target was a local arch-enemy of the Taliban, an Alikozai commander who served in the local police. Over one hundred civilians were killed, the highest toll for any single Taliban attack to date.

Their strategy now was clearly to escalate the campaign of terror, systematically targeting moderates on both sides of the border. The most prized objectives were military bases, government ministries and compounds where foreigners gathered. But as the Arghandab attack showed, the Taliban were equally happy to slaughter ordinary citizens.

———

Just over two weeks after the Serena attack, on January 29, 2008, the *New York Times* published a letter from Munir Akram, Pakistan's permanent representative to the UN, in which he stated that "suicide bombing is a phenomenon imported from Iraq and Afghanistan, alien to Pakistan." It was an insult to the intelligence of everyone involved with counterterrorism: just about every suicide bombing in the region featured an attacker or commander who'd undergone training in some part of Pakistan, usually Waziristan or Karachi.

In February, less than two weeks after Akram's *New York Times* letter was published, Pakistan's ambassador to Afghanistan, Tariq Azizuddin, was kidnapped in broad daylight in his own country while en route from Islamabad to Kabul. He had been taken in Khyber Agency near Ali Masjid, on the approaches to the famous pass. Following his release, at his home in Ankara, Turkey, he related to me the story of his ninety-seven-day captivity, along with some broader observations about the Taliban.

"The Taliban were playing cat-and-mouse games with the Pakistani government," he recalled. "[Pervez] Musharraf was desperately trying to avoid getting into direct conflict with [them] on his own home territory. . . . What Musharraf was doing was [simultaneously] guarding the Taliban's leadership and locking them up." (This much was true, though my own conclusion is that the guarding outweighed the locking up by a healthy margin.) "By 2008, the number of people locked up was rather large," he added. "[The Pakistani Taliban] were feeling the pinch of losing their leadership. Plus Musharraf also had captured a lot of the Afghan Taliban leadership, and that was pinching them on the other side as well."

The Taliban launched a campaign to secure the release of their con-
federates. Instead of kidnapping soldiers or members of the Frontier
Corps or the Frontier Constabulary, who were exchanged on a one-for-
one basis, they would hunt bigger game. The decision had been made
by Pakistani Taliban leader Hakimullah Mehsud to go for higher-value
targets—bishops instead of pawns, in other words.

On February 11, 2008, Hakimullah sent out five teams of kidnappers as part of a fishing expedition. Before they'd kidnapped anyone,
the Pakistani government caught wind of the operation and asked
for negotiations. Having gotten Musharraf's attention, Hakimullah
ordered the operation aborted. But that message never made it to the
Taliban who seized Tariq Azizuddin. "These bastards didn't have the
right phones," he recounted to me. The kidnappers said to him, "You
had this fancy vehicle with a red licence plate and big aerials on its
bumper. So we thought, Somebody big. We thought you were a diplomat." And they were right.

The Taliban moved Azizuddin away from the site of the kidnapping almost at once. They then spent nineteen days in Tirah—at the
meeting point of Kurram, Orakzai and Khyber agencies—and then
the rest in Hakimullah's home village in South Waziristan, near the
border with North Waziristan. Throughout Azizuddin's captivity, his
guards had referred to him as *mama*, a term of respect for elders that
was the equivalent of "uncle." This was only one of the odd aspects of
this hostage situation: later on, Hakimullah himself asked Tariq for
forgiveness—which the ambassador refused to give.

At one point, a group of seven Afghan Taliban and five Pakistanis
were offered up for release as part of an exchange. But the United
States apparently objected to such generous terms. Finally, a second
list, consisting only of Pakistani Taliban, was proposed. Hakimullah
quickly accepted this deal.

Tariq described the denouement this way: "It was afternoon, summer, hot. Their walkie-talkie was leaning against the wall, crackling
away with all kinds of funny conversations. And my bodyguard says,

'Listen to it carefully. . . . They said, "Get the guest ready." Did you hear it, *Mama*?"'

Tariq first insisted on polishing his shoes. Later that day, he was released.

———

Islamic Revolution Day dawned clear and calm in Kabul, an annual opportunity for Northern Alliance veterans and fellow mujahidin to celebrate their return to the nation's capital. It was a chance for old fighters to stick their chests out. Despite all the discouragements of the season, this year's parade festivities were set to be the most impressive military display that Kabul had seen since the appearance of Soviet hardware in the 1980s.

The celebration of Saur 8—April 28 in the Gregorian calendar— dates back to that day in 1992, when the mujahidin finally overthrew the Communist-backed government in Kabul. As many cynics point out, the same date also effectively marks the beginning of the brutal civil war that destroyed much of Kabul and eventually brought the Taliban to power. (By sheer coincidence, the date also happens to correspond to the butchering of President Mohammad Daoud Khan and his family in 1978.) Most observers would have preferred to see the old factional cannons permanently spiked, rather than being trotted out on parade. But as a matter of protocol, my attendance was mandatory.

As guests took their places, the parading units drawn up in front of the Eid Gah Mosque were flanked by huge photographs of Afghanistan's leaders, from Hotaki dynasty founder Mirwais Khan Hotak (1673– 1715) and Durrani emperor Ahmad Shah Durrani (1722–73) to Daoud, mujahidin-era Hazara leader Abdul Ali Mazari and Northern Alliance commander Ahmad Shah Massoud. Like "Washington" or "Lincoln" in America, these names were the stuff of legend, honoured in the names of Kabul's streets and traffic circles.

New commando units and police were on parade, living testimony to the accelerated Western-backed security training program. Something about the sight sent my mind racing to dark places, and I leaned over to remind Sir Sherard Cowper-Coles, the British ambassador, of the officers who had jumped out of a similar parade formation in 1981 and ended Anwar al-Sadat's life in Cairo. (Cowper-Coles had been in the Egyptian capital at the time as a young diplomat.) There was nervous chuckling as he and US ambassador Bill Wood digested the parallel, not altogether amused.

In the first few years after 2001, the lines of dusty, beturbaned men in this parade had been a moving sight (though in 2005, some diplomats boycotted when Mohammad Fahim insisted on parading Soviet-built Scuds, complete with fuel and warheads). More recently, it had become less nostalgia-tinged and more a showcase for demonstrating the growing might and professionalism of Afghanistan's fledgling army. At 10 a.m., President Hamid Karzai appeared on his dais in the grandstand. The national anthem sounded. Then the president and Defence Minister Abdul Rahim Wardak rode out, erect in the turrets of new Humvees, to receive salutes and three cheers from the troops. There were speeches and martial music. At last, the artillery began its deafening tribute; diesel engines from Soviet-built T-54 tanks roared to life, belching black exhaust.

At first, amid all these other sounds, the muffled *tack-tack* of distant small-arms fire was hard to place. Then it got louder, paused, and echoed again, sounding out across Eid Gah Square, closer now. Presidential guards looked nervously over their shoulders. The shots were coming in semi-automatic bursts, interrupting the regular thud of the twenty-one-gun salute.

Sensing that the rounds were live, several rows of police on parade crouched. Cadets and infantry broke their lines; flag-bearers and guardsmen made themselves smaller marks as the presidential security detail mobilized.

There was a flurry of movement in the government box; the president was rushed away. Cabinet ministers, parliamentarians and tribal elders were suddenly gone. Army and police units, lacking ammunition, were scurrying away in undignified streams. The rattle of a PK heavy machine gun boomed out as security teams returned fire against what, to me, was still an unseen menace.

The parade was over before it began. US Army general Dan McNeill, the ISAF commander, at first remained defiant at the front of the bleachers, his gaze focused on a nearby three-storey building. But eventually he yielded to his security team's pleas. The two of us were among the last to move back behind the concrete grandstand. Moments later, a spray of bullets shattered glass by the aisle through which we had just filed, pitting the wall with small cavities.

Behind the grandstand, generals in full dress uniform commingled with protocol officers and deputy ministers, none visibly nervous, all grateful for hard cover. We were all wondering how, with the city virtually locked down, the gunmen had got within shooting distance.

After fifteen minutes, the attack had run its course. In all, five people had been killed, including one Wolesi Jirga member and the leader of the Qizilbash community in Kabul. It was an embarrassing tragedy. But it could have been much worse.

The attackers launched their fusillade from an apartment in the three-storey building I'd seen General McNeill eying. An Uzbek had rented it weeks before, masquerading as a carpet trader. He and his fellow gunmen had kept to themselves inside the apartment for days, avoiding searches by chaining the door shut from the outside. They had waited in isolation for the hour to strike, ready to die. As we later learned, the cell recruiter was connected to the Serena attack. He had infiltrated the police as a captain, paying bribes at high levels to secure his commission. After the incident at the parade, he skipped town for Peshawar, and then presumably on to Waziristan.

I had attended the parade in the place of our new special representative, Kai Eide, who was present at the Serena on January 14. A veteran member of the Norwegian Foreign Service, he'd become one of the most respected envoys in the UN stable, having both led the UN mission in Bosnia in 1997–98 and been special envoy to Kosovo in 2005. We had worked closely together during his previous visits to Afghanistan, and I welcomed his appointment.

At his first meeting with reporters at Kabul's airport, on March 28, Eide pledged to show respect for the "culture, religion and history" of Afghanistan. He also promised to improve coordination and show "visible results" for Afghans. But his most memorable comment that day was aimed at putting to rest recent controversies: "I may not be Paddy Ashdown," he said, "but don't underestimate me." Even with strong support on all sides, he would have to fight hard for two years to live up to those carefully chosen words.

Eide's first job was to ensure that Afghanistan and the international community had a common game plan. He was rightly concerned that the West's obsession with security issues, however understandable, was obstructing progress on other goals, such as institution building.

There also was palpable distress over the slow implementation of the Afghanistan National Development Strategy, which had been agreed to in interim form at the 2006 London Conference. It was a vast bureaucratic enterprise, involving a mind-numbing series of inter-ministerial and provincial consultations. The overall plan's eight pillars were divided into seventeen distinct sectors plus six cross-cutting ones, as well as annexes for each major government institution—thirty-seven in all—not to mention provincial development plans for all thirty-four provinces. Such detail was not an unusual feature of major projects in Western countries. But it was unprecedented for an impoverished nation such as Afghanistan.

Eide's intention was to drive the Afghan government to complete the development strategy, with ample assistance from UNAMA, while working with Karzai and his international partners to specify new priorities for the coming years. It was a tall order—the first major reordering of priorities since the Afghanistan Compact (agreed at the London Conference).

By this point, some members of the NGO community were becoming discouraged by the lack of success in Afghanistan. The Afghanistan Compact had mandated the creation of a national voter registry, a large-scale reform of the justice system, and electrical connections for 65 percent of urban households and 25 percent of rural ones. None of these goals was being realized.

But there were a few bright spots. One of them was the Afghanistan Reconstruction Trust Fund (ARTF). Since its founding in May 2002, it had become the largest pooled, multi-donor trust fund in World Bank history, and would later be emulated in South Sudan, Timor-Leste, Iraq and Gaza. The World Bank team in Kabul, with more than eighty staff, was now one of the strongest anywhere in the world.

The central concept behind the reconstruction fund was that donor nations should be putting their resources to use through a common plan, coordinated through the Afghan national budget, as opposed to funding their own piecemeal initiatives. "We installed PricewaterhouseCoopers as the monitoring agent for the last eight years," ARTF manager Hugh Riddell told me, proud of the professionalism that marked his institution. "They allow the ARTF to reimburse what donors would want us to be reimbursing. And where they find expenditures 'ineligible,' the ministry basically pays the ARTF back."

The ARTF had succeeded by getting a few principles right: a single treasury account, one unified budget process, three-month turnaround for all paperwork, no cherry-picking by donors and a monitoring agent. The system had proven watertight. Even after six years, there was still virtually no evidence of corruption in ARTF-funded programs.

Unfortunately, instead of reinforcing this sort of success, Afghanistan's Finance Ministry had instead lapsed into off-budget spending. Moreover, the current finance minister, Anwar ul-Haq Ahady, simply didn't enjoy as much trust as his predecessor, Ashraf Ghani. As a result, foreign donors began avoiding the middleman entirely, funnelling their money through their own Provincial Reconstruction Teams. A related problem was that the military situation had become more urgent, and so on-the-ground spending decisions increasingly were being made on the basis of month-to-month crisis management, as opposed to top-down long-term planning.

For perspective, I asked Minna Jarvenpaa, former head of UNAMA's policy and planning unit, and founder of the Afghanistan Analysts Network, how she found the partnership between government and donors upon her arrival in 2007. "There's always been lots of rhetoric about partnership," she said. "[But] there was a crisis in terms of trust—a sense in which the Afghans had failed us, and we had failed the Afghans." It had put everything at risk.

The major mistake made by both sides, she added, was "the assumption that you could go into full state-building mode when there was still a war going on." Everything we had tried in 2006 and 2007 had been focused on halting this deterioration. Yet by spring 2008, security was still worsening, while distrust had grown.

How could the resulting fragmentation be overcome? The goal was to agree on priorities that would create common cause on all sides. Then we needed to put resources behind them. Implementation had to be a shared effort at the local level, bringing together elders, officials and donors. In Afghan policy circles, this came to be called the "integrated approach." But even after the London Conference and the massive bureaucratic effort that had followed in its wake, the priorities that would inform this approach were still in flux thanks to the fluid situation on the ground.

All of us were doing our best to ensure that the major issues would be settled in time for the next international-development conference, this time to be hosted by France in June 2008. But we knew we were running out of time. The world would not go on holding such conferences indefinitely.

———

The Conférence internationale de soutien à l'Afghanistan, as it was called, began on June 12 in Paris, hosted by President Nicolas Sarkozy and Foreign Minister Bernard Kouchner. President Karzai, in particular, seemed moved by the proceedings. At one point, our summary of Afghanistan's progress since 2001—set out in fifteen one-page summaries collectively entitled *Afghanistan Moving Forward*—brought him to tears.

The event was attended by representatives of sixty-eight states and eighteen international organizations. It raised over $26 billion in pledges and provided a showcase for the new Afghanistan National Development Strategy. It also set an agenda for the next two years, one that actually was followed.

The tone was set by Sarkozy himself, who gave the best speech on Afghanistan I have heard to date by a foreign political leader. He saw two potential hurdles:

> The first obstacle is the violent action of armed groups, too often supported and armed from outside. To these groups located in Afghanistan, or in Pakistan, I would like to address a simple message: we will not permit you to undo the achievements of these last years. We will not let the schools we have financed burn or be looted by people who do not respect anything. And you will not wear down the determination of the international community. Even if Afghans today in the violent opposition accept dialogue and reconciliation, I am certain they will find their place in the new Afghanistan. It is up to Afghan authorities to determine the modalities that will govern their return to democracy in Afghanistan. As for Pakistan, it must implement every measure to ensure partisans of violent action do not find on their soil a refuge which allows them to undermine our efforts in Afghanistan with impunity. We need Pakistan to engage in a determined fashion in the service of a free Afghanistan.
>
> The second obstacle is the drug trade, controlled to a large extent by the extremist sphere. Drug traffickers rot the economy, corrupt society, even sometimes the Afghan administration. Drugs are

fuelling the war. Drugs are fuelling venality. Drugs in Afghanistan as elsewhere are a threat to peace. At the base of it is, of course, cultivation of poppy by farmers seeking resources. But there are also mafia networks that prosper from the traffic. . . . To hesitate would be to be complicit with the traffickers and the armed groups that threaten the stability of the country.

In the preparations for Paris, the single issue that had generated the most rancour was corruption. Karzai and some in his cabinet blamed the international community for fuelling the problem with generous subcontracting, loose tendering practices and insufficient project oversight. At the same time, donors were now seeing what ordinary Afghans saw: a rising tide of petty corruption by civil servants, combined with larger abuses and misappropriations at the highest levels, in some cases linked to narcotics, in others not.

In fact, corruption flourished in Afghanistan for at least three interrelated reasons. First, the country's inexperienced law-enforcement agents—even the clean ones—were incapable of investigating complex and politically sensitive white-collar crimes, so the criminals knew there was little chance of being caught. Second, the power struggle in Kabul had turned corruption into a partisan weapon: most cases that came to public light were politically motivated, which meant the accusers were often dirtier than their targets. Third, the climate of impunity forged before Bonn, then reconfirmed by the provision of amnesty for Afghanistan's worst criminals, had encouraged the idea that the only justice well-connected people would face would be in the next life.

Overall, however, even this thorny issue had not prevented Paris from being a resounding success. I saw signs that the atmosphere of distrust between Afghan and Western leaders was starting to thaw.

Although Paris had restored some confidence in the political agenda, it had not stopped the military conflict from intensifying. On June 13, the day after the conference, Taliban fighters blew the gates off Sarpoza Prison in Kandahar, freeing over nine hundred inmates and detainees. The city of Kandahar, already reeling, lurched toward chaos. It was the most serious challenge to civil authority in the area since September 2006, when Operation Medusa had narrowly prevented a Taliban takeover. The damage would take years to reverse.

The new pattern of attacks continued in Kabul as well. On July 8, an assault on the Indian embassy by an explosives-laden vehicle and multiple attackers resulted in 58 deaths and injuries to 141. Among those killed were the defence attaché, Brigadier Ravi Datt Mehta, and Counsellor Venkateswara Rao, close friends and valued colleagues for many of us. Experts quickly agreed that the attack bore all the hallmarks of a Pakistani intelligence operation.

Despite such setbacks, Afghanistan's cabinet met frequently over the summer to move forward on the Paris priorities. In July 2008, President Karzai authorized the High Office of Oversight to supervise work on the government's anti-corruption strategy, which a commission had been developing since August 2006—not long after Richard Holbrooke had spooked several ministers with his candid talk at my dinner party.

The impetus for the project had been Chief Justice Abdul Salam Azimi, whose integrity was beyond question. Unfortunately, he was the exception. The same don't-rock-the-boat principle that too often had marred the work of the country's Attorney General's Office would also govern the new High Office, which was run by a well-meaning bureaucrat named Mohammad Yasin Usmani. In the close-knit political world of Kabul, neither he nor the country's justice officers would have the authority to target big fish.

As the conflict worsened, the civilian population was bearing the brunt of the carnage. According to UNAMA statistics, approximately 1,500 civilians were killed in 2007. In 2008, the number rose to 2,100—55 percent by insurgents and 39 percent by international forces.

In the worst incident on the pro-government side, US forces in Herat's Shindand district called in air strikes on several village buildings on August 22, 2008. More than seventy-five people, mostly women and children, were killed. US forces initially denied the heavy toll. But video footage of the lifeless bodies recorded with mobile phones in the immediate aftermath confirmed the accounts of eyewitnesses. As a direct consequence, Shindand tilted further into the Taliban fold.

But the main force driving insecurity was still across the border in Pakistan, where political horse-trading following the country's February elections had slowed formation of a government. Security in the country's tribal regions was deteriorating even faster than in Afghanistan, as the Pakistani Taliban showed their teeth.

Over the summer of 2008, US patience was wearing thin. As George W. Bush put it in his memoirs, "I was tired of reading intelligence reports about extremist sanctuaries in Pakistan." On September 3, US Special Forces undertook an unsuccessful covert action near Angoor Adda in the Pakistani region of South Waziristan, near the place where Uzbek militants had first broken the peace years earlier, prior to the long series of ceasefires. Pakistan noisily accused Washington of causing civilian casualties and violating its sovereignty.

As an alternative to such risky on-the-ground operations in Pakistan, Bush authorized intensified drone strikes against terrorist targets in Waziristan and other parts of the loosely controlled Federally Administered Tribal Areas. In the four years from 2004 to 2007, there had been only nine such strikes against targets on Pakistani soil. In the first seven months of 2008, they came at the rate of about one per month.

In August 2008, there were five drone strikes; in September, six more. In the final months of 2008, there was one every three days. Many of them found their mark. It was the first serious blow against senior terrorist leaders that al Qaeda, the Haqqanis and their allies had sustained since retreating to Waziristan in 2001. The impact on security in Kabul was immediate: suicide attacks levelled off.

In response, the Taliban and Haqqani forces in Waziristan tried to move to new bases of operation out of harm's way. Turi tribesmen in Kurram Agency, who had battled for months to protect their villages from Taliban encroachment from Waziristan, came into the line of fire. Hundreds of them were killed in 2008 alone. The ISI-abetted chaos in Waziristan was starting to flow to other parts of Pakistan.

Although they provided some benefit on the battlefield, the drone attacks underlined the awkwardness of US policy toward Pakistan. On one hand, Washington gave lip service to the fiction that Pakistan was an active participant in the war on terrorism. On the other hand, the US military was striking known terrorist clusters on Pakistani soil, signalling to all concerned that the Pakistani military wasn't willing or able to do its job. Meanwhile, many of the more Western-oriented Pakistani officials who made a great show of decrying the drones' encroachment on Pakistani sovereignty privately applauded American actions. There was hypocrisy all around.

Bush realized the status quo was untenable, and he authorized a wide-ranging policy review for the region under Lieutenant General Doug Lute, who had met with us over the summer as the 2008 presidential election approached. During this period, the war in Afghanistan had become a major campaign issue stateside. On July 16, then presidential candidate Barack Obama hawkishly declared: "Al Qaeda has an expanding base in Pakistan that is probably no farther from their old Afghan sanctuary than a train ride from Washington to Philadelphia." He committed himself to "finishing the fight."

———

On September 9, 2008, Asif Ali Zardari, widower of two-time Pakistani prime minister Benazir Bhutto, who'd been assassinated in December 2007, was sworn in as his country's president. Karzai was invited to the ceremony. Leaders in both governments were at least trying to forge a better relationship.

But whatever good intentions came in with Zardari, the new government remained virtually powerless in the face of the violence engulfing Pakistan itself, meaning that Afghanistan's problems were at best a secondary concern for politicians in Islamabad. On September 20, 2008, the Marriott in Islamabad, one of the capital city's two top hotels, was struck by a major truck bomb, killing at least fifty-three people. Two days later, Afghanistan's ambassador-designate to Pakistan, the former consul general in Peshawar, was kidnapped at gunpoint.

The consensus among informed observers remained that Pakistani military support for the insurgency inside Afghanistan was continuing unabated. Incidents along the border were spiking. Internal displacement within Pakistan now affected 300,000 people.

In Kabul, meanwhile, Karzai was doing what he could to restore trust with international donors, putting competent, well-regarded reformers back into key roles. On October 11, he named National Solidarity Programme head Asif Rahimi as the new minister of agriculture, irrigation and livestock, a key portfolio for a largely rural nation such as Afghanistan. Haneef Atmar became interior minister, and Farouk Wardak moved from the Office of Administrative Affairs to take his place at education.

Reforming the Interior Ministry was an especially important project. Long considered the "key to Kabul"—even more than the Defence Ministry—it had been repeatedly infested by warlord interests. When officers responsible for abuses were flagged by UNAMA, ministry insiders would lobby to clear their names.

Zarar Ahmed Moqbel, Atmar's immediate predecessor at interior, had taken some steps toward reform, instituting, for instance, a merit-based selection process for captains and majors in 2007. But he also was vulnerable to pressure from factional groups, some of which were no more than thinly disguised drug lobbies. Police positions at key border crossings or on major highways were bought and sold behind the scenes.

It was painful to watch the wheels of cynical self-enrichment grind against the imperatives of public service. Yet when the issue was raised with Karzai, he often reacted defensively. Having been briefed against us by his advisors, he would accuse "foreigners"—and at times me personally—of "interference" in Afghan affairs.

Quite apart from the question of corruption, there was also a question of basic competence among ministry officers. Counter-narcotics policing and the investigation of IED attacks, in particular, required knowledgeable specialists. Riot police and basic gendarmes had to know how to maintain security without hurting innocent bystanders. Atmar grasped these nettles, arguing for better police training and pay, expanded recruitment and elimination of corruption. His colleagues were impressed, and support for the Interior Ministry began to grow.

Within one year, Atmar had produced a five-year strategic framework for policing, a blueprint supported by France, the United Kingdom, Canada and other Western nations. The EU Police Mission also provided assistance. With the additional commitments later announced by President Barack Obama, a massive influx of US trainers began. Everyone had seemed to realize, at about the same time, that Afghanistan couldn't be saved without better grassroots policing.

———

After a violent spring and summer, the security situation remained precarious in late 2008. But there were some promising signs. The United States had pledged two additional brigade combat teams, which would add 10,000 troops to the 56,000-strong ISAF force, in addition to the 13,000 or so troops still operating under America's own Operation Enduring Freedom.

In Kandahar, a new governor was installed—Major General Rahmatullah Raufi, a former senior commander in the Afghan National Army. His predecessor, Asadullah Khalid, while still respected, had lost face following the high-profile killing of important elders in Arghandab district. The Taliban remained a wholesale threat in Kandahar, as well as in neighbouring Helmand. Yet the countrywide security collapse that many feared never materialized. Instead, the first signs of a shifting stalemate were plain to see: by turns the Taliban would increase their presence in one area of the country, then retreat when the Afghan government and Western forces moved in, only to pop up in another area.

On October 25, my team took part in a meeting with officials in Wardak province, south of Kabul, to review progress on an innovative social-outreach program conceived as an attempt to recruit local tribesmen to play an active role in securing their districts. It would rely on the authority of elders, who received a stipend for their support. The scheme was controversial and risky.

Despite all the bad news from different parts of the country, the mood in this critical area had actually improved. For nearly two years, worsening security had prevented us from travelling there by car. But the new governor was upbeat about his outreach efforts. More important, the availability of some new resources at local level had convinced elders there was still hope for their government.

Since the previous winter, my own instincts had been telling me that progress toward stability would not come without three things: improved Afghan governance, higher troop levels and action against sanctuaries in Pakistan. I saw grounds for hope in each of these areas.

First, the reinforced UNAMA, backed by the shared priorities emanating from Paris, had tipped the government into a new reform phase that seemed to be continuing into 2009. (In December 2008, for instance, Karzai promoted another reformer, Wahidullah Shahrani, to be commerce minister.) Second, the two new brigade combat teams authorized by George W. Bush, combined with Obama's apparent hawkishness on Afghanistan, held out the prospect of sufficient forces, both for counter-insurgency and for training. Third, the drone attacks in Waziristan and the new government in Islamabad held out hope (albeit theoretical) that the Musharraf-era see-no-evil policy toward Afghanistan would eventually become a thing of the past.

On November 26, 2008, members of the US National Security Council discussed the results of the regional policy review conducted by Lieutenant General Doug Lute, a document noting that the Taliban and their allies now had demonstrated capability in nearly half of Afghanistan. On the same day, the Lashkar-e-Taiba terrorist group attacked Mumbai. Over 150 people were killed, including six Americans. For those of us who had endured the 2008 attacks in Kabul, it was another reel from the same film. Yet ISI director General Ahmad Shuja Pasha had the temerity to claim to CIA director Mike Hayden that his agency was not involved. As the evidence that later emerged would indicate, it was another flagrant lie.

The next day, NATO secretary-general Jaap de Hoop Scheffer met in Kabul with the United Nations Security Council—an unprecedented event—and reassured its members that ISAF would remain accountable for its actions, and that it would seek to win back any legitimacy it had lost among Afghan civilians. He also stressed that military efforts needed political support.

On December 10, 2008, I accompanied President Karzai on stage at a Radio and Television of Afghanistan event to celebrate International Human Rights Day. True to the occasion, he placed himself with the victims of the many crimes that had plagued his nation in living memory. He showed emotion, pledging that the peace we all sought would be one in which such atrocities would never be repeated. He asked victims to forgive their assailants—to embrace an era of reconciliation.

Unfortunately, the audience that most needed to hear this message, the Taliban, wasn't listening.

CHAPTER ELEVEN

DANCE OF WAR

Do not allow the enemy to string his bow while
you are able to pierce him with an arrow.

—*The Baburnama*

On January 1, 2009, a grey speck seemed to hover, then whirl, in the winter air above Wana, the capital of the Pakistani border region of South Waziristan. Moments after the unmanned aircraft emitted a few pulses of light, a building exploded in the nearby village of Karikot, killing two senior al Qaeda veterans and two other militants.

One of the victims, Usama al-Kini, had been a senior al Qaeda leader in Pakistan since 2007. Together with his deputy, who also was killed, he'd helped mount the first attempt on Benazir Bhutto's life after her return to Pakistan, as well as the Marriott Hotel bombing a year later. Both men were Kenyans and had been involved in the US embassy bombings in Africa in 1998.

George W. Bush had warned Islamabad on August 4, 2008, of "serious action" if the Taliban sanctuaries continued to operate with impunity. Since then, US drones had eliminated al Qaeda's operations chief in Pakistan's Federally Administered Tribal Areas (FATAs), as well as the overall al Qaeda commander for Afghanistan and a top bomb maker.

After the swearing-in of President Asif Ali Zardari in September 2008, Pakistan had continued to bristle at US military actions on its side of the border. A few weeks after Zardari took office, a military spokesperson said Pakistan reserved the right to self-defence and to "retaliate if the [United States] continues cross-border attacks." Covert American ground operations were suspended. But the all-seeing drones continued to fly.

This was not the first time that Pakistan had been on the receiving end of this sort of military campaign. During its occupation of Afghanistan in the 1980s, the Soviet Union launched scattered attacks inside Pakistan. The Northern Alliance had also tried a few cross-border raids during its battle against the Taliban in the 1990s, albeit to little effect.

The US campaign that took shape in the later Bush years, and that would continue under Barack Obama, dwarfed these previous efforts. Certainly, there were plenty of targets from which the Americans could choose. The infrastructure of the Pakistani-based insurgents—training camps, safe houses and supply networks—had been in place since the 1970s. In some cases, it dated all the way back to the British frontier policy of the late nineteenth century, when parts of the borderlands were used as staging areas in the Great Game.

Al Qaeda's fighting retreat in 2001 had made the unassuming villages of Waziristan one of the undeclared capitals of global terrorism. Plans to attack Madrid, London, Mumbai, Istanbul and many other targets all were in part hatched here. As I've described, North Waziristan Agency was also the headquarters of the terrorist campaign in Afghanistan, where the complex attacks that had begun with the Serena Hotel operation in 2008 were now running at the rate of about one a month.

Pakistan's leaders wanted to deflect the spirit of jihad outward. But their strategy wasn't working. Since 2007, Waziristan had also become a refuge for various groups whose declared enemy was the Pakistani state itself, which in their view had betrayed the cause at Lal Masjid.

As 2009 began, this FATA-based "Islamic Emirate," as the constellation of Taliban and Taliban-allied Islamist groups grandly called themselves, was stronger than ever and had seeded growing operations in other parts of the country. The Pakistani army had already launched an offensive against Taliban elements in Bajaur Agency. But elsewhere, the jihadis were unscathed, with active recruitment and training facilities in all major cities, particularly Karachi.

Even with this expanded operation, however, the Taliban were having difficulty making headway in Afghanistan, notwithstanding the spectacular nature of the largest attacks. According to our UN statistics, the number of successful suicide strikes in Afghanistan in 2008—incidents in which the bomber actually had detonated explosives—was down from 2007. Only ten districts inside Afghanistan remained entirely beyond Afghan government control. Afghan officials had difficulty accessing 165 more districts, but this figure had not grown much since 2007. The stalemate was real.

The Taliban were finding it harder to expand their sphere of influence because Afghanistan's expanded security forces, backed by ISAF troops, were finally able to reinforce their presence substantially in provinces around Kabul and in the southern part of the country. By dividing its effort among several fronts, the Islamic Emirate—emboldened as it was—was having trouble overcoming the stiffening military resistance from Afghan troops and their Western allies.

From where I sat, there was a surreal aspect to the conflict. With drone attacks being launched from Afghanistan against Pakistan, and Taliban strikes coming from the other direction, one might have thought the two countries were on the brink of all-out war. Yet on the surface, the diplomacy was often very cordial. Pakistan's chief of army staff, General Ashfaq Parvez Kayani, sat down with his Afghan and American counterparts on January 2, 2009, at a scheduled meeting of their Tripartite Commission. According to Pakistani news reports, "The participants showed satisfaction in the existing level of cooperation."

My own sense was that Pakistan's ISI was in a state of confusion. The colonial playbook it was using had worked against the Soviets—and it had expected until quite recently it would work against Hamid Karzai. What it didn't understand was that Afghanistan, once an ignored backwater, now had the backing of sixty donor nations and forty military contributors. The US will to succeed, in particular, was hardening. Whatever Barack Obama's differences with George W. Bush, his views on Afghanistan were unambiguously resolute.

By early 2009, there was a prevailing view that some cardinal mistakes had been made at Bonn in 2001. UN mission head Lakhdar Brahimi acknowledged that the three dozen Afghans he'd gathered for that event had not been fully representative of the country's wider population. He regretted not having made a more concerted effort to bring the Taliban into the process from the start, when they were weak and dispersed.

Would such a scenario have been possible? I put the question to one of my veteran UNAMA colleagues, Talatbek Masadykov, a Kyrgyz national who had first come to Kabul in the late 1980s as a young Soviet adjunct to the Afghan Academy of Sciences. With his fluent Pashto, he had been an early recruit to UNAMA, first as a junior officer in Kandahar, then later as head of office. In 2008, we made him head of political affairs for the entire mission.

Masadykov recalled to me the first report he had written from Kandahar at the end of August 2002. "On the basis of our contacts with many elders, they all understood that the reconciliation process should start now because sooner or later these people [the Taliban] would come back," he had argued. "If not, these people may be taken in other directions."

At the time, the elders of the south would have been willing to make such a reconciliation process happen, to ensure that the Taliban peacefully reintegrated into their home villages. But the then governors of Kandahar and Helmand, Gul Agha Sherzoi and Sher Mohammad Akhundzada, both inveterate enemies of the Taliban, would hear none of it. As a result, early outreach to the Taliban was never seriously pursued. Masadykov himself made a few exploratory visits to the Quetta region, on the Pakistan side of the border, where most of the Taliban now were living, but later he was asked to suspend these contacts.

In his meetings in Quetta at the time, Masadykov found Taliban representatives had no inkling that any comeback might be in the offing. Most assumed they'd be returning to the pastoral life they'd known before taking up arms in the 1990s. Instead, Taliban leaders rekindled their relationship with al Qaeda and borrowed the terrorist group's nihilistic tactics. By the time Masadykov became head of UNAMA's Kandahar office in April 2003, the execution of Red Cross worker Ricardo Munguía in Oruzgan province the previous month— the first killing of a foreign aid worker in Afghanistan since 9/11—had already signalled the Taliban's descent into wanton terrorism.

The jihadis began methodically activating their old networks. "The Taliban were first activated in Kandahar, then in Zabul, then in Oruzgan, only last in Helmand," Masadykov told me. "The story in every region was the same. People came to villages from other parts, bringing satellite telephones and money, and urging their old comrades to get back in the fight—and if not them, then their sons. Those who refused were told they'd be turned over to the Americans as Qaeda agents and sent to Guantanamo. On the local level, the ISI's involvement in the campaign was common knowledge."

In Kandahar and Helmand, the anti-Taliban governors also mobilized their old networks. Popular support was with the government. Even as late as 2005, ordinary people who knew of planted IEDs were reporting them to the authorities before they exploded.

But then ordinary people saw arrested jihadis being released in return for bribes. Police with axes to grind punished innocent people, then demanded money for their release.

ISAF forces too began to make mistakes. "They did not respect Afghan traditions," Masadykov told me. "They started to do things that bewildered the locals. . . . You cannot go into an Afghan house without warning or an invitation. . . . On top of that, they started entering the *women's* side of the house, and started to search." Even the Soviet forces had mostly avoided inflicting such indignities.

In April 2003, Masadykov made the long road trip to Baghran district, in the far north of Helmand, for talks with the locals. Governor Sher Mohammad and Ahmad Wali Karzai, the president's brother, had warned against the journey, joking that Mullah Omar was still there. The shops in the area were playing Taliban music—voices without instrumental backing. The locals greeted Masadykov and his escort with sullen suspicion, serving them only tea. Several in the UNAMA delegation feared they would come under attack.

Conversations with elders went on through the night, with Masadykov insisting that the UN was committed to peace. By the next day, the elders had warmed slightly to Masadykov and his government escorts, and slaughtered a sheep. But nothing substantive came of the discussions. The next day, the UNAMA team left—and no UN political mission had yet returned to the district. "They were living peacefully in their little kingdom, cut off from everyone," Masadykov said. But even then, in 2003, the madrassas were being reopened to Taliban loyalists.

In the years following, Helmand and Kandahar both witnessed major military engagements between Taliban and coalition forces, several of which I have described. By early 2009, the situation remained in military flux. Every authority figure was a potential target for Taliban assassins, as was anyone suspected of being an informant. By January 2009, 24 members of the 150-strong Kandahar Ulema Shura had been assassinated. ISAF forces were under constant threat of running into IEDs.

The deadly challenges I've described apply to most of Afghanistan. But the region of Kandahar and Helmand is unique in one important sense: unlike the rest of the county, it was never given a chance to recover from Taliban repression, the miseries of civil war or the trauma of Soviet occupation. There simply was too little time between the arrival of American troops in late 2001 and the revitalization of the Taliban in 2003.

When Barack Obama was inaugurated in January 2009, my UNAMA colleagues and I were invited to watch the ceremony on big screens set up for the occasion in the foyer of the new US embassy. There was a genuine buzz inside the yellow cube. The place was packed.

For the first time since my arrival, there was genuine excitement among Afghans about political events on the other side of the world. In pledging to "forge a hard-won peace in Afghanistan," President Obama made this complicated place his top foreign-policy priority. He also became the first US president to mention Afghanistan in an inaugural address. For many of us who had believed all along that peace was still possible, our hearts were in our throats.

Obama made three points that would weigh powerfully on the campaign that lay ahead. The first was addressed to allies of the United States: "Our security emanates from the justness of our cause, the force of our example, the tempering qualities of humility and restraint." The last three words were especially important in light of the legacy of Bagram prison, Guantanamo and civilian casualties. Obama was reclaiming the moral high ground.

The second point was addressed to "those who seek to advance their aims by inducing terror and slaughtering innocents," reminding them that "our spirit is stronger and cannot be broken. You cannot outlast us, and we will defeat you." This spirit of defiance was common among many Afghans. They were gratified to hear it expressed by a US president. If Afghanistan required one virtue absolutely, it was stamina.

Finally, to "the Muslim world," Obama said: "We seek a new way forward, based on mutual interest and mutual respect." Some conservatives have made a fetish of bashing Obama's conciliatory gestures toward Muslim nations, suggesting that they communicated a message of weakness. But those of us who have actually worked in Muslim lands take a different view. At a stroke, Obama's comforting words placed the counter-insurgency campaign on a firmer foundation.

At the start of 2009, ISAF had a force strength of about 55,000. US forces counted a further 14,000, and CSTC-A (Combined Security Transition Command—Afghanistan) provided 7,000 multinational trainers for Afghanistan's army and police. They would soon be joined by 3,000 additional soldiers from the US 10th Mountain Division, who mostly reinforced Logar and Wardak provinces. Morale generally was excellent among all Western troops. Thanks to the more cautious rules of engagement implemented by US general David McKiernan, civilian casualties caused by pro-government forces declined sharply over the winter.

President Obama brought Afghanistan expertise to his new national security team. Robert Gates, who had worked on the anti-Soviet jihad before becoming CIA director in 1991, stayed on as secretary of defense. Secretary of State Hillary Clinton had been a consistent congressional ally for Afghanistan. The new national security advisor, former US Marine Corps general James Jones, had been supreme allied commander Europe at NATO from 2003 to 2006, during ISAF's expansion, and was a frequent guest in Kabul.

On January 22, Ambassador Richard Holbrooke was named President Obama's special representative for Afghanistan and Pakistan. At his first high-level security meeting in Munich two weeks later, he predicted that the challenge of bringing stability to the Afghanistan region would be "tougher than Iraq" and described the situation in Pakistan as particularly dire. (Islamabad, for its part, was meanwhile emitting its usual cynical doublespeak. At Munich, Pakistani foreign minister Shah Mahmood Qureshi declared: "The territory of Pakistan will not be used for terrorist activities, while our sovereignty and territorial integrity must be respected.")

Although the Obama administration seemed committed to staying the course in Afghanistan, the situation in other Western nations, such as Canada and the United Kingdom, was more ambiguous. As casualties had mounted, public opinion swung against the war. Morale among civilian development workers in Afghanistan also was a problem. Security threats were causing them to pull back from many of the areas where they were needed most.

Meanwhile, in Kabul, Hamid Karzai was feeling even more insecure than he had during the latter years of George W. Bush's tenure.

The new American administration was inclined to see the Afghan president as a relic left over from the Republican administration. With Afghan presidential elections on the horizon, members of the Obama foreign-policy team would not be content to keep all their eggs in one basket, as Bush's team had in Afghanistan's 2004 election. When word that rival candidates were being courted in Washington filtered back to Kabul, relations between Karzai and Obama went into deep freeze.

A school of thought had emerged in the White House that progress on corruption and governance would not be possible until there was a new Afghan president. Karzai was also seen as an impediment to rapprochement with Pakistan, whose army officers (falsely) viewed the Afghan president as an Indian puppet.

Unfortunately, I would not be on hand to see with my own eyes how things would turn out in Afghanistan, for my days in the country were coming to an end. Early 2009 would bring three departures—one to take my wife, Hedvig, to Denmark for her last weeks of pregnancy, a return trip for the birth itself, then a final one at the end of May, when I left Afghanistan for good. The two of us valued every minute we spent in Afghanistan. But we both agreed that, under the circumstances, it was not the best place to raise a family.

On the morning after Valentine's Day, Hedvig and I headed north from Kabul with two friends, bound for Moscow. She was now seven months pregnant. Our friends had said we were crazy not to fly out of Kabul directly. And they had a point: the road through the Salang Pass, closed only a few days earlier by heavy snow, was still choked with long lines of traffic snaking up the switchbacks toward the mouth of the Soviet-built Salang Tunnel. Our trip over the Hindu Kush took twice as long as expected. After spending the night with UNAMA colleagues in the northern Afghan city of Mazar-e-Sharif, we left our Afghan drivers behind at Termez, crossing the Amu River into Uzbekistan.

It was February 17, 2009. The previous day had been the twentieth anniversary of the departure of the last Soviet troops across the Friendship Bridge we had just traversed. There reportedly had been a small ceremony to mark the occasion. I asked the young Uzbek border guard about it, but he responded sarcastically, referring to Valentine's Day instead. I realized there was a telling generation gap at play here: the fellow was too young to remember Major General Gromov's campaign in Afghanistan, or even the USSR itself.

We drove for twelve days to reach Moscow, a distance of about 5,000 kilometres. On the way, we saw the great monuments at the Uzbek town of Shahr-i-Sabz, where Timur had been born; Samarkand, his capital; and Turkistan, where he built a great shrine near the site of his death, in 1405.

Not far north of Aralsk, a former port now miles from the shrinking Aral Sea, the road was blocked by a sea of snowdrifts that even rugged Kamaz trucks could not negotiate. We were stuck in our Land Cruiser until 11 p.m., when a highway construction crew pulled a dozen of us out. We slept in the local tea house.

The next day, we made it to the Kazakh village of Aktyube, then Uralsk near the Russian border. We overnighted in the Russian cities of Samara and Penza before reaching Moscow—a journey marked by more monuments to the campaigns of Genghis Khan, Timur, Bati and their descendants. In this part of the world, the weight of history was inescapable. Every highway bore the imprint of ancient armies.

On March 27, 2009, Obama announced the conclusions of an Afghanistan policy review, including the proposition that "the core goal of the U.S. must be to disrupt, dismantle and defeat al Qaeda and its safe havens in Pakistan, and to prevent their return to Pakistan or Afghanistan." To achieve this, the United States would (1) disrupt terrorist networks, (2) support the Afghan government, (3) build up Afghan security forces, (4) promote constitutional stability in Pakistan, and (5) engage the international community in all these tasks. This would require a surge in both civilian and military capabilities, a step that UNAMA and ISAF had been recommending for years.

But there were some ambiguities. The end game for the Taliban was left open. Would they be fought to the last man as insurgents, or could they be integrated into the country's government? The report also gingerly avoided the subject of Pakistani army support for the Taliban.

On the same day Obama was unveiling his policy review, Russia was hosting a meeting of the Shanghai Cooperation Organization dedicated to the subject of Afghanistan—a first for the six-nation regional group. The specific focus of the meeting was drug interdiction. But the very fact that a high-level political meeting on Afghanistan was being conducted in Moscow—the first time this had happened since the end of the Cold War—was significant. It showed a new level of Russian engagement.

Russian foreign minister Sergey Lavrov reminded his guests that his country had forgiven $10 billion in Afghan debt, strengthened counter-narcotics operations and opened supply lines for the flow of non-military NATO goods. The "reset" in US–Russia relations that Obama had promised was paying some dividends.

On March 31, 2009, foreign ministers of donor countries convened in The Hague, both to refine the priorities for Afghanistan spelled out in Paris the previous summer and to discuss the results of the recently completed US strategic review. At the meeting, Hillary Clinton hit all the right notes, from institution building to reconciliation. (Hamid Karzai, for his part, publicly welcomed the US strategic review, but privately complained that Washington was looking to replace him.)

As I was preparing to leave Kabul, some friends were kind enough to host an evening party at which I was thoroughly roasted. With great sarcasm and levity, my six years of failure were compared with my namesake's three years of triumph twenty-three centuries earlier. My future in Canadian politics was confidently predicted. Then, in the middle of my speech, the phone rang. It was Hedvig calling to say that her water had broken.

The room erupted with cheers for the impending arrival. I tried to focus on this singularly important piece of news. But I was distracted by professional obligations: the whole night, I had been receiving calls from Richard Holbrooke and Kai Eide, each of whom had issues with the approach being taken by the other—a sign of their emerging rivalry.

Shortly thereafter, General Stanley McChrystal was named commander of ISAF and US forces in Afghanistan. David McKiernan, his predecessor, had been a solid commander. But he had exercised limited control over Special Forces, which now were doing much of the important fighting in Afghanistan. McChrystal, on the other hand, had commanded Joint Special Operations Command in North Carolina from September 2003 until June 2008, when he became director of the joint staff in the Pentagon. In this role, he had been intimately involved in the covert campaigns in Iraq, Afghanistan and even Pakistan.

Under Gates and Obama, the United States would spare no effort to ensure that the Afghanistan campaign was supported by the Pentagon's most capable talent. McChrystal soon would be expanding Special Forces capabilities in the country and submitting requests for additional troops. The best US staff officers were coming on stream in ISAF. At long last, the US military was sending its A-team.

As McChrystal was coming in, I was on my way out. Our daughter, Selma, was born in April in Denmark, with me on hand to witness the joy of a healthy birth. I then returned to Kabul in May for a few final weeks, when change was definitely in the air.

It was difficult to say goodbye to all the ministers, ambassadors, officers and old friends I'd bonded with. I was uncomfortable leaving with the job not yet done but confident that the resources were finally coming into place that would make success possible. Symbolizing the sense of hope in Kabul was the fact that for the first time since my arrival, much of the city now enjoyed an uninterrupted supply of electricity, thanks to a power purchase agreement with Uzbekistan and transmission lines that reached over the Hindu Kush. All those meetings I'd attended to discuss the regional electricity grid had finally borne fruit. The west of the city was now a carpet of neon at night.

By now, Karzai had at least briefly understood the message that reforming the country's mismanagement and corruption couldn't be put off any longer. And he brought in a number of ministers with impressive resumés. In many cases, their work didn't make the front pages in the West, but it did much to give Afghans a reason to trust and support their government.

Out of the many examples I could cite, just one is Agriculture and Irrigation Minister Muhammad Asif Rahimi, the man charged with turning around Afghanistan's devastated farming sector. The recent spike in wheat prices had lifted production to the point where Afghanistan could almost meet its domestic needs. But otherwise, the situation remained somewhat bleak. Irrigation systems lay in ruins. Livestock and fruit producers faced enormous obstacles. Seeds, fertilizer and finance were lacking in most parts of the country.

Rahimi threw himself into the task of creating a modern vision for the sector. When we first met in his new office, adjacent to Kabul University, the anteroom was thronged with bright young assistants and advisors. He was sober about the challenges. But he already saw a way to make agriculture a growth engine for the Afghan economy.

He grasped the need to restore research capacity in the regions; in the king's time, Afghanistan had relied on a network of experimental farms to drive productivity. Rahimi saw the private sector as an important partner. He already had support from Holbrooke.

As the 2008–09 winter ended, many Afghan villages faced malnutrition. And so the ministry delivered 74,000 tons of wheat. Rahimi was mobilizing 3,000 staff and volunteers to spray for locusts in eleven provinces. The ministry had planted 3.2 million trees in the space of only six weeks. He was under pressure from dairy producers to lease government land for their expansion. On every front, Afghans were relying on him to help keep the country fed.

Beyond the immediate crises, Rahimi faced a structural dilemma. Higher productivity was vital to unlock new markets. But mechanization and more efficient farms risked leaving much of the rural labour force idle. Moreover, water and land resources had been damaged by drought, neglect, deforestation and warfare. How much growth could rural areas support? Where would the funds for investment come from? In a world beset by climate change, would the precipitation that once had fed plentiful water to the country's breadbasket ever return? It was a litany of policy woe.

In those early months under Rahimi, the ministry had no more than $20 million available to spend. Within less than a year, I later learned, he'd managed to bring in another $126 million. The experimental farms, ignored since 1992, were being revived, just as he planned. Saffron and pomegranate exports were rising.

Again, this was not the stuff of front pages. But it was critically important nonetheless. To reach the destination of its campaign for peace and reconstruction, Afghanistan would need to march on its stomach—just like any country on a mission.

———

On June 5, 2009, Obama made his historic speech to the Muslim world at Cairo University. As he'd done at his inauguration, he made several crucial points that touched on the war in Afghanistan. First, he rebutted the false accusation that the United States and its allies were at war with Islam: "I've come here to Cairo to seek a new beginning between the United States and Muslims around the world, one based on mutual interest and mutual respect, and one based upon the truth that America and Islam are not exclusive and need not be in competition." Second, he proposed that both sides overcome their misconceptions: "Just as Muslims do not fit a crude stereotype, America is not the crude stereotype of a self-interested empire." Third, with regard to the conflict engulfing Afghanistan, he reiterated that "America's commitment will not weaken."

This new resolve already was becoming clear on the ground when McChrystal assumed command on June 15. In spring and again in the fall, US Marines launched offensive operations in the Nauzad district of Helmand province, successfully ousting a Taliban cadre and restoring government authority. Other operations followed. By December 2009, Operation Moshtarak was under way in Helmand's Marja district, the largest combined Afghan and international operation in Afghanistan to date. It would take time to produce results.

McChrystal's initial military assessment, reported in *The Washington Post* on August 30, identified Kandahar as the enemy's strategic centre of gravity. It called for a buildup of US forces to protect the population in major centres. McChrystal issued new guidance stressing that civilian casualties were unacceptable. Every innocent life lost at the hands of ISAF was a tactical victory for the Taliban. He also authorized an intelligence review, rejecting existing US intelligence sources as mostly useless. It was a sobering message.

Pakistan was also rousing itself against the Taliban, albeit on a selective basis. On March 1, 2009, the army had announced the successful conclusion of an anti-Taliban campaign in Bajaur Agency that had commenced in August 2008. In May 2009, the army moved against militants in the Swat district, where they stood just sixty kilometres from Islamabad.

But Pakistan was not yet truly at *war* against the Taliban. These had been merely isolated operations against the subset of Taliban militants pursuing open jihad against the Pakistani state. When the army launched Operation Rah-e Nejat in South Waziristan in June 2009, for instance, it targeted mostly the Tehrik-e-Taliban Pakistan (TTP) and its leader, Hakimullah Mehsud (who was killed in a drone attack). But other areas of South Waziristan, and all of North Waziristan, were left in the hands of networks waging terrorism on the Afghan side of the border. Nothing fundamental had changed in the Islamic Emirate's order of battle.

--•--

By late spring, Hamid Karzai was the front-runner for the August 20 election, although he faced competition from two heavyweights: former finance minister Ashraf Ghani and former foreign minister Abdullah Abdullah.

Ghani crafted an impressive platform but had trouble attracting support beyond the educated urban elite and his own tribal kinsfolk. Abdullah, a veteran of the Northern Alliance, managed to attract more widespread attention. As Abdullah's star vaulted upward during July and August, the president's team remained complacent. Karzai was simply not campaigning, while Abdullah was travelling the country, tapping into reservoirs of disenchantment. The crowds that met him were enthusiastic, at times rapturous. By mid-summer, polls were showing Karzai struggling to stay above 40 percent, whereas Abdullah had conquered 30 percent and showed signs of rising further.

Of late, the president had been courting controversy with the West but avoiding it at home. With international support uncertain and the youth vote turning to Abdullah, Karzai now sought to renew bargains at all levels with old-guard tribal elders and commanders, often using governors to impose their influence at a local level. His strategy of keeping other major candidates out of the field—most by co-option—meant Ghani was the only serious Pashtun to challenge Karzai.

For first vice-presidential running mate, Karzai selected Mohammad Fahim, the former Tajik warlord and Northern Alliance commander he had earlier discarded under pressure from Washington and London in 2004. Karzai thereby showed Afghanistan he was nobody's poodle while simultaneously dividing the Northern Alliance bloc, whose supporters Abdullah had hoped to attract en masse.

Karzai's strategy was especially successful among Afghanistan's Uzbek minority, which had backed warlord Abdul Rashid Dostum as presidential candidate in 2004. By keeping Karim Khalili on his ticket as second vice-president, and pushing Mohammad Mohaqiq out of the race, Karzai retained a reasonable chance of winning most Shiite Hazara votes as well. These two groups would offer him crucial support.

The president's greatest challenge was that security would be poor for election day, especially in the southern part of the country, where his Pashtun supporters were concentrated. Participation rates in large, insecure provinces such as Helmand and Paktika would prove to be especially pitiful. Many people were simply too afraid.

In the end, Karzai won, but his victory was marred by allegations of ballot stuffing. All of the top four candidates are believed to have engaged in fraud. But Karzai was the most heavily implicated in subsequent investigations.

Once the most obviously fraudulent ballots were thrown out, Karzai was proclaimed the winner with 49.64 percent of all votes cast. Abdullah, who won 30.59 percent of the vote, topped the polls in eleven provinces. Karzai won twenty-one. Yet Karzai's vote tally was just 2.3 million, a far cry from the 4.4 million he'd won in 2004. And his margin of victory was 875,000 votes, well down from 3 million in 2004.

Karzai and Abdullah could each point to five provinces where they'd received over 100,000 votes. Karzai had eight more where he had received over 50,000; Abdullah had only four. Together with Faryab in the northwest, the four neighbouring eastern provinces where Karzai out-polled Abdullah by more than 50,000 votes—Nangarhar, Kabul, Kunar and Laghman—accounted for nearly half his overall margin. All had two features in common: strong Hazara, Pashtun or Uzbek populations, and decent security.

In all, eighteen police and thirty civilians were killed by Taliban attacks on election day. Nevertheless, despite the violence, most of the safeguards established to keep the process credible—disqualification of strongmen, a media commission, supervised counting at the district level and an electoral complaints commission—performed admirably on a bureaucratic level. It was at the level of politics that the process became discredited.

The first reason for this was that Afghanistan's Independent Election Commission (IEC) did not take allegations of internal wrongdoing seriously enough. Evidence emerged of influence peddling, manipulation and corruption within the IEC, even by senior staff. Second, President Karzai himself was unable to believe that he had not won a majority. He accused almost all the main actors of conspiring against him, before agreeing to a second-round runoff vote, which was cancelled after Abdullah Abdullah dropped out, declaring that a "transparent election is not possible." Third, at just the moment when it should have been exercising careful leadership, UNAMA's voice was divided. Kai Eide welcomed the election result, whereas Peter Galbraith, my successor, criticized the process much more comprehensively and spoke darkly of a conspiracy to steal the election. Galbraith was dismissed from his position soon thereafter, but not before significant damage was done to the UN in the eyes of Afghans.

Margie Cook had been chief electoral advisor both to Kai Eide and to Afghanistan's IEC since June 2008. She also had evaluated the results of the 2005 parliamentary elections in Afghanistan, which led to a raft of revisions to management and safeguards in advance of 2009. Cook was an Australian with rich experience in the field of democracy building, including the inevitable controversies. She had been a principal player, for instance, in the flawed Kenyan elections in 2007.

After the 2009 Afghan elections were over, I asked her for an assessment.

"Operationally, it was an achievement," she said. "We were not necessarily guaranteed to pull it off—getting materials into the country, getting people trained up, getting ballot materials out to the provinces and so on. The UN had only been able to operate in certain provinces and had to rely on military support."

What was the bottom line? "From a development perspective I don't think we took any great steps forward; politically, it was very problematic because we were working with an institution that was way too closely aligned with the government."

She was speaking about the IEC, whose politically appointed leaders had been repeatedly accused of siding with the palace. "It's not unique [to] Afghanistan," she said. "That's something that people forget. The chairman and commissioners are appointed by the president—that's been the situation in every electoral commission I've ever worked with."

"When push came to shove with regard to the results, the commission collapsed," Cook added. "They more than buckled—they really collapsed." The most glaring symptom: Chief Electoral Officer Dr. Najafi had asked for results to be changed—in the tally room itself—a gesture that couldn't fail to ring alarm bells among opposition candidates.

The Electoral Complaints Commission, which responded to those alarm bells, was a five-member body, with three international members. Chaired by Grant Kippen, a Canadian, it took weeks to address the ballot-stuffing issue, but ultimately, the body adjudicated the complaints competently. It had been a plus to have a truly independent group in charge of such a sensitive issue, but the perception that foreigners were calling the shots remained unpalatable nonetheless.

The stage for controversy had been set early. When Cook arrived in June 2008, the Afghan Interior Ministry was already in a tug-of-war with the IEC over the voter-registration process. In July, it was decided to undertake a partial registration, to target new voters or those who had moved or lost their cards. Nearly 4 million voters were added to the rolls in this way. But the data for other voters was outdated or nonexistent and so could not serve as a basis for a voters list. This perpetuated a weakness of the 2004–05 elections, when 13 million cards had been issued but no authoritative list compiled.

The 2009 campaign itself had been freewheeling; big rallies generally proceeded peacefully—"as healthy as you could expect in this kind of environment," Cook told me. Media had been robustly diverse, with a media commission that even took state broadcasters to task—at some risk—for favouring the incumbent.

Unfortunately, the voting process itself was not subject to the same strict safeguards. In insecure areas of the country, containing roughly

20 percent of all polling stations, arrangements to safeguard ballots were weak or non-existent. It was in these places where the most flagrant instances of fraud occurred. In some parts of the Pashtun belt, high numbers of ballots were returned for areas in which turnout was known to be light.

"The fraud was pretty naively done," Cook said. "A lot of photographs were taken of ballot sheets not even removed from the stubs, clearly signed in the same hand, rolled up with an elastic band around it and placed in the box. That's not an intelligent way to commit fraud because a ballot paper, to be valid, has to be torn off from the stub."

It was this widespread fraud, more than the scattered attacks or the relatively high voter turnout, that became the story (not to mention the cause of my UNAMA successor's firing after only seventy days on the job). It was the greatest blow to the Afghanistan government's standing in the world since Bonn.

Later on, I sat down with Abdullah's campaign manager, the former governor of Kapisa province, now a successful cement and construction magnate named Abdul Sattar Murad. His campaign had been the best run of the bunch, he believed, but it had been undermined by international backing for Karzai: "The world decided to work with the devil they knew, rather than an angel they did not," he said.

Murad concluded that the messages that resonated the most with voters were clean governance, social justice and what he called "the people's participation in security." Without involving elders and officials at the local level, there could be no stability in Afghanistan—even if the whole world contributed troops to ISAF.

But the election itself had been unpleasant. "You were lucky you left your position before the election," Murad told me.

He alleged that IEC chair Azizullah Lodin had been complicit in the fraud, arranging for provincial election officers to work in cahoots with the Karzai campaign. (Lodin had of course denied these charges.) Still,

Murad had not lost hope for democracy in Afghanistan. "In spite of all that, we decided not to oppose [Karzai's legitimacy]," he said, "even though constitutionally we could have protested.

"We have even decided to help him now," Murad added. "We need to put the interests of Afghanistan ahead of every other agenda." The past was the past, in other words.

For his part, Karzai also was saying the right things, at least in public. His post-re-election inauguration speech, focusing on good governance and institution building, was his all-time best.

In the meantime, the counter-insurgency campaign was gathering force. By August, the Afghan army had reached a strength of 93,000 men—ahead of schedule. Some of us even dared hope that the war might soon be brought to a negotiated end. On November 26, 2009, Karzai called for "urgent negotiations" with those Taliban willing to reconcile.

By the end of 2009, Obama had settled on the details of his Afghanistan policy. He would send 30,000 more troops to the country, and start bringing them home in summer 2011. In a speech to cadets at West Point on December 1, he articulated several objectives: "We must deny al Qaeda a safe haven. We must reverse the Taliban's momentum and deny it the ability to overthrow the government. And we must strengthen the capacity of Afghanistan's security forces and government so that they can take lead responsibility for Afghanistan's future."

The military surge would accelerate a transition to Afghan leadership, backed by a stepped-up civilian effort. And he made it clear that tough love would be part of the program:

> This effort must be based on performance. The days of providing a
> blank check are over. President Karzai's inauguration speech sent
> the right message about moving in a new direction. And going
> forward, we will be clear about what we expect from those who
> receive our assistance. We'll support Afghan ministries, gover-
> nors, and local leaders that combat corruption and deliver for the
> people. We expect those who are ineffective or corrupt to be held

accountable. And we will also focus our assistance in areas—such as agriculture—that can make an immediate impact in the lives of the Afghan people.

The people of Afghanistan have endured violence for decades. They've been confronted with occupation—by the Soviet Union, and then by foreign al Qaeda fighters who used Afghan land for their own purposes. So tonight, I want the Afghan people to understand—America seeks an end to this era of war and suffering. We have no interest in occupying your country. We will support efforts by the Afghan government to open the door to those Taliban who abandon violence and respect the human rights of their fellow citizens. And we will seek a partnership with Afghanistan grounded in mutual respect—to isolate those who destroy; to strengthen those who build; to hasten the day when our troops will leave; and to forge a lasting friendship in which America is your partner, and never your patron.

On October 9, as Afghanistan's election drama was still playing out, the Nobel committee announced that Obama was the peace laureate for 2009. When the US president delivered his speech in Oslo two months later, he used the opportunity to return yet again to the issue of the war in Afghanistan and the high moral stakes it entailed:

Agreements among nations. Strong institutions. Support for human rights. Investments in development. All of these are vital ingredients in bringing about the evolution that [JFK once] spoke about. And yet, I do not believe that we will have the will, or the staying power, to complete this work without something more—and that is the continued expansion of our moral imagination; an insistence that there is something irreducible that we all share.

In a year that had begun with an intensified drone campaign and ended in bitter electoral controversy, Obama's four speeches—at his inauguration, in Cairo, at West Point and in Oslo—pointed the way forward in Afghanistan. For the foreseeable future, America would be supplying both the political will and the resources necessary to sustain the war effort.

Yet for all Obama's uplifting words, reality kept rearing its ugly head. On the last day of 2009, a Jordanian doctor entered US Forward Operating Base Chapman in Khost province, which had been named for the first American solider killed in the country. Approaching the gym, he detonated a suicide belt, killing seven CIA officers and wounding five others.

It was al Qaeda's payback for the drone strikes inside Waziristan, and a signal that the campaign in Afghanistan was far from over.

CHAPTER TWELVE

LOST ARTS

Everyone knows that men who get
Angry without good reason will
Conciliate without gifts.

—Christopher Logue, *War Music*

B y 2010, signs of Afghanistan's progress were obvious to every foreign visitor, starting from the moment you stepped off the airplane
in Kabul. The newly constructed terminal, funded by the ever-
generous Japanese government, was bright and vast. Security and customs staff had been trained by the Americans and British, and offered
travellers the same level of professionalism you'd expect at Heathrow
or LAX.

Most of my friends were still in their old jobs, though many were
preparing to leave. Even after the punishing stress of the electoral crisis the previous autumn, the mood was surprisingly upbeat. Afghans
were decidedly buoyed by Obama's surge, which indirectly had provided a stimulus for the Afghan economy and, more important, held
out the prospect of rolling back the insurgency.

On January 26, 2010, President Hamid Karzai travelled to Istanbul for
the "Heart of Asia" summit, which brought together all of Afghanistan's
neighbours and most of its major strategic partners. Held without much
fanfare, this was an unprecedented event—the first multilateral meeting
in an Asian capital focused on measures to buttress Afghanistan's stability attended by both the Afghan and the Pakistani presidents.

Two days later, the international community gathered at Lancaster House in London, almost four years to the day after the Afghanistan Compact had been adopted. In 2006, the challenge had been to ensure that donors were brought in for long-term investments. That commitment now needed renewal.

UN secretary-general Ban Ki-moon, NATO secretary-general Jaap de Hoop Scheffer and Hillary Clinton all were present in London. Karzai and his defence minister made major speeches. But the day's best oratory came from the host, Prime Minister Gordon Brown, who hoped the conference would add wind to his luffing political sails. (It didn't. Three months later, his government was defeated at the polls.)

The conference did succeed in putting the issue of reconciliation with the Taliban front and centre (though the issue received only a vague and passing mention in the final communiqué). As a student of the region's history, I felt it was fitting that this should unfold in London: the ghosts of three Anglo-Afghan wars had never quite been put to rest. Thanks to the long memories of many Afghans—who quibbled when the first British forces arrived at Bagram—London's relationship with Afghanistan remained fraught even after 9/11, and the imbroglio over Ashdown's appointment and Michael Semple's departure from the country in late 2007 had merely added insult to a prevailing sense of injury.

Early 2010 brought some good news on the battlefield. On February 13, US Marines began to press home their advantage in the Marja district of Helmand, near Lashkar Gah. Then Mullah Abdul Ghani Berader, the top Taliban commander in the south, was captured in a joint US-Pakistani operation in Karachi. A few days after that, a pair of Taliban shadow governors were arrested near Akora Khattak on the Indus. Mullah Abdul Kabir, the head of the Peshawar Shura, also was detained, as was Mohammad Younis Khalis, a liaison between the

Quetta and Waziristan shuras, and shadow governor of Zabul province. Meanwhile, drone attacks in North Waziristan were eliminating a variety of other high-profile militants.

What was going on? On the surface, it seemed like a windfall. But the reality was different. Many of these figures had been key interlocutors in Kabul's nascent effort to reconcile with the Taliban. Berader, for instance, was known to have a long-standing open channel to Ahmad Wali Karzai, the Afghan president's younger half-brother (and a fellow Popalzai tribesman). In the run-up to London, such contacts had been intensifying, with Berader indicating he might be prepared to leave the struggle. Now he was a Pakistani prisoner.

Islamabad had taken Berader and his friends off the street—or helped the United States to do so—because a comprehensive reconciliation would have destroyed Pakistan's leverage in Afghanistan. To the extent there would be peace between Karzai's government and the Taliban, the ISI and its political masters wanted it to be on Pakistan's terms.

Karzai, meanwhile, was having a difficult time balancing his diplomatic outreach efforts with mutually suspicious regional neighbours, most notably Pakistan and India, whose emissaries each came calling to enlist Karzai's support against the other. In early March, US defense secretary Gates visited Kabul to discuss the US surge, including plans for expanded training of the Afghan army and police, as well as ways to reintegrate the Taliban (a prospect that still was regarded with great skepticism by many in Washington). The very same day, somewhat awkwardly, Iranian president Mahmoud Ahmadinejad paid his first-ever visit to Afghanistan. Fresh from suppressing a democratic uprising in his own country, the Iranian leader accused Washington of playing a double game in Afghanistan, claiming that the United States had created terrorists it was now pretending to fight.

A few weeks later, on March 27, Barack Obama himself visited Karzai at his Kabul palace. He had already refused the Afghan leader a scheduled visit to Washington the previous fall. Arriving after dark, the US president minced few words, demanding action on improved governance, anti-corruption and drugs. Karzai seethed with resentment at the frank talk, especially when the financial indiscretions of his family members were raised.

At some points during this period, Karzai seemed close to cracking up entirely. He had never stopped lashing out at Westerners he suspected of engineering the controversy over election fraud and the need for a second round of voting. But now he also started expressing skepticism about the intensifying US military effort, particularly night raids by Special Forces. On April 6, Karzai was quoted by Nangarhar parliamentarian Farooq Meranai to the effect that if foreign pressure on his presidency continued, he might himself join the Taliban.

Predictably, the remark touched off a firestorm of controversy. On May 10 and 11, Obama and Clinton made a huge effort to repair the damage by receiving Karzai and twenty of his ministers. In meetings at the White House, the visitors impressed on Obama the fact that Pakistani support for the insurgency had only grown.

On May 18, a major Taliban suicide attack on a military convoy near the Darulaman Palace in Kabul killed Canadian colonel Geoff Parker, US colonel John McHugh, Lieutenant Colonel Paul Bartz and Lieutenant Colonel Thomas Belkofer, as well as their two drivers. Eighteen Afghan civilians also were killed. With these deaths, the number of Americans killed in Afghanistan now exceeded 1,000. Over half of these victims had died in the past two years alone. A few days later, insurgents mounted a bold ground assault on Kandahar airfield, a repeat of an assault they'd tried at Bagram in early April.

At his inauguration, then again at the London Conference, Karzai had vowed to hold a national consultative peace jirga. After frantic preparations, it finally took place from June 2 to 4 under the big tent near the polytechnical campus in Kabul. Attended by over 1,600 delegates, it was the fourth national jirga since 2002. In the end, the Taliban declined to attend, citing the presence of foreign forces in Afghanistan. But a decision was taken to form the High Council for Peace, which was mandated to pursue reconciliation with Afghanistan's antagonists across the border.

Despite the presence of legions of security staff, an attacker managed to fire a rocket (harmlessly) at the jirga during Karzai's speech. Police then intercepted a group of suicide bombers, who detonated before arriving at their target. Then another rocket exploded, again harmlessly. The attacks had produced no casualties, but Karzai was deeply embarrassed nonetheless. It seemed there wasn't a square inch of the country that the Taliban couldn't reach.

In the wake of the jirga, there was a witch hunt within Karzai's entourage to assign blame. At one point, Karzai became convinced the United States had allowed the attacks in order to sabotage his bid for peace. The president also lashed out at spy chief Amrullah Saleh and Interior Minister Haneef Atmar, both of whom tendered their resignations.

The episode was symbolic of a larger trend: Karzai's headlong rush to reconcile with the Taliban was costing him support among even his closest allies. Women were particularly uncomfortable with the spectre of the Taliban being welcomed into government. It seemed to be a case of concession without gain. Saleh and Atmar were merely the first major casualties in Karzai's new post-electoral political order.

———

On June 15, in an appearance before a US Senate committee, General David Petraeus, head of US Central Command and earlier US commander in Iraq, briefly fainted under questioning from Senator John McCain. Little did those in attendance know that this man would soon be running America's war in Afghanistan.

In an article published in *Rolling Stone* magazine, General Stanley McChrystal, the senior military commander in Afghanistan, was quoted as uttering ungracious remarks about Obama, Vice-President Joe Biden, Holbrooke and others. By the end of June, the general had tendered his resignation, becoming the second four-star US general replaced within a single year. Petraeus, who formerly had overseen compilation of the army counter-insurgency manual and had been the key architect of the successful US surge in Iraq in 2007–08, was named his replacement in Kabul, with augmented authority.

Under McChrystal, the tempo of special operations had increased across the country, particularly in Kandahar and Helmand, and the rate of civilian casualties and air strikes had declined. Additional forces continued to move into the south, with the 101st Airborne Division replacing Canadian units in the Kandahar districts of Zhari and Arghandab. In July, a new military command was created for southwest Afghanistan, reflecting a new scale of international military commitment. By August, US forces in Afghanistan numbered 98,000, nearly three times the level of January 2009.

The surge meant ground was no longer being lost to the Taliban. But the military stalemate in the south had not yet been overcome. Of course, Taliban safe havens in Pakistan remained untouched by conventional ground operations. Despite endless meetings with Pakistan's army chief, General Ashfaq Pervez Kayani, McChrystal and his supporting team in Washington had failed to jolt Islamabad out of its habits of intransigence and denial. The Americans remained particularly concerned about the Haqqani network in North Waziristan, which Admiral Mike Mullen, chairman of the Joint Chiefs of Staff, described as the "most lethal force" involved in the Afghan insurgency.

Much of the problem came down to Kayani himself, a man who encapsulated all of the maddening neuroses and ambitions of Pakistan's military establishment. Kayani had been director-general of the ISI under Pervez Musharraf throughout the post-9/11 period, when the Taliban had withdrawn its allies from Afghanistan, then built up its insurgent forces inside Afghanistan. A chain smoker who appeared cool and measured in meetings, Kayani was motivated by the near-paranoid obsession with India that haunts most Pakistani military men of his generation. Like Musharraf, he considered the Taliban's downfall in 2001 a disaster for Pakistan's national interest and had seemed determined to ensure that they returned to power—or at least a share of it—in Kabul.

In the middle of the summer, nature added another complication to Pakistan's multi-faced policy. From July 27 to 30, torrential downpours inundated much of Punjab, Khyber Pakhtunkhwa (the new name for the North West Frontier province) and Sind. The city of Risalpur, home to the Pakistan Air Force Academy, received 415 millimetres of rain—a foot and a half. The Indus and its tributaries swelled drastically, inundating their floodplains. Across whole regions, people were left homeless, and as floodwaters worked their way down the course of Pakistan's giant river systems, crops were ruined over much of the country's arable land.

All of a sudden, calls for operations against militants in North Waziristan and elsewhere were drowned out as "relief" became the word on everyone's lips. Afghan army helicopters were deployed to Pakistan to deliver food and tents. The US military and ISAF also pitched in. Richard Holbrooke, the special representative for Afghanistan and Pakistan, visited camps, calling publicly for massive aid.

Several months later, in September, Afghanistan went to the polls again, this time to elect the country's Wolesi Jirga, or People's Chamber. Afghans cast 4.2 million valid votes, only slightly fewer than the 4.6 million cast in the 2009 presidential elections. Over 2,000 candidates contested 249 seats.

The results, certified on October 31, showed a majority of incumbents, including many old-guard warlords, had been defeated. The new parliament was younger but not necessarily better qualified. In an unexpected development, one ethnic contingent had done astonishingly well. Hazaras, though representing only about 10 percent of the country's population, would make up 25 percent of the newly elected lower house thanks to low turnout in some Pashtun-majority provinces with politically active Hazara minorities.

On the battlefield, meanwhile, Petraeus reportedly was ready to cross the border, and Kayani knew it. When NATO forces fired on a border post near Kurram Agency on September 30, Pakistan retaliated by permitting NATO's supply convoys to come under attack while traversing

the roads from Pakistan's ports into Afghanistan. Kayani saw the vul-
nerability of these convoys as a trump card. As one unnamed senior
Pakistani military official put it, Petraeus was "checkmated."

Throughout it all, Karzai was pursuing his goal of ending
Afghanistan's conflict through reconciliation. At one point, it even
appeared as if the president had managed to attract a high-level
Taliban delegation to visit Kabul for negotiations—flown in by ISAF,
no less. Later, it turned out that the man claiming to be Mullah Akhtar
Mohammad Mansour, shadow governor of Kandahar and architect of
the Taliban's suicide-attack campaign, was actually a shopkeeper from
Quetta. The whole thing had been a hoax. In November, the Taliban
explicitly rejected reconciliation, promising reprisals against anyone
who broke ranks on the issue. Karzai, no doubt, was heartbroken at
the news. After five years of trying, reconciliation had yet to produce a
decisive result.

In less than one year, Kayani had won four straight rounds of the
new Great Game he was playing with Kabul. He had ended the Taliban's
unauthorized contacts with Kabul in February. He had engineered the
resignation of the insurgency's most effective opponents in the Afghan
cabinet in June. He had resisted massive US pressure for action against
Pakistan's terrorist proxies in July. Finally, he had watched Karzai tip
his hand and embarrass himself in a set of dummy reconciliation talks
with a fake Taliban representative. By the final months of 2010, there
remained little doubt but that the Pakistan army would be the dominant player when and if reconciliation occurred.

But Kayani's gamesmanship could not alter the fact that America's
Afghan surge was changing the battlefield. For the first time since
2002, the Taliban were clearly losing ground, including in Kandahar,
the Taliban heartland. US forces had themselves taken heavy casualties, but they had given a master class in counter-insurgency. In
regard to Kandahar, an October 20 *New York Times* headline was
unequivocal: "Coalition forces routing Taliban in key Afghan region."

Just as the need for a political breakthrough with Pakistan was becoming urgent, there was tragic news, this time from Washington. In a meeting in Hillary Clinton's office on December 17, Richard Holbrooke suddenly found himself in extreme discomfort. Doctors diagnosed a torn aorta. Within forty-eight hours, he was dead.

Holbrooke had been a champion of civilian capacity building in Afghanistan. He also had deepened US engagement with Pakistan. While Petraeus and Kayani faced off across conference tables, Holbrooke quietly and subtly had built leverage with both Karzai and his Pakistani counterpart, Asif Ali Zardari. The loss of his skilful diplomacy, both in Asia and in the corridors of Washington, was a great blow to all those who were working to stabilize Afghanistan.

On December 15, Admiral Mullen completed his twenty-first meeting with Kayani. In public, he expressed "strategic impatience" with Pakistani inaction, while acknowledging "strategic patience" was required in the overall relationship. It was a muddled statement to match the muddled relationship between the two nations.

In an annual policy review, Obama acknowledged that progress in relations with Pakistan had been substantial but uneven. The document noted Pakistan's costly military operations in six of seven agencies of the Federally Administered Tribal Areas but did not mention Baluchistan, to the south, from which much of the infiltration was taking place. Regarding Afghanistan, it said Taliban momentum had been "arrested in much of the country and reversed in some key areas."

In Pakistan, 2011 began with more tragic news. On January 4, Punjab governor Salman Taseer, who had been in office since 2008, was assassinated for giving public support to Asia Bibi, a Christian Pakistani who had been condemned to death for blasphemy. His assailant, Malik Mumtaz Hussain Qadri, was one of his own guards. The man quickly became a national hero.

Petraeus began pressing for more authority for cross-border raids conducted in hot pursuit of Taliban fighters—apparently without success. Then, in early January, US vice-president Joe Biden made his first visit to Pakistan since entering office, to press Islamabad for action in North Waziristan. On January 14, Obama met Zardari, who was in Washington for a commemoration of Holbrooke's life, to repeat the message. Little had changed: Pakistan's government seemed more intimidated by men such as Taseer's killer than by the Americans.

On January 18, Karzai made his first visit to Russia as head of state. He called for increased Russian support for his struggle to stabilize his country, flattering his hosts by calling Russia a "great country." Karzai and Russian president Dmitry Medvedev were joined for talks in Sochi, on the Black Sea, by Zardari and Tajik president Emomalii Rahmon. Then in February, Karzai visited Delhi to meet Prime Minister Manmohan Singh. Unsure of the future of bilateral Afghan-American relations, Karzai was casting his diplomatic net far and wide.

In his State of the Union address, Obama issued this stern warning: "In Pakistan, al Qaeda's leadership is under more pressure than at any point since 2001. Their leaders and operatives are being removed from the battlefield. Their safe havens are shrinking. And we've sent a message from the Afghan border to the Arabian Peninsula to all parts of the globe: We will not relent, we will not waver, and we will defeat you."

In a few cases, the jihadis made the job easier by turning on one another. On January 22, Colonel Imam, the renowned "godfather of the Taliban," was killed on the orders of Hakimullah Mehsud in North Waziristan. He had been taken prisoner in March 2009, along with fellow ISI veteran Khalid Khwaja, who himself had been killed in April. The generation of jihad was passing.

Colonel Imam (his real name was Amir Sultan Tarar) was an iconic figure in the Taliban insurgency. He had been commissioned into Pakistan's 15th Frontier Force Regiment before being sent to Fort Bragg in 1974, where he received a green beret. He served with the mujahidin throughout the anti-Soviet jihad, playing a particularly distinguished role in the Battle for Hill 3234 in Khost alongside the forces of Jalaluddin Haqqani. He later had been a key architect of

Pakistan's policy in the 1990s, championing the Taliban at every turn. After 2001, he had urged Musharraf not to part ways with the exiled Islamic Emirate.

Colonel Imam, who once had been received in the White House by President George H.W. Bush, had held out hope for reconciliation with his captors until the very end. His passing was a genuine shock to many Taliban-friendly Pakistani officers, both serving and retired. Slowly, they were realizing that the murderous Taliban monster they'd created was now beyond their control.

The irony was that Colonel Imam still had many friends in Washington, most of them unconscious of the damage he had done to the international effort to stabilize Afghanistan. On January 22, Husain Haqqani, Pakistan's ambassador to Washington, tweeted: "On Col (R) Amir Sultan Tarar aka Col Imam's death: Prayers for the departed and for the bereaved family." He should have known better, for this was the same Haqqani who, as an academic, had provided the following testimony to a congressional committee in 2007: "[Pakistani] authorities have remained tolerant of remnants of Afghanistan's Taliban regime, hoping to use them in resuscitating Pakistan's influence in Afghanistan in case the US-installed Karzai regime falters."

Afghanistan's High Council for Peace visited Islamabad in early January and was warmly received by Pakistan's leadership. But there was no serious progress on reconciliation, despite the presence of former Taliban and Hezb-i Islami officials in the Afghan delegation. Back home in Kabul, controversy continued to swirl around the Afghan parliament as court rulings on the legality of the election in contested provinces and the election of a speaker still remained unresolved three months after the voting itself.

Then, on January 27, US diplomat Raymond Davis, an employee of the US consulate in the Pakistani city of Lahore—and, as it later turned out, a CIA contractor—shot dead two men who had been tailing him on motorbikes. The next day, multiple attackers detonated themselves in the Finest Supermarket in Kabul, killing at least eight people, including Hamida Barmaki, an Afghan human rights commissioner. It was the first major attack in Kabul since the Darulaman bombing nine months earlier. On February 12, multiple attackers hit the Kandahar police headquarters, killing nineteen—bloody testimony to the fragility of any gains in the south.

By far the most dangerous of these new developments concerned Davis, who was arrested and would remain in Pakistani detention until the payment of blood money to the victims' families in March. Pakistan had been doing its best to block expanded US operations in Waziristan and elsewhere. US officials involved in such work, such as Davis, were watched closely. The next round of trilateral talks in Washington was postponed because of the Davis controversy, and Pakistan's foreign minister was removed from the country's new cabinet after showing weakness on the issue.

All in all, it seemed to me that the "heart of Asia" was beating alongside a "heart of darkness"—dusty highlands and labyrinthine urban slums where the networks supporting the Islamic Emirate of Afghanistan prepared for another year's campaign. For Afghanistan, they were an existential threat. Yet in Pakistan, they were considered a "strategic asset." How long could this situation continue?

As 2011 opened, the Afghan economy was in trouble. Growth was at 8 percent—high by Western standards but too low for a poor nation requiring rapid growth. The rush of foreign money, meanwhile, had boosted inflation to double-digit levels, an especially dangerous development given the role of high food prices in triggering revolts in other poor nations. Although tax revenues were up, an important IMF program that ended on September 25 had not been renewed, pending the winding-up of Kabul Bank, where fraud and losses had led to a run on deposits in the fall. It marked the first time since March 2004 that Afghanistan was off an International Monetary Fund–endorsed development program. Pakistan was now in the same boat—or even worse off.

Meanwhile, Karzai's great dream of reconciliation remained a dead letter. Petraeus's counter-insurgency tactics, combined with Kayani's covert proxy war, heralded confrontation between the United States and Pakistan, something neither country wanted. For now, the politics of peace and bilateral rapprochement remained lost arts.

THE SEVENTH ROOM

It may be said of the present system that it precludes the possibility of peace.

—Winston Churchill, *The Story of the Malakand Field Force*

In *The Seduction of Yusuf*, a painting produced more than five centuries ago, the legendary Persian artist Kamaleddin Behzad depicted the lustful Zolaykha as she makes a dramatic lunge for Yusuf the Prophet—a fragment from an ancient story of romantic pursuit made famous many times over by Muslim poets. The two are situated in the top half of the frame, on an upper floor of Zolaykha's palace, with Zolaykha rushing into an alcove in which Yusuf, startled, is stepping away. Counting upward from the bottom of the mythical mansion, which is depicted in cross-section, they are in the seventh room.

In Persian tradition and Sufi doctrine, this seventh chamber is considered a place of spiritual insight—of mystical union with the divine. Zolaykha's love opens the door to this room, but the price of entry is the rejection she suffers from Yusuf. According to the complicated, metaphysical way in which this story has been interpreted, Behzad's seventh room shows Zolaykha's earthly passions being transformed into noble spiritual longing. It was a very Afghan tale.

Behzad lived and worked in what is now the city of Herat, in western Afghanistan. In the seven rooms he depicted in *The Seduction of Yusuf*, I see a metaphor for Afghanistan's story over the last decade. The sprawling house is not unlike the huge mud wall–encircled *qalas* one still finds in many parts of the country, with their great labyrinths of halls and rooms filled with giggling children, deep-pile carpets and brocaded pillows, clucking elders, the embers of cooking fires, strutting roosters—all the rustic theatre of rural life.

Afghanistan was ushered into its first post-9/11 room with the rapid fall of the barbaric Taliban regime, then the Bonn Agreement and Hamid Karzai's inauguration as chairman of the country's interim authority. The new government had real legitimacy, and the prevailing sense of euphoria in the country helped embolden the United States and the United Kingdom to move boldly on to Iraq.

The second room—spanning 2003 and 2004, the time when I first arrived in Kabul—was a period of neglect.

Thankfully, neglect did not translate into complete civilian and military disengagement by donors and troop contributors. But the scale of our effort was paltry in light of the country's challenges. Moreover, the al Qaeda and Taliban brain trust in Pakistan, which had brought down the Twin Towers and was now preparing fresh outrages in London, Madrid, Istanbul, Indonesia, Yemen, the Maghreb and elsewhere, had free rein over the borderlands.

In the third room, these militant networks went back on the attack. Throughout 2005 and 2006, they re-entered southern Afghanistan and the country's eastern border region, while preparing to expand their influence in the west and around Kabul. They deployed new tactics to subvert state building, including suicide bombing, a weapon borrowed from Sri Lanka, Iraq and other Arab lands.

In the fourth room, encompassing 2007 and 2008, the Taliban and its allies were beaten back—but not defeated. The Afghan government, ISAF and the civilian actors operating under UN leadership prosecuted a counter-insurgency campaign with scarce resources. But militants opened a second front—in Pakistan—which has continued to widen ever since.

Only once Barack Obama implemented his troop surge did we move on to the fifth room: in 2009 and 2010, our inadequate response gradually improved to the point where the Afghan government, not the Taliban, held the initiative. Still, the insurgency did not end.

The year 2011 has marked Afghanistan's emergence into a sixth room, which some describe as a new kind of stalemate. The insurgency is still active but no longer is a source of panic. No one imagines that they will wake up to find Taliban legions laying siege to Kabul. Moreover, institution building inside Afghanistan is finally occurring on a serious scale. Even in Pakistan, the policy of denial and duplicity is now under scrutiny more than ever. A light is being shone on the shadow Afghan government that is run out of Waziristan, Baluchistan, Abbottabad, Punjab and Karachi, which is destabilizing not only Afghanistan but great swathes of Pakistan itself. For the first time since the 1960s, voices within Pakistan are calling into question the country's policy of sending proxies into Afghanistan.

But the seventh room still lies ahead: the stage at which true peace is achieved—a peace not only among factions but also between Afghanistan and Pakistan. It would be a peace in which the whole region would have a stake, a sort of Central Asian version of the 1648 Treaty of Westphalia, which gave Switzerland its borders after years of war.

The question of borders remains crucial. No deal with the Taliban will stick unless they and their backers abandon their goal of reconquering Afghanistan by force. Twenty-three years after the Geneva Accords that led to the withdrawal of Soviet forces but did not end the conflict in Afghanistan, the proxy war still being waged by regional powers must end. Pakistan should definitively part ways with insurgents. In return, Afghanistan should extend the political recognition that borders require to have any prospect of being secure. Afghan romantics, never far from the mainstream of politics in Kabul, must dispense with their dangerous dream of a triumphant Pashtunistan, with Peshawar and Quetta reverting to Afghan control. In other words, a bilateral settlement between two sovereign nations is desperately needed—one that would match an end to cross-border interference with an end to implicit irredentism. The latest round of interference began in 1979; irredentism has dogged their relations since at least 1879. But both countries stand to gain immeasurably from a move beyond these hackneyed positions.

Looking on from the comfortable vantage point of Toronto or Frankfurt, decision makers in donor countries not surprisingly have lost confidence in the Afghan project, which seemed so worthy in the early years following 9/11. They have been besieged with images of suffering and violence. They have been told that Afghanistan's new institutions are rotten to the core. The pundits seem to proclaim with one voice: Afghanistan will never change.

Yet it *has* changed. The last decade has seen a dramatic shift in the country's human landscape. Over 5 million Afghans have returned home, mostly from Iran and Pakistan. Per-capita income has grown, by some measures, sevenfold. A new road system is the backbone for a reviving economy, with agriculture, handicrafts, telecom, construction and even mining all booming.

Take a typical village in Ghor province, smack in the middle of the country. There may be Taliban lurking nearby, funded from Quetta. There may be drug traffickers lording their money over local officials. But chances are the village also has a community development council that has received a block grant from the National Solidarity Programme. Microfinance loans are available. There is likely a new school, perhaps two or three, all built since 2002. A rural road may have been straightened or graded. A new mosque or community centre will in most cases have been built. Seed and fertilizer were probably supplied in the past year. There is almost certainly a clinic within walking distance furnishing advice from a nurse and a few hygienic supplies. If the village is not terribly remote, it will have mobile telephone service and a television or two. Irrigation channels will have been cleaned or repaired, or new ones dug. New orchards will be growing in many stream-fed valleys. On the hills nearby, knots of livestock will have grown into herds.

To a casual observer, these changes are invisible. We in advanced economies do not easily distinguish between the standard of living of a country that was next to last on the human development index in 2004 and one that is sixteenth from the bottom now. In both cases, they seem—to use those all-purpose adjectives thrown around so casually by experts—primitive and medieval. But for Afghans, these changes matter. They have sustained hopes in the face of waves of violence. They also have laid the groundwork for functioning institutions and a national economy.

This investment is not only worth protecting; it is worth *celebrating*.

Whatever the pernicious influence of the drug trade, however unscrupulous the leadership at Kabul Bank may have been, the vast majority of Afghans have put aside self-interest in order to start building a better country for future generations. For those of us who had the privilege of living through this formative period, it has been a moving spectacle: Afghans rebuilding their homes; government officials delivering results on a shoestring; parliamentarians, often women, turfing the old guard—military commanders, even—to make way for reformers. The three plagues of Afghan life since the Soviet withdrawal—factions, drugs and terrorists—are now all in stasis or retreat.

This path has not been a straight line, and it has been punctuated by individual tragedies. When Ahmad Wali Karzai, the president's brother, was assassinated in July 2011 by a once-loyal retainer, he had apparently been on the verge of leaving Kandahar. Instead, he died almost the same death their father had endured in Quetta in 1999.

The awful truth is that thousands of people have laid down their lives to make this emerging Afghanistan a reality. Everyone wishes the cost had been lower, the long way back to peace less tortuous. But at every step of the way, we underestimated the entrenched forces arrayed against a stable Afghanistan, their roots planted deep in the history of the region. As I have made clear in this book, the victims of violence over the last decade have lost their lives, either directly or indirectly, because of a misguided Pakistani policy that treats Afghanistan as a mere pawn in an ongoing battle for regional supremacy against India. Conflict will not yield to peace in Afghanistan unless and until this policy is abandoned.

It is perhaps no accident that Osama bin Laden was taken down by US Special Forces in a town named for one of Sir Henry Lawrence's young men, a group who were in many respects the architects of the Frontier Policy—the oscillating influence and interference—that governs Pakistan's approach to Afghanistan even today. With US Navy SEALs obliged to eliminate the world's most wanted terrorist within a stone's throw of the Pakistan Military Academy, where most of Pakistan's officers had been trained, the resilience of this policy over two centuries has been brought starkly to light.

The UN, ISAF, NATO and the United States have not been fighting independent terrorists in Afghanistan. They have been fighting proxies carefully nurtured on Pakistani soil. The failure to describe this conflict in its true terms has simply prolonged it. Our inability to censure this behaviour in the strongest political terms has merely encouraged it further. This appeasement must end.

Some counsel patience, arguing that the deeper issues between Afghanistan and Pakistan cannot be solved until India and Pakistan resolve the status of Kashmir. Or they defend the policy of appeasement: bringing the Taliban—and with them, Pakistani influence—into Afghanistan's government through some sort of power-sharing arrangement. (Hezbollah's gradual takeover of Lebanon shows where such power-sharing schemes with ruthless terrorist groups eventually lead.) I argue for a more principled and urgent approach. No nation on earth should have to permit continual military interference from a neighbour.

I hasten to repeat that it is not just Pakistanis but Afghans too who must agree to put aside old disputes about borders and dreams of a reunited Pashtunistan. Indeed, border grievances have infused patriotic rhetoric in Afghanistan for generations.

On March 14, 2011, I gave a talk to a group of students at Glendon College in Toronto. Their professor told me they had voted the previous week on the question of whether Canada should remain engaged in Afghanistan. Thirty or so had favoured disengagement; only a dozen wanted Canada to stay involved.

My talk went on longer than I expected. Over two hours, I took them through the story since 2001. I described the misery and repression to which Afghanistan had been reduced under the Taliban. Then I introduced Yusuf and Zolaykha, using the metaphor of the seven rooms to tell the story of our partnership with Afghanistan. I did not predict peace. But I argued that it was still possible if Pakistani interference was curbed, then ultimately ended, allowing Afghans to finish building the credible institutions they so plainly crave. There were many questions.

It was a knowledgeable and very diverse audience. Some of the students were children of officers who had served with the Soviet army in Afghanistan. Others had their own family roots in Afghanistan, Pakistan, Iran or India. They knew how high the stakes had been in the Cold War, and how, before that, partition had left a deep political wound in the heart of South Asia.

The next week, the professor phoned me to report that the students had voted again. This time, more than thirty wanted us to remain engaged in Afghanistan until peace was achieved. A dozen or so still favoured a pullout. A few more had abstained.

That phone call reaffirmed my conviction, which constitutes this book's animating spirit, that ordinary people will be more willing to support our effort in Afghanistan if they hear the experience of those who have worked, first-hand, in the struggle to rehabilitate that country. There are now many of us, and this story should be told and retold in all its facets, dimensions and aspects.

For Afghanistan, it has been a long way back from its abyss under the Soviet occupation, the civil war of the 1990s and the Taliban regime that followed it. Unfortunately, the words of the Afghanistan Compact continue to apply: "Afghanistan's transition to peace and stability is still not assured."

We now know what it will take to reach Afghanistan's seventh room. To everyone reading this book, in Afghanistan and outside, I say: Let's walk those final steps together.

ACHNOWLEDGEMENTS

In all conflicts it is just as fatal to underrate the difficulties
of your enemy as to overrate your own.

—Erskine Childers, *The Riddle of the Sands*

This book sprang from a conviction that despite a continuous barrage of reporting and published works, Afghanistan's story since 2001 has yet to be properly told. I hope this modest contribution will serve as a reminder to others of our obligation to bear witness to these extraordinary events—if only to show succeeding generations of Afghans, as well as a broader global audience, what was attempted, and what achieved.

My first debt of gratitude goes to all who worked with me in the Canadian embassy and in Canada's Task Force Kabul from 2003 to 2005. For professionalism and dedication, they were second to none, making the "3-Ds"* mantra a reality, while never losing sight of our goal—to bring peace, stability and a more prosperous future to Afghans.

Exceptional Canadians populate every aspect of this story. Nipa Banerjee and Eileen Olexiuk, who may have done more to frame Canada's exemplary effort than any other individuals, have my special praise, as do Lieutenant General Andrew Leslie and General (ret'd.) Rick Hillier, whose leadership within ISAF set a standard their successors were hard pressed to match. Canada's Task Force, Battle Group, Strategic Advisory Team and other commanders, together

---

*   Defence, development and diplomacy.

with the tens of thousands of men and women deployed from across the Canadian Forces, left a singular legacy. They were the epitome of courage, competence, teamwork, finesse, tenacity and clarity of vision. I would also like to thank the embassy's Military Security Guards (2003–05)—*Securitas*!

But this was never a single nation's mission. Like the Persian, Macedonian, Kushan and even Soviet campaigns of old, the forces deployed since 2001 have been multinational, and they were often ill-prepared. But NATO's campaign has taken a fresh path. Thanks to countries from Mongolia to Iceland (with even Macedonia back after two millennia!), ISAF has brought together a strong plurality of the world's deployable armies. It has also—thanks to British, Canadian and German leadership until 2006, and US thereafter—expanded its capabilities every year, restoring Afghan capacity along the way. I wish to salute all the men and women of ISAF with whom it was a true privilege to serve—and to pay tribute to the memory of those who did not make it home.

The diplomatic corps, though smaller in number, was every bit the equal of this military machine for ingenuity and sheer commitment. Over six years, I was constantly amazed by the qualities of my colleagues—from the EU's Francesc Vendrell, Russia's Zamir Kabulov, France's Jean de Ponton d'Amécourt and the UK's Dame Rosalind Marsden and Sir Sherard Cowper-Coles to Italy's Ettore Sequi, Pakistan's Tariq Azizuddin and India's Vivek Katju, Rakesh Sood and Jayant Prasad, as well as the Aga Khan Development Network's Aly Mawji and the US quartet of Zalmay Khalilzad, Ron Neumann, "Chemical" Bill Wood and Karl Eikenberry. Thrusting aside (most days!) the siren call of the Great Game, they made this a team effort. This book draws only indirectly on our shared experience. I am grateful to them all for their friendship, trust and wisdom.

From my earliest days in Kabul, one of Afghanistan's greatest post-Taliban treasures was the United Nations Assistance Mission in Afghanistan (UNAMA). It had Afghan and international talent in spades. Its political judgment was the best on offer. Sadly, from 2006 to 2009, when it was finally starting to become large enough to fulfil its mandate, its impact as a civilian organization was blunted by the reality of war. But I would like to congratulate the UN Country Team—all the agencies, funds and programs operating in Afghanistan—for their high principles, and thank UNAMA's heads—Brahimi, Arnault, Koenigs and Eide (and their deputies, Grandi, Haq and Asplund)—for their leadership. Afghanistan owes a great deal to UNAMA's pluck, resilience and acumen. It was an honour to serve with these men and women; I hope this slender volume does some small measure of justice to their effort. They have all understood how this story is ultimately about protecting ordinary people from violence, impunity and want.

My deepest thanks must go to all my Afghan friends and colleagues. It is fashionable to tar Afghan leaders indiscriminately with the brush of corruption. The reality is much more complex—and reassuring. Throughout this enterprise, Afghanistan has had a president, ministers, officers, business leaders, *ulema*, women parliamentarians, political leaders, writers, musicians and tribal elders of rare quality. While far from perfect, they each faced obstacles unimaginable to most outside the country. This is their story. Life in Afghanistan was for me uplifting and meaningful only because of them.

From 2009 until 2011, I conducted over 150 interviews for this book, which of necessity reflects only a fraction of the material gleaned. I am grateful to all my friends and colleagues for their confidences, which have shaped my judgments. In particular, I wish to thank Aly Mawji, Saad Mohseni, Ashraf Ghani, Tahoora Moheb and Haneef Atmar, as well as my former drivers, Zia and Akhtar.

I would like to thank my agent, Michael Levine, and HarperCollins editors Jennifer Lambert, Alex Schultz and Noelle Zitzer for their patience in bringing a first-time author into print. Senior publicist Lindsey Love, copy editor Judy Phillips and proofreader Janice Weaver also have my gratitude. I especially wish to thank editor Jonathan Kay for his collaboration, without which this book would not have the focus its subject so richly deserves.

Since I wrote this book, the electors of Ajax-Pickering have seen fit to send me to the House of Commons in Ottawa as their Member of Parliament. For years now, they have gathered on the Highway of Heroes that passes through our riding to honour our fallen soldiers. Every step of the way they have reminded me—by large gestures and small—that this project has been worth each ounce of energy expended upon it.

I am also most grateful to Prime Minister Stephen Harper for his courageous leadership, and to Minister of National Defence Peter MacKay and Minister of Foreign Affairs John Baird for their encouragement.

The mistakes and shortcomings are all mine—without exception. It has been hard to exclude so many memorable episodes. But Hedvig, Selma and I, together with all our friends from Afghanistan, will be celebrating them forevermore.

BIBLIOGRAPHY

Babur's Garden: Afghan History
The best guides to Afghan history are the chronicles and "mirrors for princes" written under the patronage of succeeding dynasties. The Avesta, Zoroastrianism's holy scripture, is the most ancient. The *Milindapanha*, a dialogue between the second-century BC Greco-Bactrian dramatist Menander and the Buddhist sage Nagasena, is another high point, as are the *Hudud al-Alam*, written in Jawzjan, and the *Shahnameh*, written in Ghazni—both in the tenth century. The latter is perhaps the most influential Afghan chronicle of all, rivalled only by the sixteenth-century *Baburnama*. The superb travel works of Robert Byron (*The Road to Oxiana*), Eric Newby (*A Short Walk in the Hindu Kush*) and Peter Levi (*The Light Garden of the Angel King*) are infused with this legacy.

Frontier Policy
Any account of the Great Game must start with Mountstuart Elphinstone's *An Account of the Kingdom of Caubul and Its Dependencies in Persia, Tartary and India* (London, 1815), as well as Alexander Burnes's *Cabool: Being a Personal Narrative of a Journey to, and Residence in That City, in the Years 1836, 7 and 8* (London, 1842)—written before the first Anglo-Afghan war. The account of Burnes's native Indian secretary, Munshi Mohan Lal, entitled *Life of the Amir Dost Mohammed Khan, of Kabul* (London, 1846), may be the

best of all. Charles Allen's *Soldier Sahibs: The Daring Adventurers Who Tamed India's Northwest Frontier* (London, 2000) tells the story of the absorption of Punjab. Henry George Raverty's *Notes on Afghanistan and Part of Baluchistan* (London, 1878) gives the deeper story of the frontier policy and Afghanistan's emergence as a buffer state. There are numerous military memoirs on which to draw: Field Marshal Earl Frederick Roberts's *Forty-one Years in India* (London, 1898) is justly the most illustrious. Churchill's own *The Story of the Malakand Field Force: An Episode of Frontier War* (London, 1898) is equally revealing, as is George Nathaniel Curzon's *Russia in Central Asia in 1889 and the Anglo-Russian Question* (London, 1889). But the Afghan perspective is best conveyed by M. Hassan Kakar's *Political and Diplomatic History of Afghanistan (1863–1901)* (Leiden, 2006) and *Government and Society in Afghanistan: The Reign of Amir 'Abd al-Rahman Khan* (Austin, TX, and London, 1979). While Vladimir Minorsky, Vasily Barthold, René Grousset and C.E. Bosworth all deserve attention on the broader picture, there is no greater overview of the geopolitical rivalries from which modern Afghanistan emerged than Jonathan Lee's *The "Ancient Supremacy": Bukhara, Afghanistan and the Battle for Balkh, 1731–1901* (Leiden, 1996), though I am told that Mir Ghulam Mohammad Gubar's *Afghanistan dar Masir i Tarikh* [Afghanistan in the course of history] (Kabul, 1967), which has not to my knowledge been translated into English, is also excellent, even if the scholarship is tinged with the prevailing socialism of his era.

Pakistan, Russia and Jihad
"Strategic depth" still awaits a competent treatment. But the shape of Pakistani interference in the 1980s is nowhere more lovingly described than in Brigadier (ret'd.) Mohammad Yousaf and Mark Adkin's *The Bear Trap: Afghanistan's Untold Story* (London, 1992), though George Crile's *My Enemy's Enemy: The Story of the Largest Covert Operation in History; The Arming of the Mujahideen by the CIA* (New York, 2003) and Milt Bearden and James Risen's *The Main Enemy: The Inside*

Story of the CIA's Final Showdown with the KGB (New York, 2003) are also essential reading. The Soviet experience has been chronicled in *The Soviet-Afghan War: How a Superpower Fought and Lost* (Kansas, 2002), Artyom Borovik's *The Hidden War* (New York, 1990) and M. Hassan Kakar's *Afghanistan: The Soviet Invasion and the Afghan Response, 1979–1982* (Berkeley, 1995). More recent analysis has come from Gregory Feifer's *The Great Gamble: The Soviet War in Afghanistan* (New York, 2009) and Rodric Braithwaite's *Afgantsy: The Russians in Afghanistan 1979–89* (London, 2011). Pakistan's continuing reliance on irregular warfare and terrorism as instruments of state policy are covered in Husain Haqqani's *Pakistan: Between Mosque and Military* (Lahore, 2005), Ayesha Siddiqa's *Military Inc.: Inside Pakistan's Military Economy* (London, 2007), Tariq Ali's *The Duel: Pakistan on the Flight Path of American Power* (New York, 2008), Shuja Nawaz's *Crossed Swords: Pakistan, Its Army and the Wars Within* (Oxford, 2008) and Bruce Riedel's *Deadly Embrace: Pakistan, America and the Future of the Global Jihad* (New York, 2011). John Lewis Gaddis's *Surprise, Security and the American Experience* (Cambridge, MA, 2004) does not even mention Pakistan, though as we now know, bin Laden had moved from the frontier to Abbottabad that very year.

Al Qaeda, the Taliban and Terrorism
British pro-consuls on the frontier, such as Sandeman (Baluchistan), Cunningham, Warburton and Caroe (NWFP), richly deserve full-length biographies. Charles Allen's *God's Terrorists: The Wahhabi Cult and the Hidden Roots of Modern Jihad* (London, 2006) and Alan Warren's *Waziristan: The Faqir of Ipi and the Indian Army; The North West Frontier Revolt of 1936–37* (Oxford, 2000) are useful reminders of modern terrorism's local antecedents despite "masterful inactivity" and "closed doors." Overall, the early literature on al Qaeda and the Taliban is painfully short of connections to the preceding Raj and Pakistani policy, making the books of Peter Bergen, Jason Burke, Steve Coll, Jonathan Randal and Lawrence Wright much less satisfying in

retrospect. The same holds true of Robert Crews and Amin Tarzi's *The Taliban and the Crisis of Afghanistan* (Cambridge, MA, 2008); Antonio Giustozzi's *Koran, Kalashnikov and Laptop: The Neo-Taliban Insurgency in Afghanistan* (New York, 2008) and *Decoding the New Taliban: Insights from the Afghan Field* (New York, 2009); and Syed Saleem Shahzad's *Inside al-Qaeda and the Taliban: Beyond bin Laden and 9/11* (London, 2011). But Ahmed Rashid's *Taliban* (London, 2000) still stands up to scrutiny, as does Abdul Salam Zaeef's *My Life with the Taliban* (New York, 2010), which is refreshingly frank about Pakistan's role.

Treading Lightly (2001–04)
The best account of these years is in the records of the conferences at Bonn, Tokyo and Berlin, as well as the emergency and constitutional loya jirgas. The military campaign is detailed, from the CIA side, in Gary Berntsen's *Jawbreaker: The Attack on bin Laden and al-Qaeda* (New York, 2005) and Gary Schroen's *First In: An Insider's Account of How the CIA Spearheaded the War on Terror in Afghanistan* (New York, 2006), and from the special forces side in Robin Moore's *The Hunt for bin Laden: Task Force Dagger; On the Ground with the Special Forces in Afghanistan* (New York, 2003) and Dalton Fury's *Kill bin Laden: A Delta Force Commander's Account of the Hunt for the World's Most Wanted Man* (New York, 2008). Bob Woodward's *Bush at War* (London, 2002) and George W. Bush's *Decision Points* (New York, 2010) give the view from Washington. But the most lucid accounts of the real story are James Dobbins's *After the Taliban: Nation-Building in Afghanistan* (Dulles, VA, 2008) and Sarah Chayes's *The Punishment of Virtue: Inside Afghanistan After the Taliban* (New York, 2006), though Rory Stewart's *The Places in Between* (New York, 2004) still takes the laurels for evocation of place. Chris Johnson and Jolyon Leslie's *Afghanistan: The Mirage of Peace* is slightly depressing, though on many issues their diagnosis still rings true. The concept for institution-building followed by Afghan reformers in those years is

laid out in Ashraf Ghani and Clare Lockhart's *Fixing Failed States: A Framework for Rebuilding a Fractured World* (Oxford, 2008).

Hanging Fire (2005–07)

As the insurgency hit, "Helmand and Kandahar Lit" sprang to life. Sebastian Junger's *War* (New York, 2010) is in a league of its own because of the hammering intensity of the fight in the Korengal valley of Kunar province. But my favourite book from this sub-genre, for its humanity and its clear-eyed turn of phrase, is Christie Blatchford's *Fifteen Days: Stories of Bravery, Friendship, Life and Death from Inside the New Canadian Army* (Toronto, 2008), though Chris Wattie's *Contact Charlie: The Canadian Army, the Taliban and the Battle That Saved Afghanistan* (Toronto, 2008) is also first-rate. On the British side, there are Patrick Bishop's *Ground Truth: 3 PARA Return to Afghanistan* (London, 2009), Stephen Grey's *Operation Snakebite: The Explosive True Story of an Afghan Desert Siege* (London, 2009), Stuart Tootal's *Danger Close: Commanding 3 PARA in Afghanistan* (London, 2009), Sam Kiley's *Desperate Glory: At War in Helmand with Britain's 16 Air Assault Brigade* (London, 2009), James Fergusson's *A Million Bullets: The Real Story of the British Army in Afghanistan* (London, 2008) and Patrick Hennessey's *The Junior Officers' Reading Club: Killing Time and Fighting Wars* (London, 2009). The mixed outlook for the country is well chronicled in Geoffrey Hayes and Mark Sedra's *Afghanistan: Transition Under Threat* (Waterloo, ON, 2008), Sally Armstrong's *Bitter Roots, Tender Shoots: The Uncertain Fate of Afghanistan's Women* (Toronto, 2008) and Sean Maloney's *Confronting the Chaos: A Rogue Military Historian Returns to Afghanistan* (Annapolis, MD, 2009). The first decent overview of the reinforced jihadi networks in Pakistan was Muhammad Amir Rana and Rohan Gunaratna's *Al-Qaeda Fights Back Inside Pakistan's Tribal Areas* (Islamabad, 2008). Once again, the best account of the overall strategic picture—as well as the slide in security on both sides of the Durand Line—came from Ahmed Rashid, whose sprawling *Descent into Chaos: The United States and the Failure of Nation Building in Pakistan, Afghanistan and Central Asia* (New York, 2008) is still unrivalled.

Bolder Strokes (2008–11)
As the US moved to end the Iraq War and refocus on Afghanistan, we had Seth Jones's *In the Graveyard of Empires: America's War in Afghanistan* (New York, 2009), David Kilcullen's *The Accidental Guerrilla: Fighting Small Wars in the Midst of a Big One* (New York, 2009), Gretchen Peters's *Seeds of Terror: How Heroin Is Bankrolling the Taliban and al Qaeda* (New York, 2009) and Michael O'Hanlon and Hassina Sherjan's *Toughing It Out in Afghanistan* (Washington, 2010). There was also an even larger slew of conference and think-tank reports. Some of the best analysis of the insurgency came out of the Institute for the Study of War. But the critical account of the strategy and debate behind the surge is still Bob Woodward's *Obama's Wars* (New York, 2010). There are also offerings from some of the key international actors: Kai Eide's *The Power Struggle Over Afghanistan: An Inside Look at What Went Wrong—and What We Can Do to Fix It* (New York, 2011) and Sherard Cowper-Coles's *Cables from Kabul: The Inside Story of the West's Afghanistan Campaign* (London, 2011). For a stimulating read from one of the US officials who knows Afghanistan best, see Peter Tomsen's *The Wars of Afghanistan: Messianic Terrorism, Tribal Conflicts, and the Failures of Great Powers* (New York, 2011). This period also saw the publication of Thomas Barfield's *Afghanistan: A Cultural and Political History* (Princeton, NJ, 2010)—now the best one-volume introduction to Afghanistan in English, alongside two classics: Martin Ewans's *Afghanistan: A Short History of Its People and Politics* (London, 2001) and Willem Vogelsang's *The Afghans* (Oxford, 2002).

INDEX